Deviant Sex and Buddhism

Emerging Perceptions in Buddhist Studies
(ISSN 0971-9512)

1-2. An Encyclopaedia of Buddhist Deities, Demigods, Godlings, Saints & Demons — with Special Focus on Iconographic Attributes; by Fredrick W. Bunce. 2 Vols. (ISBN 978-81-246-0020-7; set)

3. Buddhism in Karnataka; by R.C. Hiremath; with a foreword by H.H. the Dalai Lama (ISBN 978-81-246-0013-9)

4-5. Pāli Language and Literature: A Systematic Survey and Historical Study; by Kanai Lal Hazra. 2 Vols. (ISBN 978-81-246-0004-7; set)

6. Maṇḍala and Landscape; by A.W. Macdonald (ISBN 978-81-246-0060-3)

7. The Future Buddha Maitreya: An Iconological Study; by Inchang Kim (ISBN 978-81-246-0082-5)

8. Absence of the Buddha Image in Early Buddhist Art; by Kanoko Tanaka (ISBN 978-81-246-0090-0)

9. A Few Facts About Buddhism; by Gunnar Gällmo (ISBN 81-246-0099-6)

10. Buddhist Theory of Meaning and Literary Analysis; by Rajnish K. Mishra (ISBN 978-81-246-0118-3)

11. Buddhism as/in Performance: Analysis of Meditation and Theatrical Practice; by David E.R. George (ISBN 978-81-246-0123-5)

12. Buddhist Tantra and Buddhist Art; by T.N. Mishra (ISBN 978-81-246-0141-9)

13. Buddhist Art in India and Sri Lanka: 3rd Century BC to 6th Century AD — A Critical Study; by Virender Kumar Dabral (ISBN 978-81-246-0162-4)

14. The Tibetan Iconography of Buddhas, Bodhisattvas and Other Deities: A Unique Pantheon; by Lokesh Chandra & Fredrick W. Bunce (ISBN 978-81-246-0178-5)

15. The Dalai Lamas: The Institution and Its History; by Ardy Verhaegen (ISBN 978-81-246-0202-7)

16. The Tibetan Tāntric Vision; by Krishna Ghosh Della Santina (ISBN 978-81-246-0227-0)

17. The Buddhist Art of Kauśāmbī From 300 BC to AD 550; by Aruna Tripathi (ISBN 978-81-246-0226-3)

18. Mahāmudrā & Atiyoga; by Giuseppe Baroetto; Translated from Italian into English by Andrew Lukianowicz (ISBN 978-81-246-0322-2)

19. Theravāda Buddhist Devotionalism in Ceylon, Burma and Thailand; by V.V.S. Saibaba (ISBN 978-81-246-0327-7)

20. Faith and Devotion in Theravāda Buddhism; by V.V.S. Saibaba (ISBN 978-81-246-0329-1)

21. Sects in Tibetan Buddhism: Comparison of Practices Between Gelugpa and Nyingmapa Sects; by Vijay Kumar Singh (ISBN 978-81-246-0330-7)

22. Emptiness and Becoming: Integrating Mādhyamika Buddhism and Process Philosophy; by Peter Paul Kakol (ISBN 978-81-246-0519-6)

23. Buddhist Ethics in Impermanence; by M.V. Ram Kumar Ratnam and K. Srinivas (ISBN 978-81-246-0562-2)

Emerging Perceptions in Buddhist Studies, no. 24

Deviant Sex and Buddhism

Wadinagala Pannaloka

DK PRINTWORLD
Publishers of Indian Traditions

Cataloging in Publication Data — DK
[Courtesy: D.K. Agencies (P) Ltd. <docinfo@dkagencies.com>]

Pannaloka, Wadinagala, 1974- author.

Deviant Sex and Buddhism / Wadinagala Pannaloka.
pages cm. - (Emerging perceptions in Buddhist studies ; no. 24)
Includes bibliographical references.
ISBN 9788124610039

1. Paraphilias. 2. Sex — Religious aspects — Buddhism. 3. Sensuality — Religious aspects — Buddhism. 4. Tipiṭaka. Suttapiṭaka — Criticism, interpretation, etc. 5. Tipiṭaka. Vinayapiṭaka — Criticism, interpretation, etc. I. Title. II. Series: Emerging perceptions in Buddhist studies ; no. 24.

LCC BQ4570.S48P36 2019 | DDC 294.3422 23

ISBN: 978-81-246-1003-9
First published in India in 2020

Printed and published by:
D.K. Printworld (P) Ltd.
Regd. Office: "Vedaśrī", F-395, Sudarshan Park
(Metro Station: E.S.I. Hospital), New Delhi - 110015
Phones: (011) 2545 3975, 2546 6019
e-mail: indology@dkprintworld.com
Website: www.dkprintworld.com

Dedicated to

Emeritus Prof. P.D. Premasiri

who inspired a generation of students

to seek moral and intellectual excellences

at the Department of Pali and Buddhist Studies,

University of Peradeniya, Sri Lanka

Preface

THE current world is attempting to liberalize traditional values in the sphere of sexuality. Sexual practices which are traditionally accepted as non-conforming to social, cultural or other sorts of values and judgements are being questioned and certain groups try to prove that some sexual practices are not deviant.

Within the last two decades, few researches have attempted to explain the Buddhist scriptural views on sexuality. This work undertakes the task of looking into the cases and views regarding non-conforming sexual practices mentioned in the Pali Sutta and Vinaya sources which belong to the Theravada Buddhism.

In understanding the early Buddhist view on this controversial aspect of human behaviour, the book first examines the early Buddhist doctrinal foundation under the concept of sensual desire (*kāma-taṇhā*) and other psychological factors which lie at the root level. Then a detailed examination is carried out on the views about human body, seen as the source of pleasure, as reflected in the Pali literature. Deviant sexual behavior is categorized into three aspects, normal, pathological and sociological. The research gathers data found in the primary Buddhist sources corresponding to these three categories and reveal the textual views on them.

The implication of the research is twofold: sex within

marriage is acceptable and all the other forms of sexual practices are considered as immoral. Any sexual act violating the norms of chastity and celibacy within the Buddhist community comes to be identified as deviant sexual act; no stigma is inflicted upon the deviant but treated as capable as any normal person in actualizing spirituality.

Rev. Wadinagala Pannaloka

Contents

Acknowledgements

I MUST immensely thank the supervisor of this work Emeritus Prof. P.D. Premasiri, University of Peradeniya, for his valuable advice, thought-provoking comments and constructive criticisms. Also, I would like to thank Prof. G.A. Somaratne, Centre for Buddhist Studies, University of Hong Kong for his highly useful instructions, suggestions and encouragement to make this work a success. I love to remember Venerable Nun, Dr Xing-yi Shi, the former Dean of Yuan Kuang Buddhist Research Institute, Taiwan, for her keen interest in this book, and for her suggestions and inputs.

I owe my gratitude to my friends Venerable Nalagama Dhammavansa, Venerable Dr Hindulwala Punnaji, and Venerable Dr Toong Herng, Associate Professor, Yuan Kuang Buddhist Research Institute, Taiwan.

Finally, I am so happy to appreciate the sincere efforts of D.K. Printworld (P) Ltd. in publishing the book with critical editing.

Abbreviations

AA	*Aṅguttara Nikāya Aṭṭhakathā*
Abhi	*Abhidhānappadīpikā*
AN	*Aṅguttara Nikāya*
BD	*The Book of Discipline*
CDB	*The Connected Discourses of the Buddha*
DN	*Dīgha Nikāya*
DA	*Dīgha Nikāya Aṭṭhakathā*
Dialogues	*Dialogues of the Buddha*
Dh	*Dhammapada*
DhA	*Dhammapaṭṭhakathā*
Dhs	*Dhammasaṅghani*
DPPN	*Dictionary of Pali Proper Names*
DSM-IV	*Diagnostic and Statistical Manual of Mental Disorders (4th edn)*
ESB	*Encyclopedia of Sexual Behavior*
GS	*Gradual Sayings*
It	*Iti-Vuttaka*
J	*Jātakam*
KhA	*Khuddakapāṭha Aṭṭhakathā*
KS	*Kindred Sayings*
LODB	*The Long Discourses of the Buddha*

Miln	*Milindapañha*
MN	*Majjhima Nikāya*
MA	*Majjhima Nikāya Aṭṭhakathā*
MLDB	*The Middle Length Discourses of Buddha*
ND	*Niddesa I & II*
PED	*Pali-English Dictionary*
Pv	*Petavatthu*
PvA	*Petavatthu Aṭṭhakathā*
SN	*Saṃyutta Nikāya*
SA	*Saṃyutta Nikāya Aṭṭhakathā*
Sn	*Sutta Nipāta*
SnA	*Sutta Nipāta Aṭṭhakathā*
Th.I.	*Theragāthā*
ThagA	*Theragāthā Aṭṭhakathā*
Th.II	*Therigāthā*
ThigA	*Therigāthā Aṭṭhakathā*
Ud	*Udāna*
Vv	*Vimānavatthu*
VvA	*Vimānavatthu Aṭṭhakathā*
Vin	*Vinaya*
VinA	*Vinaya Aṭṭhakathā*
Vism	*Visuddhimagga*

1

Introduction

Introduction to Deviant Sexual Behaviour

THE concept of deviant sexual behaviour deals with the sexual practices that are considered as going against social and cultural expectations and violation of norms and values on sexuality established by traditional social systems. Conceptualizing certain sexual acts as unnatural or deviant is grounded on the assumption that heterosexual penile–vaginal sex within the institution of marriage is morally acceptable and natural. Sexual taboos and prohibitions are involved in various aspects of the human being at personal level and at social in that they have become an inevitable field of research and discussion.

Among the most distinctive features of human sexuality are the number of prohibitions and the importance attached to sexual behaviour. Violations of sexual prohibitions are regarded as one of the more serious infractions an individual can commit. It seems that the large amount of valuation that occurs with human sexuality is a reflection of the importance of human sexuality to the well-being of the individual and of the species, as well as the potential of sexual misbehaviour to result in serious harm to others. Owing to this problematic nature of the behaviour, the study on the concept of deviant sexual behaviour has become a multi-disciplinary subject of discussion in the modern world. This multi-disciplinary approach has given rise to a host of theories, arguments, views and explanation on the topic.

The diversity of views and the impact of this type of human behaviour create an interest in the researcher's mind to look for different sources of human knowledge connected with the subject. I find it quite interesting and useful to make an investigation into this topic as found in the Buddhist scriptures. Buddhism has been established with its own doctrinal tenets and ethical system aiming at the release of human kind from suffering. Buddhism explains human being and his behaviour on the theoretical basis of cause and effect accepting conditionality of the phenomena. Being subject to be conditioned is seen as the reason of suffering or the issue. The Buddha in the first step recognizes the issue and its cause, then, prescribes a way to reach the solution of the issue. The set of doctrinal teachings expounds the nature of human problem (*dukkha*) and its cause (*avijjā* and *taṇhā*) and the ethical system shows how to get rid of the problem. The present study will be based on these two lines of doctrinal and ethical teachings because the information on sexuality found in scriptures has been produced in relation to them. The *Sutta Piṭaka* and the *Vinaya Piṭaka* of the Pali canon that belong to the Theravada school of Buddhism have been selected as the main sources for the study considering the nature of their contents. That is, the *Sutta Piṭaka* includes the doctrinal aspect of the Buddha's teaching and the *Vinaya Piṭaka* includes corresponding ethical blueprint aimed at realizing the goal of *nibbana* (ultimate solution for suffering).

This issue is concerned with what is deviant sex and what is normal sex. Sexologists, sociologists, medical scientists, anthropologists, and religious theorists are only a few that are trying to explain and analyse it. The penile–vaginal sexual intercourse between man and woman, who are legally married to each other, is universally accepted as normal sexual behaviour. In addition to this form of sexual expression, there can be seen a variety of practices such as masturbation, pederasty, exhibitionism, etc. utilized by human being to gain sexual gratification. It is accepted that to define a sex act as normal or deviant is very difficult because this phenomenon is understood in relative to society, culture, place, person, etc. One has to follow many restrictions, cultural values, religious restraints, social expectations and legal prohibitions in talking about sex and engaging in it. Religious teachings and sexuality are seen as two integral phenomena. Buddhism, Christianity, Islam, Hinduism and Judaism, the five main world religions have expounded their own views on sexuality.

Sensuality and Sexuality in Buddhism

The early Buddhist discussion on sensuality is worthy to be examined to understand the nature of sexuality because it belongs to the domain of sensuality. In this context, the term *kāma* has to be examined. The Buddha's understanding gained about the issue of *saṁsāra* and the way to get out of it is briefly expressed in the formula of four noble truths. The second noble truth *dukkha samudaya sacca* explains the cause of suffering. Thirst (*taṇhā*) is given in three aspects as the root of all suffering. The three aspects of it are:

i. *kāma-taṇhā* (desire for sensual pleasure),

ii. *bhava-taṇhā* (desire for existence), and

iii. *vibhava-taṇhā* (desire for annihilation) — *Vin* I.10

Kāma-taṇhā is described as the desire for the gratification derived through five senses eye, ear, nose, tongue and body. The *Mahāsatipaṭṭhānasutta* defines the sensual pleasure including mind as the sixth sense:

> What things in this world are dear, what things are pleasant, the sense of sight, the sense of hearing, the sense of smell, taste, touch, and imagination — these are the things in this world that are dear, that are pleasant.
>
> — *Dialogues* II.342

The pleasure of sensual gratification leads the individual to remain in the sāṁsāric existence as it is meant by the term *bhava-taṇhā*. The theory of cause and effect (*paṭiccasamuppāda*) expounds that grasping (*upādāna*) is the cause of continuation of the existence (*bhava*). *Upādānas* are fourfold:

- *kāma* — grasping of sensual pleasure
- *diṭṭhi* — speculation
- *sīlabbata* — beliefs in rites
- *attavāda* — belief in the soul theory — *DN* II.58; *MN* I.51

The first item represents thirst (*taṇhā*) and ignorance is represented by the latter three. These are the very basic reasons to remain in the *saṁsāra*. It is clear from this short reference to the philosophical doctrine of *paṭiccasamuppāda* that sensual desire is directly related to suffering of rebirth and death.

As to the psychological aspect of the term *kāma*, the concept of *āsava* and *anusaya* is noteworthy. *Kāma* is given both as one of *āsava* (*DN* II.84) and *anusaya* (*DN* III.254). *Āsavas* are the most binding and deeply entrenched of all misplaced tendencies needing to be "rooted out" (Hamilton 1996: XXV). These are given as lists of three or four in the *Sutta Piṭaka*. The *Sammādiṭṭhisutta* mentions of three: the *āsava* of sense desire (*kāmāsava*), *āsava* of desire for continuous becoming (*bhavāsava*) and *āsava* of ignorance (*avijjāsava*) (*MN* I.55). The fourth is the *āsava* of holding views (*diṭṭhāsava*). It is clear that these form the very basis of human psyche and dominate both affectional and cognitive aspects of the individual. These exist as latent tendencies in the consciousness and function as intoxicants of the mind (*PED*, pp. 114-15).

The Buddhist understanding of latent tendencies of *āsavas* can be seen by their being given as the cause of *avijjā* (ignorance) in the canon. Ven. Sāriputta states that as *āsavas* arise, ignorance arises, and as *āsavas* become extinct, ignorance also becomes extinct.[1] The extinction of these brings about enlightenment (*khīṇāsava*).

A similar emphasize can be seen on the other list of mental biases of *anusaya*. They have been translated into English as bent, bias, proclivities, the persistence of dormant or latent disposition, predisposition and tendency (*PED*, pp. 114-15). These are given as seven in several places in the canon. They are: proclivity of sense desire (*kāmarāgānusaya*), proclivity of anger (*paṭighānusaya*), proclivity of view (*diṭṭhānusaya*), proclivity of doubt (*vicikicchānusaya*), proclivity of conceit (*mānānusaya*), proclivity for rebirth (*bhavarāgānusaya*) and proclivity of ignorance (*avijjānusaya*). We can see four of *anusayas* similarly found among the list of *āsavas*, sensual desire, desire for continued existence, views and ignorance. The profundity of *anusayas* is suggested by their being mentioned together with the *āsavas*.

These two categories of *āsava* and *anusaya* jointly represent "part of human nature". Cyclically reinforced over many lives, they have become embedded in an individual's psychological make-up (Hamilton 1996: 77). From this short reference made to Buddhist psychological explanation, it

---

[1] *āsava samudayā avijjā samudayo, āsavanirodhā avijjā nirodho* — *MN* I.54

becomes clear that sensual desire has been understood as a deep-rooted psychological phenomenon. The term *kāma* has occurred in the canon in combination with the words such as *rāga*, *chanda*, *āsā* and *nandi*, all of which are connected with grasping.

According to Buddhist cosmological mapping, three plains of existence are accepted, viz. the world of sensual desire (*kāmaloka*), the world of fine matter (*rūpaloka*) and the world of non-matter (*arūpaloka*). Terms like *kāmāvacāra*, *kāmabhava* and *kāmadhātu* refer to the same cosmological state as the first world mentioned above. The world of desire is composed of six divine abodes, the human world and four hells (*SN* II.151). Beings in these eleven places are led by desire for pleasure of the senses (*kāmanīta* — *J* II.214-15) and they are dependent on it (*kāmanissita* — *Miln* 11). An individual led by the desire for worldly pleasure seeks every possible ways and means to get what he wishes. Sometimes, he has no regard for morality or immorality involved in the act done in search of enjoyment of the senses (*Vism* 573-74). Such a person goes blind by passion (*kāmandha*) (*Ud* 76).

To distinguish sexual pleasure from sensual pleasure, as one shade of the term *kāma* is used in the Buddhist scriptures, seems to be somewhat controversial. K.N. Jayatilleke has clearly distinguished sexual pleasure from sensual pleasure admitting that *kāma-taṇhā* refers to sexual pleasure and recognizing it as of independent nature. To quote Jayatilleke (1980: 233):

> We get satisfaction from time to time by gratifying our desire for sensuous pleasures and sex (*kāma-taṇhā*).

Ven. Hammalawa Saddhatissa, discussing the term *kāma* in the third precept, says that it signifies abstinence from indulgence in all the five sense objects, viz. sight, sound, smell, taste and touch. As he interprets, the term *kāma* includes all kinds of sensual gratification (Saddhatissa 1987: 92). I feel that it is useful to refer to Rhys Davids and W. Stede in connection with the interpretation of the third precept:

> *Kāma* as sensual pleasure finds its most marked application in the sphere of the sexual: *kāmesu micchācārin*, transgressing in the lusts, sinning in the lusts of the flesh, or violating the third rule of conduct equivalent to *abrahmacariyā*, inchastity Pug 38, 39; It 63, etc. *itthi-kāmehi paricāreti* "he enjoys himself with the charms of woman" S iv.343. *Kāmesu brahmacariyavā* practising chastity *Sn* 1041. *Kāmattha* for sexual amusement *A* III.229. – *PED*, p. 204

When we examine these contexts in the canon, it seems that Jayatilleke's interpretation is acceptable.

Buddhist teaching accepts that sensuality and sexuality are a barrier to enlightenment. Buddhism has made a methodological approach to its discourse on sexuality. This methodology consists of three aspects:

i. *assāda* – enjoyment,

ii. *ādīnava* – consequences (adversive), and

iii. *nissaraṇa* – getting rid of the problem.

The application of this methodology in this context is found in the *Kāmasutta* of the *Sutta Nipāta*. In the first step, if an individual obtains what he wishes, he becomes enraptured in mind. In the second step, if the individual loses what is loved, he is hurt as though pierced by a barb (*sallaviddhova ruppati*). Due to this problematic nature of attachment to sensuality, a mindful person should always avoid sensual pleasures (Norman 1993: 90).

Buddhism consists of doctrinal understanding connected with a practice leading to the final goal. While the Dhamma represents the doctrinal analysis, the Vinaya follows the practice. The path that leads people to the final goal of *nibbana* is recognized as an ethical one that should be followed by both the monk and lay communities. The doctrinal teachings are common to both categories of followers. In contrast to this equality regarding Dhamma, the degree of emphasis upon the practice bears two different attitudes towards the ecclesiastical society and the lay society.

The *bhikkhu-bhikkhuṇī* community is entirely committed to the pursuit of the religious life whereas the laity is offered freedom to work for the goal at some ease. However, both the groups must adhere to basic ethical promulgations. The twofold attitude towards the ethical restrictions becomes clearer in the context of sexuality. For the monks and nuns, sex is completely prohibited but for the laity, it can be enjoyed at one's will within the ethical frame. As the Buddhist life is supposed to be ethically right, every action should necessarily be in accordance with the ethical system.

Ethically, the Buddhist lay life is based on the five precepts. The third precept is concerned with one's sex life and it prohibits sexual misconduct. The norm for the lay people's sexual life is found in this precept. Marriage life is necessarily involved here and sexuality within the institution of marriage is considered as normal and acceptable for the laity. Any violation of the third precept, according to the Buddhist value system, falls into immoral behaviour and eventually can be classified under deviant sexual behaviour.

The moral system is inevitably connected to the theory of *kamma* and rebirth that prophesies rewards and punishments for one's moral and immoral deeds. In Buddhist scriptures, the moral or immoral nature of one's sex life is accepted as a factor that determines the place of birth (pleasant or unpleasant) in the next life. The Buddhist attitude towards deviant sexual behaviour discussed in the present thesis is based on this point of view.

As for the Buddhist monastic community, it was mentioned above that sex is completely impermissible. The *Vinaya Piṭaka* details every practice applicable to the monastic life. The four grave offences connected with the life of the monk entail expulsion from the order in case of their commitment. Sexual conduct with opposite sex, stealing, killing a human being and lying about superhuman attainments form the top category of Vinaya rules. The first rule indicates the adherence to celibacy as the ground of noble conduct (*brahmacariya*).

Abstinence from sexual behaviour is a common practice among Indian mendicants who had given up household life in search of eternal freedom from worldly suffering. So, celibacy was the norm for the Buddhist monastic community too, concerned with sexuality. One of the major criticisms of the Buddha was directed against the contemporary trend in his society for self-indulgence (*kāmasukhallikānuyoga*). The first violation of the norm of celibacy within the Buddhist monastic order is reported to have been committed by the elder Sudinna with his former wife (*Vin* III: 18). Following this incident, the Buddha lay down the first Vinaya rule in the legal form against the sexual conduct by the Saṅgha (*Vin* III: 21). There can be seen a range of violations related to the rule appearing within the community. The *Suttavibhaṅga* is a rich source to study those episodes.

According to the norm established for the community of

monks and nuns, any conscious sex act is a sexual deviation. Nevertheless, a closer examination into the nature of severity attributed to certain sex acts differ from one category to another. This fact is important in a discussion on deviant sex among the clergy. The bulk of information on deviant sexual behaviour in the Pali Sutta and Vinaya sources are entwined with several aspects of human life and thinking ranging from the very basic sex act to deep psychological, philosophical, ethical and societal phenomena.

Defining Deviant Sexual Behaviour

The concept of deviant sexual behaviour is involved in the nature of naturalness and unnaturalness of sex acts of human beings. Heterosexuality, which is procreative, is universally accepted to be normal. Procreative sex is involved in penile-vaginal intercourse between male and female. Yet, there exist a number of variations of sexual practices such as masturbation, homosex and incest which have been labelled deviant or unnatural.

Historically, we can see attitudinal changes regarding sexual customs in the course of time. If we look back to Western history, the first discussion on natural and sterile sex is traceable to Plato. Plato in his *Symposium* deals with the relative merits of heterosexual and homosexual love, and the relation between (erotic) love and other goods such as knowledge. It classifies homosexuality as "unnatural" because it is sterile. The next evidence of laws against deviant sex can be found in the Old Testament of the Bible. All the sexual acts that are currently legislated against in the criminal law owe their stigma to the Judeo-Christian religious tradition (Gagnon 1968: 216).

During the medieval time, in England, Holland and

some other Western countries, extramarital sexual activity including fornication, adultery, concubinage, homosexuality and prostitution were repressed (Posner 1992: 16). In the nineteenth century, the Victorian science discovers child sexuality as a menace to society. Specially, masturbation came to be known as a cause of feeble-mindedness, insanity, criminality, homosexuality and sterility. In traditional Catholic thought, masturbation is a mortal sin because it is a form of non-marital, non-procreative and, therefore, "disordered" sex.

In the nineteenth century, the study of sexuality became a wider field and was divided into two streams as speculative and empirical (ibid.: 18). Richard von Krafft-Ebbing (1886) and Sigmund Freud (1972) had done their researches on a speculative basis and Havelock Ellis and Magnus Hirschfield had conducted empirical researches. Modern sexology is a multi-disciplinary subject mingled with psychology, biology, anthropology, sociology and some other fields of study on human behaviour and sexuality. Among the sexological studies that appeared during the mid-twentieth century, the two works produced by Alfred C. Kinsey et al., *Sexual Behavior in the Human Male* (1948) and *Sexual Behavior in the Human Female* (1953) are valuable sources that reveal deviant sexual practices existing in American society in addition to the normative penile–vaginal sex among married couples.

Parallel to the constant attempt to repress sexual acts denied by social, cultural, religious and other institutional forces, the maintenance of such behaviour is also evident in human social history. On the other hand, there is no universally accepted value system to judge a sexual act as normal or undesirable. The acceptability or denial is dependent on a variety of factors such as culture, place and religious value system. In relation to the existence of variable sex acts, a frequently raised question is "What are the reasons for the attachment to prohibitory rules, coupled with the failure to apply sanctions?" The answer to this question is involved in several aspects of human life.

Sex is accepted as a strong biological drive that needs to be fulfilled. Another assumption is that all of the variance of sexual behaviour is attributable to social and psychological factors. But this assumption is found to be unacceptable since there is a lack of data on the relation between these elements and the biological facts. It has been accepted that both basic biological characteristics and differential socialization practices are equally influential factors that give rise to some of the differences between the overt sexual behaviour of males and females (Gagnon 1968: 216).

To explain sexual perversions, Sigmund Freud introduced the theory of psychosexual development undergone by children. This developmental process passes through five stages: oral, anal, phallic, latency and genital. Each stage has a predominant erogenous zone of development. Each stage gives rise to certain kinds of conflict and inadequate or excessive gratification in any stage can lead to fixation in that age and the development of traits and sexual preferences characteristic of that stage. *Three Essays on the Theory of Sexuality* (1972/1905) by Sigmund Freud carries on his discussion on this matter in relation to infantile sexuality tracing the cause of sexual aberration into childhood.[2]

[2] A good proportion of the deviations from normal sexual life which are later observed both in neurotics and in perverts are thus established from the very first by the impressions of childhood — a period which is regarded as being devoid of sexuality. – Freud 1972/1905: 148

→

Modern psychologists refer to sexual deviations by the term paraphilia and they emerge in one's personality due to obstructed prenatal, post-natal aspects in the development of the child (McKinney 1994: 395-96).

Prior to proceeding with the discussion of definitions of deviant sexual behaviour, let us examine the etymology of the term "deviant". It has come into vogue during the period of Middle English (1350–1400) and has been derived from the late Latin stem of *devians*, present participle of *deviare* to deviate. The term deviant functions both as an adjective and as a noun, and adjectivally it means deviating or departing from the norm characterized by deviation. As a noun, it means "a person or thing that deviates or departs markedly from the accepted norm".[3]

The verb deviate (transitive) occurs in the meanings of to turn aside as from a route, way, course, etc. to depart or swerve, as from a procedure, course of action, or acceptable norm, and to digress, as from a line of thought or reasoning. In the use of the noun, deviate means "a person whose sexual behaviour departs from the norm in a way that is considered socially or morally unacceptable".[4] This dictionary meaning seems to be the best applicable to the present study.

← A perversion in childhood, as is well known, may become the basis for the construction of a having a similar sense and persisting throughout life, one which consumes the subject's whole sexual life.

– Freud, 2001 (1919): 192

[3] *Random House Unabridged Dictionary*, p. 543; Morris' *The American Heritage Dictionary* (1985), p. 389: One that differs from a norm, especially a person whose behavior and attitudes differ from accepted social standards.

[4] *Random House Unabridged Dictionary*, p. 543.

SEXOLOGICAL DEFINITIONS

The article published by Clifford Allen on sexual perversions in *The Encyclopedia of Sexual Behavior* defines sexual perversion as follows:

> Sexual perversions (also called sex deviations, paraphilias, or psychosexual abnormalities) are ways in which sex gratification is obtained, mainly or exclusively, without penile–vaginal intercourse. Perversion may occur by the individual's selecting an abnormal sexual object or by engaging in abnormal relations with usual sex objects.
>
> – Allen 1961: 802

From the biological point of view, the primary aims of sex are pleasure and reproduction and include, at some stage, coitus between a man and a woman. When these aims are entirely sidetracked and out of fear or fixation, the usual modes of heterosexual intercourse are completely omitted, then the individual's behaviour is considered deviant. The deviant's choice of sexual object may be someone of the same sex (homosexuality), an immature person (infanto-sexuality), or an animal (bestiality), or if his choice of object is heterosexual, his deviation may take the form of fetishtic attachment to or injuring of another person (sadism), being injured (masochism), or oral–genital or anal–genital relations used as an exclusive substitute for penile–vaginal coitus (Allen 1961: 802).[5]

---

[5] This article has given a list of perversions with a brief account on each of them. The writer makes his classification based on the assumption that a sexual perversion can occur either by wrongly behaving to the right object or by selecting a wrong object. So, classification is made under two headings as "disorders of sexual expression" and "disorders of the instinctual object".

1. *Disorders of Sexual Expression:*

→

The definition of Clifford Allen has considered almost all aspects of sexual deviation in accordance with the

---

← i. Sexual oralism — fellatio and cunnilinctus

ii. Sexual analism — the use of anus for sexual purposes

iii. Other forms of abnormal orificial sexuality — using fissure beneath the breast, the armpit and the folds between the thighs

iv. Coprophilia and coprophagia — abnormal interest in excrements and a desire to eat secretions and excretions

v. Masochism — male and female (wish to hurt and to be hurt = sadomasochism)

vi. Frottage — rubbing against strangers

vii. Scoptophilia and Exhibitionism — observing others' genitals and showing one's own in public

2. *Disorders of the Instinctual Object:*

i. Homosexuality — sex between the members of the same sex

ii. Transvestism — sexual ratification from dressing in the clothes of opposite sex

iii. Transsexualism — wish to change one's sex

iv. Infanto-sexuality — the use of an immature person as a sexual object

v. Bestiality — the use of an animal as a sexual object

vi. Autosexuality — perversions used on oneself (masturbation)

vii. Necrophilia — use of a dead body as a sexual object

viii. Gerontosexuality — use of an elderly person as a sexual object

It should be noted that most of these behaviours are considered perversions only when they become fixated or main way of getting sexual excitement.

understanding of the subject in the 1950s and 1960s. Specially, the *Diagnostic and Statistical Manual of Mental Disorders* (*DSM*-I: 1952 and *DSM*-II: 1968) published by the American Psychiatric Association (APA) defined homosexuality as deviant (Milner and Dopke 1997: 394f). The *DSM*-III (1980) did not include homosexuality in the classification of paraphilias (the word "deviant" was dropped from the *DSM*-III assuming the term "paraphilia" is more scientific) (Mckinney 1994: 395) and included "ego dystonic homosexuality" as paraphiliac (Suppe 1987: 112). This shows that perception of deviation is changeable from time to time and from the biological aspect of sex, deviation can occur in homosexuality by being away from the aim of procreation. According to this definition, adultery or fornication can be accepted as normal, which are unacceptable in Buddhism, Christianity and other religious systems. Williams Simon defines sexual deviance as follows:

> Sexual deviance might be defined as the inappropriate or flawed performance of conventionally understood sexual practices. – Simon 1996: 117

In Clifford Allen's definition, the terms paraphilia, deviation and psychosexual abnormalities are used as synonyms for "sexual perversions" (see fn. 5). In contrast to this view, Simon sees sexual deviance and perversion as two aspects and their distinction depends on larger categories of social practice than those that are specifically sexual. Rape is an act of transsexual deviation that is rarely defined as an act of perversion. Simon defines perversion as:

> Perversion can be thought of as a disease of desire, not only in the sense that it appears to violate the sexual practices of a time and place, but also it constitutes a violation of common understandings that render current sexual practice plausible. – 1996: 118

Perversion is a form of desire too mysterious and sometimes too threatening to the elementary definitions of desire and satisfaction to be tolerated. The "pervert's behaviour is psychologically problematic to the society" (ibid.).

The *Encyclopaedia Britannica Micropaedia's* entry on sexuality defines deviant sex as:

> Sexual deviation is defined here as any pattern of behaviour including a habitual, preferred, compelling need for sexual gratification by any technique other than willing coitus between man and woman and involving actions that directly result in genital excitement. — Stroller 1982: 601

According to this definition, any sexual act with the exception of penile–vaginal intercourse is a deviation if that is characterized as being habitual, preferred and compelling. This definition implies that occasional experience of the variable sex acts cannot be classified as deviations. The second part of the definition considers mutual willingness between a man and a woman as constituting an acceptable sex act. By that, any forcible sex act is considered to be deviant.[6]

The definitions examined above were taken from sexological studies. Two definitions (of Allen and *Encyclopaedia Britannica Micropaedia*) emphasize sexual intercourse (penile–vaginal) between man and woman as acceptable. Fixation, preference and will of the partner are decisive characteristics of deviation. Deviation can arise by wrong behaviour to the right object and by the selection of a wrong object. Simon sees convention as a decisive factor in judging deviation.

---

[6] The degree of consent of the partner is a factor that decides deviance of a sex act.

SOCIOLOGICAL DEFINITIONS

Let's examine a few definitions from sociological studies. John H. Gagnon's definition is:

> Deviance is traditionally conceived of as being antithetical to the values of the larger social system, although it is thought to have value punishment of it reinforces conformity.
>
> – Gagnon 1968: 217

As this writer says, any form of deviation is an opposite phenomenon to the value system of the larger society, but it has some benefit by being conducive to reinforce the "accepted" behaviour. This definition has been made on a basis of functionalism. Christopher Hensley and Richard Tewksbury in collaboration discuss how to determine a sexual act to be deviant:

> A sexual act is commonly perceived as deviant according to one or combination of the following conditions: i. the degree of consent, ii. the nature of sex object, iii. the nature of the sex act, or iv. the setting in which the sex act occurs.
>
> – Hensley and Tewksbury 2003: 5

In addition to these conditions, sociologists recognize two other dimensions in determining which activities are deviant (Wheeler 1960): the degree of outrage felt by others concerning a certain behaviour and how common the activity is practised in general society (Hensley and Tewksbury 2003: 5). Hensley and Tewksbury further defining sexual deviation say:

> When most people hear the phrase "sexual deviance" they assume that it involves some form of pathology or psychological disorder. In reality, however, sexual deviance can have little to do with either. Sexual deviance

> merely refers to socially disapproved characteristics and behaviours that incite negative reactions, punishments, ostracism, or ridicule. – Ibid.: 3-4

These authors distinguish sexual deviation from the common understanding of paraphilias as deviant sexual expressions. Deviation is solely explained as social construction. The sociological definitions necessarily view violation of norms as deviant behaviour (Levin 1994: 368).[7]

MEDICAL SCIENTIFIC DEFINITIONS

In Medical science, sexual deviance falls into the category of mental disorders. Defining a mental disease or a mentally unhealthy condition is still found to be a difficult task among the mental health professionals. Medical researchers on deviant sexual behaviour point out that there exists a lack of well-supported criteria upon which to distinguish permissible or healthy sexual behaviour from unhealthy and deviant behaviour. It is difficult to provide clear demarcations to distinguish normal from abnormal behaviour (Laws and O'Donohue 1997: 1). The existence of abnormal sexual behaviour is accepted. To have an idea about this, let's refer to how the *Diagnostic and Statistical Manual of Mental Disorders* (*DSM*) (1994) of the American Psychiatric Association (APA) defines a mental disorder:

> a clinically significant behavioural or psychological syndrome or pattern that occurs in an individual and that is associated with present distress (e.g. a painful symptom) or disability (i.e. impairment in one or more important areas of functioning or with a significantly increased risk of suffering death, pain, disability or an important loss

[7] Norms means, widely accepted rules for behaviour that apply to specific social situations.

> of freedom. In addition, this syndrome or pattern must not be merely an expectable and culturally sanctioned response to a particular event, for example, the death of loved one. Whatever its original causes, it must currently be considered a manifestation of a behavioural, psychological or biological dysfunction in the individual. Neither deviant behaviour (e.g. political, religious or sexual) nor conflicts that are primarily between the individual and the society are mental disorders unless the deviance or conflict is a symptom of a dysfunction in the individual as described above (pp. xxi–xxii). –Laws and O'Donohue 1997: 2

By the authors of *DSM*-IV (1994) of the APA, sexual deviance has been regarded as a mental disorder because it is a *symptom of a dysfunction*[8] *in the individual.* There are three types of dysfunctions: behavioural, psychological and biological. Sexual disorder or paraphilia is judged by the following criteria in the *DSM*-IV:

> The tendencies, sexual urges, or behaviours cause clinically significant distress or impairment in social, occupational, or other important areas of functioning.
>
> – Laws and O'Donohue 1997: 2-3

The first part of the criterion states that an individual must be distressed by his or her sexual fantasies, urges, or behaviour. The second half explains that there should be impairment in social, occupational or other important areas of functioning. This aspect is something unable to be diagnosed and it is more societal than scientific. This criterion has taken into consideration both mental health and social well-being.

---

[8] Dysfunction in an individual may be (i) distress, (ii) disability, or (iii) a significantly increased risk of suffering death, pain or an important loss of freedom.

There can be seen a historical evolution of the process of classifying sexual disorders by the psychiatrists (Suppe 1987: (11-36). The *DSM*-IV has classified sexual disorders under mental disorders, and sexual disorders are referred to as "paraphilias"[9] instead of deviations in order to give a scientific basis. The sexual paraphilias listed in the *DSM*-IV are as follows:

i. *Exhibitionism* — sexual excitement obtained by exposing one's own genitals to an unsuspecting stranger; seems to occur in males exposing themselves to females.

ii. *Fetishism* — use of non-living objects as the preferred or exclusive method of obtaining sexual arousal

iii. *Frotterism* — touching and rubbing against non-consenting person; this usually occurs in crowds.

iv. *Paedophilia* — sexual activity with children.

v. *Sexual masochism* — sexual excitement caused by one's own suffering — being humiliated, beaten, bound, or otherwise made to suffer.

vi. *Sexual sadism* — sexual excitement caused by making someone else suffer.

vii. *Transvestic fetishism* — heterosexual male cross-dress as female and masturbates while imagining himself to be both the male and female subject of his sexual fantasy.

viii. *Voyeurism* — looking or "peeping" at naked or disrobing

---

[9] A diagnostic category used by the American Psychiatric Association to describe atypical sexual patterns of sexual arousal of behaviour that become problematic in the eyes of the individual or society such as fetishism or exhibitionism. The urges are recurrent and are either acted on or are distressing to the individual. (From Greek roots meaning "to the side of" [*para-*] and "loving" [*philos*].

individuals, usually strangers for sexual excitement.

– Schewe 1997: 424

In addition to these, the *DSM*-IV provides a list of sexual disorders named as not otherwise specified (NOS). This category is used to classify sexual disorders that occur either very infrequently or have not been sufficiently described in the literature to warrant a separate category.

Uncommon Paraphilias:

i. *Telephone scatologia* — sexual arousal associated with exposing a victim to sexual and obscene language over the telephone. Frequently, the caller will masturbate while talking to the victim.

ii. *Necrophilia* — a variation of fetishism and dead human bodies are the sexual object. Necrophiliac acts or fantasies are differentiated between "genuine" necrophiles and "pseudo necrophiles" based on the existence of "a persistent sexual attraction to the corpse".

iii. *Zoophilia* — intense and repetitive urges, fantasies, or sexual activity with animals.

iv. *Coprophilia and urophilia* — the use of feces or urine to obtain sexual arousal. These types of activities are sometimes incorporated into sadomasochistic rituals.

v. *Partialism* — a variation of a fetish and consists of exclusive arousal to a specific body part usually not associated with sexual activity.

vi. *Klishmaphilia* — giving or receiving enemas as the preferred method of sexual arousal.

– Penix 2008: 420-23

The short discussion implemented on the definitions on sexual deviance in the fields of sexology, sociology and medical science examines following three aspects:

1. Sexology is based on the idea of maintaining issue-free existence of sexual gratification so far as a sexual act is not problematic to the actor (subject) as well as to the acted (object) is accepted as normal. Perversion is subject to change its validity due to frequency of occurrence, age of the object and relationship to the object.[10] This proves that to decide a sex act as normal or perverted it should fulfil several conditions and the criterion is very flexible.
2. Sociology is concerned with social value system and considers sexual deviation as a socially constructed concept and sees as conducive to conformity in one sense.
3. Medical science is concerned with the health of the individual and it does not regard mere social, political or religious morals as criteria to judge a sexual act to be deviant but the diagnostic symptoms and clear impairment in many aspects of the individual's life.

It is clear that these subjects have taken into consideration certain limits in the enjoyment of sex in order to avoid harmful effects upon the individual and society from a value-free approach to sex. These studies make their approach from a secular viewpoint, whereas Buddhism holds a bifocal approach to sex, that is, sex as a worldly pleasure and a sex-free state achieved through the removal of basic tendencies

---

[10] It must be emphasized that sexual oralism, analism and other extravaginal forms of coitus are by no means perverted or neurotic under all or even most circumstances. They are part of mammalian heritage. It is only, therefore, when extravaginal forms of sexual behaviour become highly fetishtic, fixated, exclusive, obsessive-compulsive, or disorganized that we can correctly speak of a clinical manifestation of abnormality or perversion. – Allen 1961: 804

in the individual for lust, hatred and ignorance.

It is interesting to see in the Buddhist story of the genesis of the earth, and the evolutionary development of human institutions, the very first act of sex that took place between man and woman was considered to have been subjected to public protest. Sexuality has started as a deviant act. In this context, the Buddha is reported to have said that an act which was at one time considered as *adhamma*, now has come to be considered as *dhamma* (*DN* III.89). This statement is evident for admission of the relativity of popular attitudes towards human activities. Throughout social history, it can be seen that the change of value system from time to time determines desirability or undesirability of sexual matters and this is more evident in the late two or three centuries. The Buddhist discourse on sex runs beyond the present life and sees it as a cause of rebirth. And there is a doctrinal and ethical system to regulate sexual behaviour and finally to root out it. The attitude regarding deviant sex in the Pali Sutta and Vinaya has been formed on this basis.

Previous Studies

Within the last two–three decades, there have appeared a considerable number of researches on Buddhist sexuality. Pali, Sanskrit, Chinese, Tibetan and Japanese Buddhist scriptures have been sources for scholars to seek views on sexuality and gender. L.P.N. Perera has attempted a technically valuable research on sexuality based on the Pali *Vinaya Piṭaka*. He has tried to recognize variations of sexual behaviour included in the *Vinaya Piṭaka* in the light of modern sexological studies, and monastic terminology is explained in comparison with sexological terms. Perera reveals the nature of Indian sex life during the Buddha's time and before and after one–two centuries of Him. The episodes found in the *Vinaya Piṭaka* are examined by way of case-histories which were used by the sexologist, Alfred C. Kinsey in the explanation of his data. Perera says:

> The data we have dealt with are partly in the shape of case-histories. And case-histories, Kinsey and his associates state, do not reveal everything that people think or do. It has also been noted that sexual terminology itself bears the monastic stamp. – 1993: 248

The assertion is made that Buddhism arose in an urban social background wherein sexual stimuli were abundant. An attempt is made to prove the use of "eunuch" (*paṇḍaka*) as a foreign influence from the Arabian countries upon India (ibid.: 110-63).

Chamindaji Gamage's *Buddhism and Sensuality* has discussed sexuality and sensuality as integral aspects of human life. An attempt has been made to investigate canonical views and implications on sexual taboos, the institute of marriage, abortion and contraception. Chamindaji carries out his discussion from the viewpoint of sociocultural aspect of sexuality and the ethical views on it as reflected in the canon (1998: 4).

Another noteworthy work on sexuality in Buddhism is *Buddhism, Sexuality, and Gender* edited by José Ignacio Cabezon. Cabezon introduces the text:

> The essays in this collection focus on issues related to gender and sexuality in different Buddhist traditions.
> – 1992: vii

The investigations included in this collection have touched Buddhist doctrinal views and cultural aspect in relation to its theme. This text enlarges the cross-cultural experience and understanding on sex and gender in countries such as Sri Lanka and Japan where Buddhism has been contributory in moulding ideological basis. Leonard Zwelling's article in this work has made an investigation into homosexuality in the Indian Buddhist texts. The ideas found in both Pali and Sanskrit sources are associated with regard to the theme discussed. He launches a discussion on the terms of homosexual value, such as *paṇḍaka* (eunuch) and *ubhatobyañjanaka* (hermaphrodites) and position held by Buddhist expositors regarding the spiritual capacity of this type of persons (Zwelling 1992: 203-14).

The present study aims at examining both Sutta and Vinaya sources in relation to deviant sexual behaviour. The studies mentioned earlier on sexuality in Buddhist literature have attempted to reveal the Buddhist canonical and post-canonical views in relation to heterosexual and other forms of sexual behaviour. My attempt in this study is to make an investigation based on the classification of normal sexual deviations, pathological sexual deviations and sociological sexual deviations. This classification was produced by J. Gagnon and W. Simon (Gagnon and Simon 1967 in Hensley and Tewksbury 2003: 7). Their classification is utilized in order to systematically present the data on sex in the selected sources and to understand how Buddhism in its ethical system has dealt with sexual patterns classifiable under these three categories.

The present study is carried out as a textual study and a critical, comparative and descriptive approach will be made in examining the data in the sources. For that, sexological, sociological and medical scientific views are associated where it is necessary. By this attempt, the ethical basis that explains the consequences of deviant sexual acts will be clarified. Specially, the application of *kamma* and rebirth in relation to deviant sexual behaviour will be illuminated. The second purpose is to point out the nature of sexual freedom offered to lay society in the enjoyment of sex and this is discussed in comparison with certain deviant sex acts prohibited to the monastic community. The third matter to discuss is the relationship between the human body and deviant sexual behaviour. The fourth and the final theme viewed is the Buddhist psychological explanation of the origin of sexuality and its various expressions in relation to the concept of *kāma*. Based on this inquiry, I will propose that sexual deviation is a natural phenomenon arising from the source of the psychophysical complex, and according to Buddhism, it has been subject to ethical control.

This study consists of six chapters and a conclusion. The introductory chapter deals with the concept of sensuality and sexuality in brief, definitions of deviant sexual behaviour in sexology, sociology and medical science, a brief survey of previous studies and introduction to the Theravada Pali *Sutta Piṭaka* and *Vinaya Piṭaka*.

The second chapter, "Sensuality and Sexuality in Early Buddhism", deals with doctrinal teachings which examine the psychological and philosophical discussion in relation to the origin of sensual desire, sexual desire and their impact on sentient beings. Finally, it is pointed out that deviant sexual behaviour is an outcome of psychological obsession due to sensual desire.

In the third chapter, "Buddhist Attitude to Human Body" in the Theravada Buddhism is discussed in relation to sensual desire and sexual desire. The *pañcakkhandha* analysis, constitution of the human body and the attitude of negativism expressed towards the human body is discussed to recognize the importance of the human body as a seductive power to arouse sexual desire. It is pointed out that the body is an agent of temptation and a source of deviant sexual behaviour. The conclusion drawn is that negativism towards the human body in Theravada Buddhism is a result of understanding it as a seductive agent causing obstruction to the religious practice.

"Celibacy, Chastity and Normal Deviant Sexual Behaviour", the fourth chapter, in the first part, discusses the norms of celibacy and chastity as the criteria of deciding a sex act as deviant. The second part is dedicated to examine data on marriage, adultery and the practices of monogamy and polygamy. In the last section, premarital sex and masturbation are examined. The canonical and commentarial views are critically analysed with sexological views. The moral teachings concerned with these sexual practices in relation to lay and ecclesiastical societies are clarified.

The fifth chapter, "Pathological Deviant Sexual Behaviour", discusses rape, incest, exhibitionism, voyeurism and paedophilia. The data available on these are critically analysed. The moral basis is examined.

"Sociological Deviant Sexual Behaviour", the sixth chapter, provides data analysis on prostitution, homosexuality and pornography. The social background of maintaining these behaviours is discussed. The moral teachings are examined.

In the Conclusion, I point out that any deviant sexual act is rooted in the two fundamental components of the human psyche: desire for sensual gratification (*kāma-taṇhā*), and ignorance (*avijjā*), which forms an unrealistic image as an existing entity and thereby tempts the person to gratify this image (*atta*). As the second point, I show that while Buddhism accepts sexual pleasure as the highest sensual pleasure, it prescribes to experience it within acceptable ethical confines for the laity. The norm for its clergy is complete abstinence from sex, i.e. celibacy. Violation either of chastity (norm for laity) or celibacy is a morally wrong act, and thereby it comes to be recognized as an unwholesome deed. According to Buddhism, unwholesome acts (*akusala kamma*) cause the continuation of existence. So, from the Buddhist point of view, deviant sexual behaviour is a matter connected with sāṁsāric suffering.

Vinaya Piṭaka

The *Vinaya Piṭaka* belonging to the Theravada Pali canon is concerned with the moral conduct of the monastic community (*bhikkhu-bhikkhuṇī saṅgha*). The commentator Buddhaghoṣa defines: "because this disciplines the body and speech, it is called *vinaya*".[11] According to the Theravada tradition, the Buddha's message depends on the *Vinaya* or disciplinary conduct of the *saṅgha* community. C.A.F. Rhys Davids defines the *Vinaya Piṭaka* as "a thesaurus of monastic community" (*BD* I: lxi). John C. Holt mentions:

> The *Vinaya* is the product of one highly regarded attempt to define membership in that community, a serious reckoning with the central concern of "what it means to be Buddhist".
>
> \- 1981: 30

When the purpose and the nature of the contents of the text are examined, it is evident that it bears a legal effect concerned with the members of the celibate community. It

[11] *VinA* 18: *vividhavisesanayattā vinayanato ce 'va kāyavācānam, vinayatthavidhūhi ayam vinayo vinayo 'ti akkhāto.*

has compiled rules, regulations and punishments with an evolutionary process in order to regulate the behavioural conduct of the community.

The purpose of the *Vinaya Piṭaka* is to facilitate the path of achieving supreme bliss of enlightenment by constraining the outward conduct of monks and nuns who entered the order as ardent followers. The *Vinaya* aims at both personal cultivation and constructing an ideal character in front of the lay society. The precepts and guidance included in this book have been produced to fulfil those two goals. The attention paid to the society is proven by references frequently made to the public opinion in promulgating precepts (*Vin* I.44). Considering this aspect of the *Vinaya*, modern researchers conclude that this particular collection is aimed at outward life of the community. Rhys Davids and Hermon Oldenburg state:

> The vinaya contains the regulations for the outward life of the members of the Buddhist saṅgha. — 1990, SBE vol. 13: ix

However, the role of the *Vinaya* cannot be confined only to the external behaviour because the external discipline is directly conducive to mental discipline. The path (*paṭipadā*) leading to *nibbana*, the eight noble path, embodies the threefold precepts of *sīla*, *samādhi* and *paññā*, and is identified as the *tisso sikkhā*. Of these three cardinal precepts, *sīla* (virtue) forms the basis on which the other two rest. Well practised virtue brings about concentration leading to wisdom, whereby the cankers are destroyed.[12] The purpose of the *Vinaya Piṭaka* can be put thus:

> Discipline is the ethos of Buddhist monasticism: the trail

[12] *DN* II.118: *sīlaparibhāvito samādhi, samādhiparibhāvito paññā sammadeva āsavehi vimuccati.*

> head of the path of purity leading to *nibbana* and the fibre of the community's soul, a means to salvation and the nucleus of communal identity. – Holt 1981: 1

The division of the canonical *Vinaya Piṭaka*:

i. *Pātimokkha* (*bhikkhu-bhikkhuṇī*)

ii. *Vibhaṅga* or *Suttavibhaṅga* (*Mahāvibhaṅga* and *Bhikkhuṇīvibhaṅga*)

iii. *Khandhaka* (*Mahāvagga* and *Cullavagga*)

iv. *Parivāra*

The *Pātimokkha* contains basic *Vinaya* rules. The term *suttavibhaṅga* means "analysis of the *suttas*". These two texts have been composed as a commentary to the rules given in the *Pātimokkha*, which is generally accepted as the nucleus of the *Suttavibhaṅga*. Herman Oldenburg states that the *Pātimokkha*, "is the earliest specimen of Buddhist Vinaya literature that we possess" (*Vin* I: xv-xvi). Due to the close similarity of the style of producing rules in the two texts, Oldenburg concludes:

> The whole *Vibhaṅga* is nothing more than an extended reading of the *Pātimokkha*. – *Vin* I: xvi

Based on two reasons, Oldenburg argues:

i. the *Pātimokkha* contains only a set of rules without a commentary and illustrations whereas the *Suttavibhaṅga* represents a further extension in the applicability of rules. So the *Suttavibhaṅga* points to a later origin.

ii. The *Mahāvagga* and *Cullavagga* portions of the *Khandaka* division presuppose the existence of the *Pātimokkha* and account for the origins of its recital. – Vin I: xvii-xx

The *suttavibhaṅga* has got the same contents of the *Pātimokkha* with commentary and illustrations. Miss Horner defines the term *suttavibhaṅga* as follows:

> The word *sutttavibhaṅga* means analysis or classification (*vibhaṅga*) of a *sutta*, a term here applied to each rule or cause of training in the *Patimokkha*. The word *sutta*, in the Vinaya, probably does bear the meaning of rule. — Vin I: x

Rhys Davids examines the *Suttavibhaṅga* as follows:

> The book deals with each of the 227 rules in order and following throughout one set scheme or method. That is to say it tells us firstly how and when and why the particular rule in question came to be laid down. The historical introduction always closes with the words of the rule in full. Then, follows a very ancient word-for-word commentary on the rule — a commentary so old that it was already about 400 BCE considered so sacred that it was included in the canon. And the old commentary succeeded, where necessary, by further explanations and discussions of doubtful points. These are sometimes of great historical value. - 1896: 55

These statements made by the experts on this field give a sufficient understanding of the text.

The *Khandhaka* consists of the *Mahāvagga* and the *Cullavagga*. These serve as a continuation and a supplement to the *Suttavibhaṅga*. And, they also accommodate the evolutionary changes in the *Vinaya Piṭaka*. The growth of the order necessitated more and more regulatory guidance to maintain the membership with proper conduct as persons and a community. The *Khandhakas* have fulfilled this need.

The *Parivārapali* or *Parivārapāṭha* is the last book of the *Vinaya Piṭaka*. This book consists of nineteen chapters (according to the commentary, *soḷasaparivāra*) and it is considered as a book written by a Sri Lankan *bhikkhu*. When compared with the other texts of the *Vinaya Piṭaka*, this is not considered as having much importance. Jotiya Dhirasekera (1982: 13) expresses that the *Parivāra* has not done a really worthwhile contribution to the problems of monastic discipline.

The beginning of the *Vinaya* goes back to the Buddha's time as it is evident from the *Sutta-Vinaya* sources.[13] The Buddha's time is generally accepted to be *c.*566–486 BCE. There is no argument on the fact that the major rules were framed by the Buddha. But, the attribution of the whole *Vinaya* to the Buddha is somewhat debatable. Regarding this matter, I.B. Horner opines:

> Although the framing of each major rule without exception attributed to Gautama, it has never been suggested that at the inception of the Orders he thought over all the possible cases of wrong-doing and depravity of which the monks might be capable, and propounded a ready-made body of rules to meet every conceivable contingency. It is, however, more likely that the majority of rules grew up gradually as need arose and are the outcome of historical developments that went on within the order. – *BD* I: xv

As Horner views, it is acceptable that there had been a gradual development of the *Vinaya Piṭaka*. G.C. Pande, based on his readings of Rhys Davids and Oldenburg, assumes that the *Vinaya Piṭaka* had gone through five stages to reach its present form (Pande 1995: 18). In examining the historical value of data included in the *Vinaya*, it is of use to know how long the evolutionary process of the text had continued. Sukumar Dutt states that the compilation of the *Vinaya Piṭaka* came to be finalized a little earlier than the Vesālī Council:

---

13 *DN* II.154: The *Mahāparinibbānasutta* clearly states that the *vinaya* was laid down (*paññatta*) by the Buddha himself. *MN* III.10: *Gopakamoggallānasutta* reports the recital of the *Pātimokkha*.

> *Vinaya Piṭaka* ... points unmistakably to a final *diaskeuasis* which must have been a little earlier than the Council of Vesālī.
> – Dutt 1996: 11

E. Frauwallner, being somewhat different from Dutt, concludes that the entire compilation of the *Vinaya* should have taken place shortly before or after the Second Council. He sees the Second Council providing a perfect occasion to frame an authoritative text to prevent possible disputes over *Vinaya* in future. The *Skhandhaka* was compiled to meet this necessity. He concludes:

> This enables us to reach an even closer approximation in the datation of the old *Skhandhaka* text. It must have been composed shortly before or after the Second Council. And since the tradition places event in the year 100 or 110 after the *nirvāṇa*, the composition must go back to about 100 years after the *nirvāṇa* that is the first half of the fourth century BCE. — Frauwallner 1956: 67 in Holt 1995: 44 fn. 2

According to *Mahāvaṁsa* and *Dīpavaṁsa*, Oldenburg states that the Vesālī Council had occurred somewhere about 383 BCE and the revision of the *Vinaya* must have been somewhere before this time, but not much earlier. Hence, he makes the conjecture that this period was not far from 400 BCE (*Vin* I: xxxviii–ix). Grounding on the assumptions made by these scholars, it can be considered that 400 BCE remarked the finalization of the *Vinaya* development. Then, the conclusion reacheable is that the *Vinaya* has undertaken its course of evolution for three centuries: sixth, fifth and fourth century BCE.[14] Historically, this development period of the *Vinaya*

[14] L.P.N. Perera suggests that the third century BCE too can be included since the final redaction of the entire Pali canon was made during the Aśokan period. – 1993: 29

reflects the conditions of India up to early Mauryan period.

Value of Vinaya Piṭaka for the Study

In finding data on sexuality in the Buddhist literature, the *Vinaya Piṭaka* serves as the main source in the present study. Since the *Vinaya* is mainly intended on the external behaviour (the bodily and verbal restraint), there can be seen a considerable amount of information related to sex. The *Suttavibhaṅga* (*Mahāvibhaṅga* and *Bhikkhuṇīvibhaṅga*) starts with the rule of abstinence from sex. The method used by the compilers of this text has led to produce a good deal of data on sexual deviations. The bulk of information found in the *Vinaya Piṭaka* is directly connected with the ecclesiastical or minor society belonging to Buddhism. It has to be accepted that the roots of these practices run into the major society of that period. Accordingly, we can say that the *Vinaya* reveals certain aspects of sex life existed for two–three centuries in India. As to the value of sexual data in the *Vinaya Piṭaka*, it is, says Horner,

> interesting historically, scientifically and psychologically, and even psycho-analytically. – *BD* I: xxxvii

A salient feature that is seen in the *Vinaya Piṭaka* is its way of presenting sexual matters with openness. It is possible for someone to consider this as somewhat crude. Yet, the passages dealing with sexual matters in the *Vinaya* are free from deliberate indecency and obscenity as their purpose was completely a different one. And also, Horner points out that such a characteristic is not something strange to see in ancient literatures (*BD* I: xxxvi). This open approach to sex can be generally regarded as basically the expression of a more positive and accepting attitude towards the body, its function and appetites. Thus, *Vinaya* reveals the significance of the ethological frame of reference for human sexual behaviour (Gamage 1998: 43).

Buddhism was well-conscious of the power of sexual desire and emphasized the need of practising self-control by monks and nuns who were supposed to get enlightenment quicker than the laity. Within the monastic order, the *Vinaya* records about monks and nuns who were assailed by sexual desire (*anabhiratiyā pīḷitā*). As there was no permissible way at all to release the sexual tension, certain monks and nuns happened to practise different kinds of sexual acts.

In addition to heterosexual relationships, the *Vinaya Piṭaka* records a variety of sexual acts which are recognized as deviant sexual customs by modern sexologists. The recorded events whether they were actual or imagined as possibilities within a celibate society, Buddhism recognizes them as a danger to the spiritual seeker and making blemishes to moral purity, which is the initial stage and a primary need for the furtherance of inner development.

Abstinence from sex is a basic vow (celibacy) by an entrant to the monastic institute. As the complete abstinence from sex life is considered morality, so the violation of this morality is counted to be an act entailing bad results in this life as well as in the following life (rebirth). According to medical scientific investigations, masturbation is free from psycho-physical harm and makes no harm to fellow people. But, as for a monk, it is a serious offence and an obstacle to *brahmacariya*; therefore, it is unacceptable. Moreover, it is conducive to rebirth because such an act is necessarily characterized by craving. To know the early Buddhist approach to sexual transgressions by the monastic community, the *Vinaya Piṭaka* is the richest source within the Pali canon. Particularly, the *Bhikkhuvibhaṅga* and the *Bhikkhunīvibhaṅga* serve as the major sources in recognizing the Buddhist attitude to deviant sexual behaviour because they have included a range of deviant sexual patterns in the form of case studies.

In addition to the *Vinaya* texts, I examine the *Sutta Piṭaka* to have a doctrinal and psychological understanding of sexuality. Buddhist doctrinal teachings on human sexuality and sensuality spread light on realizing the deep-rooted causes leading the individual to seek various types of ways and means to achieve sensual pleasure. Like the *Vinaya Piṭaka*, the *Sutta Piṭaka* too becomes a source for open references to deviational sex acts. The Pali commentarial, sexological, sociological and medical scientific data are used to clarify the data in the major sources.

2

Sensuality and Sexuality in Early Buddhism

Introduction

THE concept of sensuality and sexuality is comprehended under the concept of *kāma* in the early Buddhist discourses. There is a systematic analysis of the concept of sensuality in the Pali scriptures. The Buddha's position on happiness is expressed by the statement that he accepts happiness as happiness wherever it is available (*SN* IV. 228). Accordingly, sense-pleasure is recognized as a kind of happiness (*sukha, assāda*) and sensual lust as a deep-seated psychological characteristic inalienable from human personality.

Buddhism as a liberating path for human beings in suffering looks into the cause from which it emerges. In this causal examination, sensual desire (*kāma-taṇhā*) comes to be recognized as a cause contributory to the sāṁsāric problem faced by sentient beings. Moreover, it was discovered by the Buddha that desire for sense gratification outweighs the amount of pleasure over its ill-effects. As a result of this understanding, it was unavoidable for the early scriptures to talk about the problematic nature of the thirst for sensual gratification. Due to the emphatic instructions to renounce the world afflicted by desire, Buddhism seems to have expressed a pessimistic outlook regarding sensuality. In this chapter, I try to examine the teachings that have been presented with a positive outlook on leading a life of sensuality as well as the views that enunciate the ill-effects of attachment to sensuality. Attempting so, it is intended to explain the origin of deviant sexual behaviour as a phenomenon arising from man's desire for sensual gratification misdirected by ignorance.

In the early canonical material, references to five strands of sensual pleasures (*pañcakāma guṇa*) are frequently found. The discourse of *Great Mass of Suffering* defines *pañcakāma guṇa* thus:

> What ... is the gratification in the case of sensual pleasure? ... there are these five codes of sensual pleasure. What are the five? Forms cognizable by the eye that is wished for, desired, agreeable and likeable, connected with sensual desire, and provocative of lust. Sounds cognizable by the ear. ... Odours cognizable by the nose. ... Flavours cognizable by the tongue. ... Tangibles cognizable by the body that are wished for, desired, agreeable and likeable connected with sensual desire, and provocative of lust. These are the five codes of sensual pleasure ... the pleasure and joy that arise dependent on these five codes of sensual pleasure are the gratification in the case of sensual pleasures.
>
> – *MN* I.85; *DN* I.245

In certain discourses, sense pleasure is defined in terms of six senses and their corresponding objects.[1] An examination of the term *kāma* for its meanings is important here, since it is the predominant word associated with both the concepts of

---

[1] *DN* II.308: The definition of sense pleasure including the mind is similar to modern definition of pleasure: "The gratification of the senses or of the mind; agreeable sensations or emotions; the excitement, relish, or happiness produced by the expectation or the enjoyment of something good, delightful, or satisfying;–opposed to pain, sorrow, etc."

sensual and sexual pleasure in the Pali canon. Sensual desire is constituted of two aspects. They are as follows:

1. *Objective*: pleasantness, pleasure-giving characteristic, an object of sensual enjoyment.
2. *Subjective*: (a) enjoyment, pleasure on occasion of sense contact; and (b) sense-desire.

Buddhist commentaries express 1 and 2 by *kāmīyatī ti kāmo* and *kāmetī ti kāmo*. *Kāma*, as sense desire and enjoyment *plus* objects of the same, is a collective name for all but the very higher or refined conditions of life. As Rhys Davids and W. Stede point out, the term has not been analysed until the later canonical texts were composed (*PED*, p. 203). In the *Mahāniddesa* appears the twofold division of desires, i.e. desire of objects (*vatthukāma*) and subjective desire (*kilesakāma*).[2] A more logical definition is given by Dhammapāla in the *Vimānavatthuaṭṭhakathā*. He classifies:

> i. *manāpiya rūpādi-visaya* (pleasant objects), ii. *chandarāga* (impulsive desire), iii. *sabbasmim lobha* (greed for anything), iv. *gāmadhamma* (sexual lust), v. *hitacchanda* (effort to do good), and vi. *seribhāva* (self-determination). — *VvA*, p. 9

The term in most instances in which it occurs connotes sensuality in the scriptures and it can sometimes be seen to refer to sexuality too (*AN* III.229). So, it can be concluded that the teachings pertaining to sensuality are equally applicable to sexuality too as it is a major aspect of sensuality.

The early Buddhist scriptures have listed different kinds of pleasures or happiness (*AN* I.80ff.). In the list given in the *Aṅguttara Nikāya*, it is mentioned that there are two kinds of pleasure, one is sensual pleasure (*kāmasukham*) and the

---

[2] *Nid.* I.1: *kāmā ti uddānato dve kāmā vatthukāmā ca kilesakāmā ca* ।

other is pleasure of giving up (*nekkhammasukham*) (*AN* I.80). Sensual pleasure is considered as generally associated with the lay community as indicated in the expression "the white-clad laymen enjoying sensual pleasures (*gihī odātavasanā kāmabhogino*)" (*DN* III.125; *MN* I.491f.) and something not to be associated with those who have renounced household living (*agocara* or *avisaya* to the *pabbajita*).

The Buddha claimed that his approach to the concept of sensuality was considered by himself as unique. As the *Mahādukkhakkhandhasutta* reports, other contemporary religious groups questioned how the Buddha's analysis of sense pleasures, material form and feelings differs from that of theirs because they too, possess a full understanding of related matters.[3] In reply to the question, the Buddha states that if wanderers of other sects were to be questioned as to what is the gratification, the danger and the escape in the case of sensual pleasures (material form and feelings), they would fail to give an explanation about the matter, and also, they would get into difficulties (*vighātam āpajjissanti*). The reason is that it is not their province (*avisaya*). (This implies that sensuality is a subject beyond perception or understanding like *kamma*, *Buddha* and *paticcasamuppāda* as given in the *suttas*.) Further, it is mentioned that only the Buddha and his disciples or a person learned from them, can give a satisfactory answer to these questions (*MN* I.85). When the comprehensive investigation made in the scriptures regarding the role of sensuality in promoting the continuation of the sāṁsāric cycle is considered, it is clear that the Buddha may have justification for this claim.

---

[3] *MN* I.84: This question was raised from monks and was reported to the Buddha.

The methodology adopted to analyse the concept of sensuality in the canon, consists of three aspects, that is the examination of the gratification (*assāda*), the danger (*ādinava*) and the escape (*nissaraṇa*) associated with sensuality (Norman 1993: 90). Here, it notes a difference in the methods used to explain the problem of suffering (*dukkha*) and one of the reasons (*kāma-taṇhā*) contributory to it. In the formula of four noble truths, danger (suffering) is discussed first whereas the analysis of sensuality begins from positive features of the phenomenon. We can assume two reasons for this disparity in methodology. One is sensual pleasure is the most appealing to the ordinary mind and therefore its direct denial could cause a fear in the listener (*AN* IV.438ff.). The other is that sensual pleasure is accepted as a kind of happiness (*AN* IV.80ff.).

The Buddha declares that the knowledge regarding the three aspects of sensuality was the result of his own research on the six senses: eye (*cakkhu*), ear (*sota*), nose (*ghāṇa*), tongue (*jivhā*), body (*kāya*) and mind (*mana*), and their corresponding external objects of material form (*rūpa*), sound (*sadda*), smell (*gandha*), taste (*rasa*), touch (*poṭṭhabba*) and thoughts (*dhamma*). In the *Saḷāyatana-Saṃyutta* of the *Saṃyutta Nikāya*, a comprehensive investigation has been implemented on various doctrinal matters on the basis of internal the six senses and their corresponding external objects. Here, each sense organ and object has been subjected to a thorough examination.

The Buddha says that before his enlightenment, while he was still a *bodhisatta*, the question occurred to him as to what are the gratification, the danger and the escape in the case of six internal sense bases and six external sense bases (*SN* IV.7f.). The pleasure and joy that arise dependent on the eye is the gratification in the eye. The danger in the eye is that it is impermanent, suffering and subject to change. The escape from the eye is the removal and abandonment of desire and lust for the eye (*CDB*, p. 1137).

The *sutta* represents the Buddha to have said that so long as he did not directly know as they really are the gratification, the danger and the escape of these internal (and external) sense bases, he did not claim to have awakened to perfect enlightenment that it is only after gaining the knowledge of them, that he did so (ibid.). Further, he asserts that he set out seeking the gratification, the danger and the escape with respect to the sense bases (internal and external) and has seen with wisdom just how far these three aspects extend from them (*SN* IV.8ff.).

This description is significant concerning the experimental value of the views on sensuality given in the scriptures and implies that the emphasis on giving up of attachment to sensual pleasure was not a mere dogmatic injunction but was based on first-hand knowledge.

Sensory Perception and Sensuality

In order to understand the real nature of any kind of phenomenon, it is necessary to look into its original state and the causes that are contributory to its manifestation. In early Buddhism, the method applied to understand the cause of suffering is the theory of cause and effect (*paṭiccasamuppāda*). Human beings derive pleasure from six senses and therefore it is incumbent upon them to understand the psychological processes connected to sense perception. Early canonical materials have examined in detail how the sensory process produces desire in the human mind on a causal basis. Let us examine at which point of the sensory process the sensual desire comes into manifestation.

The human body is constituted of the five aggregates of material form (*rūpa*), feelings (*vedanā*), perceptions (*saññā*), volitions (*saṅkhāra*) and consciousness (*viññāṇa*) (*SN* II.3-4). A passage in the *Aṅguttara Nikāya* explains how the body comes into being through physical and psychological factors. The elder Ānanda explains that the body has come into being through food (*āhārasambhūto*), craving (*taṇhāsambhūto*), pride (*mānasambhūto*) and sexual intercourse (*methunasambhūto*).[4] The appearance of a being is believed to take place with the union of three conditions, the sexual union of parents, mother being in her proper season, and descent of the rebecoming consciousness.[5]

In the *paṭiccasamuppāda* analysis, the five aggregates are comprehended under the concept of *nāma-rūpa* (psycho-physical complex). According to the *Saṃyutta Nikāya Nidāna-vagga*, six sense bases arise with the name-and-form as condition.[6] The beginning of the process of sense perception takes place when these internal sense bases come into contact with their external sense bases. The internal sense bases are not only a part of the physical personality but also an essential part of the psychical (Kalupahana 1994: 32). The *Madhupiṇḍikasutta* presents the perception process as follows:

> Dependent on the eye and forms, eye-consciousness arises.

---

[4] *AN* II.145: *āhārasambhūto ayaṃ bhagini kāyo āhāraṃ nissāya āhāro pahātabbo, taṇhāsambhūto ... mānasambhūto ... methunasambhūto ayaṃ bhagini kāyo methuno ca setughāto vutto Bhagavatā* ।

[5] *Majjhimanikāya*, BJTS, vol. 10, pt. 1, p. 622 in Gamage 1998: 21 fn. 38: *mātāpitaro sannipatitā honti, mātā ca utunī hoti, gandhabbo ca paccupaṭṭhito hoti, evaṃ tiṇṇaṃ sannipātā gabbassāvakkanti hoti* ।

[6] *SN* II.1: *nāmarūpa paccayā saḷāyatanaṃ* ।

> The meeting of these three is contact. With contact as condition there is feeling.[7]

Even though the process continues, it is necessary to explain the term feeling (*vedanā*) for it is the most affective psychological experience. It is useful to refer to the observation made on feeling by D.J. Kalupahana:

> The inevitable result of contact (*familiarity*)[8] is feeling (*vedanā*), which introduces the emotive element, and this can be pleasant, unpleasant, or neutral. Familiarity breeds not only contempt but also admiration and indifference. For the Buddha, the emotive aspect of sense experience is most important, instead of leaving them as arbitrary decisions unrelated to the factual world. However, the Buddha was not unaware that feelings can grow into monstrous forms, overwhelming human beings to such an extent that they lose all rationality. *In other words, emotions, which are inevitable elements in our experiences, can also cause most of our confusion and suffering.* (emphasis added)
>
> – 1994: 33

If the feeling (*vedanā*) stage can cause confusion (*moha*) in the human mind, its two preceding cognitive stages (*viññāṇa* and *phassa*) should have enough substance (or emotive and cognitive properties) to culminate at the point of feeling in the process of perception. In this case Kalupahana points out that the consciousness (arising dependent on sense organ and sense object) is not a *tabula rasa* but it is part of the psycho-physical personality and hence conditioned by previous experiences and *phassa* (familiarity) breeds not only contempt

[7] *MN* I.111: *cakkhuñca paṭicca rūpe ca uppajjati cakkhuviññāṇaṃ, tiṇṇaṃ saṅgati phasso, phassa paccayā vedanā* ।

[8] This was added by me into the original passage.

but also admiration and indifference (Kalupahana 1994: 33).[9]

In the *Paṭiccasamuppāda* formula, *viññaṇa* (rebecoming consciousness) is given as conditioned by *saṅkhāra* (volition).[10] *Saṅkhāra* is understood as the aggregate of dispositions. In the definition of *saṅkhāra* as good (*puñña*), bad (*apuñña*) and imperturbable (*āneñja*),[11] we can see, the twofold lines of thought (skilful – non-greed, non-hatred and science, and unskilful – lust, hatred and ignorance), are considered as dispositions. It is clear that *viññaṇa* being conditioned by dispositions, possesses the seeds that are turned out to be likes, dislikes, concepts, etc.

If we refer to the initial factors of the perceptual process, internal sense organ and sense object, the eye has a tendency to grasp form and form has the nature of being pleasant to the eye. The Buddha explains that if there were no pleasure in the eye, beings would not become enamoured with it; but because there is pleasure in the eye, beings become enamoured with it. In the same manner, there is pleasure in the material form and therefore beings become enamoured with it.[12] Now it explains how sense perception becomes a force so afflictive upon the person to the extent that he is confused at the point of feeling (*vedanā*).

---

[9] Jayatillake (1980: 434-35) holds the idea that "*viññāṇa* is full of cognitive capacity against the theory of *viññāṇa* is not full cognition but bare sensation ..." produced by Dr Saratchandra.

[10] *SN* II.1: *saṅkhāra paccayā viññāṇaṃ* ।

[11] *DN* III.217: *tayo saṅkhārā: puññābhisaṅkhāro, apuññābhisaṅkhāro, āneñjābhisaṅkhāro* ।

[12] *SN* IV.10-12: *no cedaṃ bhikkhave cakkhussa assādo abhavissa nayidaṃ sattā cakkhusmiṃ sārajjeyyuṃ* । *yasmā ca kho bhikkhave atthi cakkhussa assādo tasmā sattā cakkhusmiṃ sārajjanti* । *no cedaṃ bhikkhave rūpānaṃ assādo abhavissa nayidaṃ sattā rūpesu sārajjeyyuṃ* । *yasmā ca kho bhikkhave atthi rūpānaṃ assādo tasmā sattā rūpesu sārajjanti* ।

Lust for sensuality and sex is a highly emotional condition in one's psychological make-up. The *Visuddhimagga* states that pleasure is included in the aggregate of feeling (*vedanā*).[13] Previously, reference was made to the canonical division of pleasure as sensual and non-sensual (*kāmasukha* and *nekkhammasukha*). From these two authorities, it comes to be seen that sensual pleasure (sensual pleasure what is the dominant in the worldly mind) assumes its identity being a component of feeling. According to the foregoing discussion with regard to the initial stages of the process of sense perception, it may be concluded that sensual and sexual emotions come to manifestation at psychical level with the appearance of feeling (*vedanā*).[14] The crucial role of *vedanā* in maintaining the being in *saṁsāra* can be understood on the basis of the statement that when one completely knows about these three feelings, one has nothing further to accomplish and attains the state of having done what has to be done.[15]

The *paṭiccasamuppāda* formula presents *taṇhā* (desire) after *vedanā*. In *vedanā*, there exist properties that can cause desire. The threefold feelings — happy, unhappy and indifferent (*sukha*, *dukkha* and *adukkhamasukha*) — by their being experienced, cause the arousal of desire to receive them continuously, which is named as *taṇhā* (ego-centric desire) (*chanda*, *rāga*, *nandi* or *taṇhā* can be used to indicate this obsessed state in consciousness). In the early Buddhist psychological analysis, the actual recognition of sensual

---

[13] *Vism* 145: *vedanākkhandhasangahitaṃ sukhaṃ* ।

[14] *AN* I.80f introduces the category of pleasure divided as *kāyika-sukha* and *cetasika-sukha*. Then pleasure is enjoyed physically as well as mentally.

[15] *SN* II.99: *tīsu vedanāsu pariññātāsu ariyasāvakassa natthi uttariṃ karaṇīyanti vadāmi* ।

desire in human psyche has been connected to *taṇhā* stage of psychological phenomena and this becomes evident in the division of *taṇhā* into three, viz. sensual desire (*kāma-taṇhā*), desire to rebecome (*bhava-taṇhā*) and desire for annihilation (*vibhava-taṇhā*) as found in the analysis of the second noble truth (*SN* V.421).

Philosophical Aspect of Sensuality

The problem of *saṁsāra* in Buddhism is explained as a consequence of the activity of the psychological roots of *taṇhā* (craving) and *avijjā* (ignorance).[16] While ignorance functions as the very basic factor of binding the individual into the round of existence, *taṇhā* is the manifestation of mind that is governed by ignorance (*SN* II.178f.). The function of *taṇhā* and *avijjā*, in producing the body and six internal sense bases whereby sense-contact is generated and in turn how pleasant and unpleasant feelings affect the individual, is explained in the following passage:

> *Bhikkhus*, for the fool, hindered by ignorance and fettered by craving, this body has thereby originated. So there is body and external name and form: thus this dyad. Dependent on the dyad there is contact. There are just sense bases and through their contact — or through the contact of a certain one among them — the fool experiences pleasure and pain. - *CDB*, p. 549 and n. 48 on p. 740

In this *sutta*, the Buddha states that since the common person has not abandoned ignorance and has not utterly destroyed craving, with the break-up of the body, the person passes on to another body whereby he becomes exposed to suffering of birth, aging and death, and he is not free from sorrow,

---

[16] *It*, p. 34: *avijjāmūlakā sabba-icchālobhasamussayā* ।

lamentation, pain, displeasure and despair (*SN* II.24). From this description, it becomes clear that *taṇhā* and *avijjā* lie at the root of psychological process by which a person becomes subject to rebirth and consequently becomes a victim to the whole mass of suffering. Further, it is given as the reason why the uneducated faces this destiny due to not having led a holy life for the complete destruction of suffering (*SN* II.24).

In order to understand the dire consequences of attachment to sensuality, the concept of sensuality has to be examined in relation to the teachings pertaining to the nature of *taṇhā* and *avijjā*. The teaching of the four noble truths establishes *taṇhā* as the cause of sāṁsāric suffering. The second noble truth, *dukkha samudaya ariya sacca*, explains *taṇhā* as producing rebirth due to desire for sensuality (*kāma-taṇhā*), desire to be reborn (*bhava-taṇhā*) and desire for annihilation (*vibhava-taṇhā*) (*SN* V.421). Ignorance is given as heading the existential process of dependent arising in the *paṭiccasamuppāda* theory (*SN* II.1). In early Buddhism, *avijjā* is accepted as the cause of forming the false view of "self" (*atta*). While *taṇhā* (craving) represents emotional imbalance of the individual's personality, *avijjā* represents intellectual or cognitive imbalance (Govinda 1991: 54). How craving in the form of sensual desire works to force the sentient being to remain in existence has been examined in the canonical material. The psychological force of ignorance functioning as the ideological basis to generate sensual desire has been referred to.

It has been clearly declared that attachment to sensual gratification is a serious hindrance to the individual aspiring to attain enlightenment or liberation. Sakka, the lord of *devas*, once asked the Buddha why certain beings do not attain *nibbana* in this very life while others do so. In response, the Buddha presents the following explanation:

> There are, lord of the *devas*, forms, cognizable by the eye, sounds cognizable by the ear, smells ..., tastes ..., touches ..., and mental phenomena cognizable by the mind that are desirable, lovely, agreeable, pleasing, sensually enticing, tantalizing. If a *bhikkhu* seeks delight in them ..., and remains holding to them, his consciousness becomes dependent upon them and clings to them. A *bhikkhu* with clinging does not attain *nibbana*. If a *bhikkhu* does not seek delight in them, does not welcome them, and does not remain holding to them, his consciousness does not become dependent upon them or clinging to them. A *bhikkhu* without clinging attains *nibbana*. – *SN* IV.102

The entire teaching of the Buddha is intended to reveal the fact that there is no permanent self as the contemporary eternalists asserted. The purpose of the doctrine of five aggregates is to disprove the validity of this false view. The six senses are also equally contributory to form the concept of "self" by misinterpreting the sense experience due to the influence of perceptual[17] and volitional formations deposited in the consciousness. In a discourse to the elder Rāhula, the Buddha clarifies why it is wrong to have the idea of self. He asks from Rāhula:

> "What do you think, Rāhula is the eye permanent or impermanent?" — "Impermanent venerable sir". –"Is what is impermanent, — suffering or happiness?" — "Suffering venerable sir" — "Is what is impermanent, suffering and subject to change fit to be regarded thus: "This is mine, this

[17] Kalupahana (1992: 18) interprets *saññā* as: Each one of our perceptions constitutes a mixed bag of memories, concepts, and dispositions as well as the material elements or the functions referred to by *rūpa*.

> I am, this is my self?" — "No, venerable sir."
>
> Are forms permanent or impermanent? ... Is eye-consciousness ... Is eye contact ... Is anything included in feeling, perception, volitional formations, and consciousness arisen with mind-contact as condition permanent or impermanent? - *SN* IV.106f.

The psychological aspect of human personality is composed of feeling, perception, volitional formations and consciousness. In this statement, it is shown that sense-contact is the condition for the psyche of human being. The argument outlined here is that if the very bases of sense-contact, the internal and external sense bases, are impermanent, how can we obtain the permanence of psychological entity? On the other hand, the danger of producing "the self" concept by sense experience is explained. The existence of sense bases and consequent psychological process are never considered as evil. As Citta once said the sense bases are not evil but when they are connected with consciousness which is the result of volitional activities, there arises a complex which produces wrong perceptions of things that are not really existing (*SN* IV.282).

The doctrinal formula of four nutriments (*āhāra*) is to be analysed to understand the role of sense gratification in the course of entangling the beings in *saṁsāra* and the cause of flourishing sense desire. The four nutriments which are necessary for the existence and continuity of beings are:

1. ordinary material food (*kabalimkārāhāra*);
2. contact of sense organs with the external world (*phassāhāra*);
3. consciousness (*viññāṇāhāra*); and

4. mental volition or will (*manosañcetanāhāra*).[18]

Although there are other conditions for being, these four alone are called nutriments because they serve as special conditions for the personal life-continuity (*ajjhattikasantatiyā visesapaccayattā*). Edible food (*kabalimkāra āhāra*) is a special condition for the physical body of those beings who subsist on edible food. In the mental body, contact is the special condition for feeling, mental volition for consciousness and consciousness for name and form. Edible food as soon as it is placed in the mouth, brings forth the groups of form with the nutritive essence; the nutriment contact brings forth the three kinds of feeling; the nutriment mental volition brings forth the three kinds of existence; and the nutriment consciousness brings forth name and form on the occasion of rebirth (*CDB*, p. 731 n. 18).

All four conditions are explained as supportive to the maintenance of the continuation of existence. The *Puttamamsakasutta* states that when the nutriment edible food is fully understood, lust for the five codes of sensual pleasure is fully understood. When lust for the five codes of sensual pleasure is fully understood, there is no fetter bound by which a noble disciple might come back again to this world.[19]

The full understanding of lust for five codes of sensual pleasure is gained as follows:

1. by realizing that the craving for tastes arisen at the

---

[18] *SN* II.98, 101; *MN* I.48: *cattāro me bhikkhave āhārā bhūtānaṃ vā sattānaṃ ṭhitiyā sambhavesīnaṃ vā anuggahāya* ।

[19] *SN* II.99: *kabalimkāre bhikkhave āhāre pariññāte pañcakāmaguṇiko rāgo pariññāto hoti* । *pañcakāmaguṇike rāge pariññāte natthi taṃ samyojanaṃ yena samyojanena samyutto ariyasāvako puna imaṃ lokaṃ āgaccheyya* ।

tongue door is the same craving that arises at all five sense doors;

2. realizing that lust for all five codes of sense pleasure arises in regard to a single morsel of food placed in the bowl (for food stimulates desire in all five senses); and
3. realizing that nutriment is the root of all five types of sensual lust, since sensual desire thrives when people are well fed. – *CDB*, p. 773

The explanation made to nutriment of material food reveals the relation between food (eaten, tasted, touched) and arising of sense desire. While material food is supportive to increase the degree of sensual desire and in turn sensual desire becomes attached to material food. The attachment to material food results in sāṁsāric continuation. The *Atthirāgasutta* explains the chain of sāṁsāric existence due to attachment to nutriment edible food as follows:

> If, *bhikkhus*, if there is lust for the nutriment edible food, if there is delight, if there is craving, consciousness becomes established there and comes to growth. Wherever consciousness becomes established and comes to growth, there is a descent of name-and-form. Where there is name-and-form, there is the growth of volitional formations. Where there is the growth of volitional formations, there is the production of future renewed existence. Where there is the production of future renewed existence, there is future birth, aging, and death, I say that is accompanied by sorrow, anguish, and despair.[20]

[20] *SN* II.101: *kabalimkāre ce bhikkhave āhāre atthi rāgo atthi nandi atthi taṇhā patiṭṭhitaṃ tattha viññāṇaṃ virūḷhaṃ* । *yattha patiṭṭhitaṃ viññāṇaṃ virūḷhaṃ atthi tattha nāmarūpassa avakkanti* । *yattha atthi nāmarūpassa avakkanti atthi tattha sankhārānam vuddhi* । *yattha atthi sankhārānaṃ vuddhi atthi tattha āyatim punabbhavābhinibbatti* । *yattha atthi āyatiṃ* →

The removal of lust for nutriment edible food entails freedom from birth and death. In the analysis of the nutriment edible food (*kabalimkāra āhāra*), one can see the integral connection of sensual attachment in the process of maintaining the existence of being and thereby causing all sorts of problems.

Early Buddhism, in its explanation of the issue of continued sāṁsāric suffering, denies the existence of an uncaused first cause for the process (*Vism* XVII: 105-07). However, ignorance of the four noble truths and the mistaken notion of self are accepted as the reasons for entanglement in the vicious cycle. The lack of understanding about the principle of causation is also recognized as a reason for the continuance of human suffering (*DN* II.55). According to the *Paṭiccasamuppāda*, all volitional actions are conditioned by ignorance. Thus conditioned volitional formations condition rebirth consciousness (*viññāṇa*) and in turn *viññāṇa* becomes a condition that is productive of the psycho-physical complex (*nāma-rūpa*) wherein the six sense organs (*saḍāyatanāni*) come into being. Sense contact (internal and external) (*phassa*) arises with internal sense bases. Feeling arises with sense contact as condition. Craving (*taṇhā*) arises with feeling as condition. According to Vasubandhu, the author of the *Abhidharmakośa*, this link is particularly associated with sexual passion at puberty (Gethin 1998: 150). Clinging (*upādāna*) is conditioned by desire. Rebecoming arises with clinging as condition. Birth takes place with rebecoming as condition and birth becomes the condition of all kinds of psycho-physical suffering ending with death (*SN* II.1).

← *punabbhavābhinibbatti atthi tattha āyatiṃ jātijarāmaraṇaṃ* । *yattha atthi āyatiṃ jātijarāmaraṇaṃ sasokantaṃ bhikkhave sadaraṃ saupāyāsanti vadāmi* ।

The philosophical understanding of the middle path is explained in the *Saṃyutta Nikāya*, in the conversation with Kaccāna Thera (*SN* II.17f.). This passage can be interpreted as the philosophical definition of ignorance too. The two extreme views, eternalism (*atthitā*) and nihilism (*natthitā*), are denied in this *sutta*. Views (*diṭṭhi*) are the basis of one's attitudes, concepts, interests, etc. Ideology constructs the world of concepts wherefrom every sort of activity on the personal level and the interpersonal level takes place. The reason for rejecting these two extreme notions is that they are based on the concept of self. D.J. Kalupahana (1977: 38) explains the basis of the Upaniṣadic concept of self as an attempt for a philosophical justification of man's desire to have permanent pleasure without end. Eternalism based on the view of indestructible self, induces human society to remain in the realm of existence to enjoy pleasure, which is according to the Buddhist point of view, the very cause of suffering.

Nihilist thinkers seeing the destruction of self in this very life prescribe the practice of any kind of action to satisfy desires (Hiriyanna 1994: 194). They have no concern about moral value of the actions, and if people were to follow such a view the consequences for the whole world would be chaotic. So, the denial of the view of eternal self can mean a paradigmatic change in the conceptual world of the contemporary India which had perceived sensuality as the very nature of being (ibid.). The emphasis made by both ideological lines of thought on sensuality is evidently of this tendency. The Buddha, realizing well how these two doctrinal views are contributory to self-indulgence, says that the five codes of sensual pleasure are dependent upon the eternalistic view (*atthitā*) and the nihilistic view (*natthitā*).[21] From this statement, the Buddha points out how sensuality is involved in ideologies formed on wrong assumptions which finally can lead to misconceptions and into mass of suffering.

Psychological Aspect of Sensual Attachment

Early Buddhist psychology is concerned with mental tendencies that function as hindrances to the realization of *nibbana* resulting in tendencies to hold on to existence. Among those tendencies, longing, hatred and confusion (*lobha, doṣa* and *moha*) are recognized as unwholesome roots (*akusala mūlāni*) in many places in the canon (*AN* I.201). All the evil actions find their basis in these three psychological roots. The ten evil deeds are given as produced by them. The wholesome activities are rooted in non-greed, non-hatred and non-delusion (*alobha, adosa* and *amoha*).

Regarding *lobha* and *dosa*, Buddhist interpreters point out that these two are different aspects of the psychological tendency. When one longs for sensual objects, it is called desire (*lobha*). Aversion to obstacles against the satisfaction of such desire turns out to be hatred. So, desire and hatred are like the two sides of the same coin (Dhirasekara 1982: 2021). These two are concerned with the emotional aspect of the personal psyche.

Moha is concerned with the cognitive faculty of personality. It can be said that sensual desire comes to manifestation as a product of these three characteristics. Confusion represents the idea of a permanent self and "I" ness whereby desire is produced to gratify the "I". The wish to gratify "I" ness is

---

[21] Norman 1993: 88: Forms, sounds, tastes, smells, contacts and all mental phenomena are desired, pleasant and lovely as long as it is said, "they exist".

called craving or desire while the attitude to barriers to this wish is expressed as hatred.

The *Dvedhāvitakkasutta* in the *Majjhima Nikāya* presents a three lines of thinking in which sensual desire is placed at the beginning. They are as follows:

i. *Kāmavitakka* (sensual desire)

ii. *Vyāpādavitakka* (thoughts of ill will)

iii. *Vihiṁsāvitakka* (thoughts of cruelty) (*MN* I.114).

These three are explained as conducive to the continuation of existence. The three opposite lines of thinking are:

i. *Nekkhamma* (thoughts of renunciation)

ii. *Avyāpāda* (thoughts of non-ill will)

iii. *Avihiṁsā* (thoughts of non-cruelty).

These are conducive to cessation of suffering. A *sutta* included in the *Saṃyutta Nikāya, Nidānavagga*, explains the source wherefrom these two opposing classes of thought arise and how they mature:

> Depending on the sensuality element (*kāmadhātu*)[22] there arises sensual perception; depending on sensual perception there arises sensual intention; depending on sensual intention there arises sensual desire; depending on sensual desire there arises sensual passion; depending on sensual passion there arises a sensual quest. Engaged in a sensual

---

[22] *CDB*, p.792 n. 234: The sensuality element is sensual thought, all sense-sphere phenomena in general, and in particular everything unwholesome except the ill-will element and the harmfulness element which are mentioned separately here. Sensual perception arises depending on the sensuality element either by taking it as an object or by way of association (i.e. when sensual perception is associated with sensual thought in the same *citta*).

> quest, the ordinary person conducts himself wrongly in three ways — with body, speech and mind. - *SN* II.151

These two classes of thoughts are included in the second item of the eightfold path, *sammāsaṅkappa* — right thought (the latter set of thoughts in the present *sutta*) and *micchāsaṅkappa* — false thought (the former set of thoughts in the present *sutta*) (*MN* III.73). If we look into the first class of thoughts mentioned here, placing the thoughts (sensual desire) first and its relation to the other two can be interpreted as follows. The nature of desire for sense-pleasure is characterized by thirst, i.e. looking for more. Due to this tendency, the sentient beings automatically fall into a competitive mental condition, necessarily giving rise to thoughts of ill will within the individual productive of conflicts at the interpersonal level, resulting in the practice of torturous acts (*vihiṁsā*).[23] So, sensual desire is recognized as the most problematic psychological characteristic in the early Buddhist discourses. It can be seen in the placing of *kāma-taṇhā* as the first out of the three types of *taṇhā* in the initial dialogue of the Buddha to the world.

The simile of "the great low-lying mass", which is compared to sensual desire as interpreted in the *Dvedhāvitakkasutta*, implies that the ordinary person is dependent on sensual desire (*MN* III.117). The removal of sense desire and thoughts of ill will and torture by cultivation of thoughts of renunciation and thoughts devoid of ill will and violence is conducive to *nibbana* (*MN* III.117).

---

[23] *MN* III.86: The *Mahādukkhakkhandhasutta* explains the origin of every type of conflicts in society as a result of desire for sensual gratification.

In Buddhist psychology, the concepts of *āsava*[24] and *anusaya* are representative of deep-lying tendencies in the consciousness. As Erich Frauwallner points out, the teaching of threefold taint (*āsava*) is more perfect than the teaching of Four Noble Truths because it includes both causes of entanglement in the cycle of being, i.e. ignorance and thirst (*avijjā* and *taṇhā*), whereas the latter emphasizes only on the thirst as the sole cause of suffering (1993: 171). The inclusion of sense desire into *āsava* and *anusaya* shows the decisive role of it in the formation of one's emotional and intellectual attitudes. *Kāmāsava* and *bhavāsava* represent the emotional aspect while *avijjāsava* represents the intellectual aspect of the psychological make-up. *Āsava* and *anusaya* overlap; however, they appear to have referred to the same state of mind.

The *āsavas* are enumerated as three or four in the *Sutta Piṭaka*. The *Sammādiṭṭhisutta* mentions of three: the *āsava* of sense desire (*kāmāsava*), *āsava* of desire for continuous becoming (*bhavāsava*) and *āsava* of ignorance (*avijjāsava*) (*MN* I.55; *It.* 49). The fourth is the *āsava* of holding views (*diṭṭhāsava*). It is clear that these form the very basis of human psyche

---

[24] Dasgupta 1992: 99-100 on *āsavas*: "Childers translates *asava* as 'depravities' and Mrs. Rhys Davids as 'intoxicants'. The word *asava* in Sanskrit means 'old wine'. It is derived from 'su' to produce by Buddhaghoṣa and the meaning that he gives to it is *ciraparivasikatthena* (on account of its being stored up for a long time like wine). They work through the eye and the mind and continue to produce all beings up to Indra. As those wine which are kept long are called 'asavas' so these are also called *asavas* for remaining for long time. The other alternative that Buddhaghoṣa gives is that they are called *asava* on account of their producing *samsāradukkha* (sorrows of the world), *Aṭṭhasālini*, p. 48. (Contrast it with Jaina *asrava* flowing in of *karma* matter). Finding it difficult to translate it in one word after Buddhaghoṣa, I have translated it as 'depravities' after Childers."

and they are predominant in both emotional and cognitive aspects of the individual. These exist as latent predispositions in the consciousness and function as intoxicants of the mind (*PED*, pp. 114-15). The Buddhist understanding of these psychological tendencies can be seen by their being given as the cause of *avijjā* (ignorance) in the canon. Ven. Sāriputta states that when *āsavas* arise, then ignorance arises, when *āsavas* become extinct, then ignorance becomes extinct.[25] The extinction of these brings about enlightenment (*khīnāsava*).

A similar emphasis can be seen in the other list of mental biases called *anusaya*. They are mentioned as seven. They have been translated into English as bent, bias, proclivities, the persistence of dormant or latent disposition, predisposition and tendency (*PED*, p. 44). These are given as seven in several places in the canon. They are: proclivity of sense desire (*kāmarāgānusaya*), proclivity of anger (*paṭhighānusaya*), proclivity of view (*diṭṭhānusaya*), proclivity of doubt (*vicikicchānusaya*), proclivity of conceit (*mānānusaya*), proclivity for rebirth (*bhavarāgānusaya*) and proclivity of ignorance (*avijjānusaya*) (*DN* III.254). We can see four of *anusayas* listed under the *āsavas*, sensual desire, desire for continued existence, views and ignorance. The importance of the role of *anusayas* is suggested by their being mentioned under the *āsavas* as well.

The *āsavas* remain until the practitioner realizes the super knowledge of destruction of cankers (*āsavakkhayañāṇa*). In the *Aṅguttara Nikāya*, it is mentioned that if one's mind is not stained by the five hindrances (*pañca-nīvaraṇāni*), it could promote concentration that leads to the destruction of cankers (*āsavas*) (*AN* II.210; III.92), with the further possibility

---

[25] *MN* I.54: *āsava samudayā avijjā samudayo, āsavanirodhā avijjā nirodho* ।

of gaining arahantship. Thus, the rejection of *nīvaraṇāni* does not suffice to bring about the removal of predispositions (*āsava*). This shows that there is a difference between the terms *kāmacchanda* (in *nīvaraṇa*) and *kāmāsava* in their function where the state of *āsava* exists as a stronger layer in consciousness. Early canonical materials recognize that these deep-rooted psychological tendencies should be removed by the employment of wisdom (*paññā*).[26] The *Vatthūpamasutta* explains how the practitioner attains the state free from *āsavas* and enlightenment as follows:

> He understands thus: "there is this, there is the inferior, there is the superior, and beyond there is an escape from this whole field of perception."[27] When he knows and sees thus, his mind is liberated from the taint of sensual desire, from the taint of becoming, and the taint of ignorance. When it is liberated, there comes the knowledge: "It is liberated." He understands: "Birth is destroyed, the holy life has been lived, what has to be done has been done, there is no more coming to any state of being." — *MN* I.39

The *Mahāmāluṅkyaputtasutta* says that *kāmānusaya* is found even in an infant. The Buddha states that one can question thus: A young tender infant lying on his back does not even have the notion "sensual pleasures" so how could desire arise in him? Emphatically he says: "Yet the underlying tendency to sensual lust lies within him" (*MN* I.434; *MLDB*, p. 538). This early Buddhist view on sensual desire is in agreement with the modern sexological views.[28]

---

[26] *DN* III.230: *āsavānam khayo paññāya sacchikaraṇīyo*

[27] *MA* I, p. 185 (Devanāgarī): The *Majjhima Nikāya* commentary interprets this passage as realizing four noble truths. According to it, destruction of *āsavas* takes place with realizing the noble truths.

[28] Nevid, Rathus and Rathus 1995: 390-400: S. Freud hypothesized that →

Ven. Walpola Rahula in his explanation of the truth of thirst in relation to rebecoming that lie in the child says that in a child all the physical, mental and intellectual faculties are tender and weak, but they have within them the potentiality of producing a full grown man (Rahula 1982: 33). Regarding the nature of both these classes of mental characteristics, it may be said that when latent tendencies are connected with the thinking process unwholesome types of behaviour can ensue unconsciously. The latent tendencies themselves are expressed in thought (and, word and deed).[29] We can find a dynamic example in the *Saṃyutta Nikāya* to understand how these tendencies lie behind both pleasurable and painful feelings experienced by the individuals.

When an ordinary person is contacted by a painful feeling, he undergoes two kinds of pains, first physical and second mental. Being contacted by that same painful feeling, he harbours aversion towards it. When he harbours aversion towards painful feeling, the underlying tendency to aversion (*paṭhighānusaya*) towards painful feeling lies behind this. Being contacted by painful feeling, he seeks delight in sensual pleasure. The reason is that the ordinary person does not

← infants also seem to derive sensual pleasure from sucking fingers, pacifier's nipples or whatever else fits into the mouth. Now it is accepted that stimulation of the genitals in infancy may also produce sensations of pleasure. Parents who touch their infants' genitals while changing or washing them may discover the infants smiling or becoming excited. Infants discover the pleasure of self-stimulation (masturbation) for themselves when they gain the capacity to manipulate their genitals with their hands. A striking discovery has been reported by Kinsey and his colleagues (1948). They noted that baby boys show behaviours that resemble adult orgasm by as early as five months; orgasmic responses in boys are similar to those in men — but without ejaculation.

[29] *AN* II.158; *SN* II.40: *asampajāno manosankhāraṃ abhisamkaroti* ।

know of any escape other than sensual pleasure. Behind seeking pleasure, there lies underlying tendency to lust for pleasant feeling (*rāgānusaya*). He cannot understand the feeling as characterized by origin and passing away as well as its gratification, danger and escape. The reason for this is the underlying tendency to ignorance in regard to neither-painful–nor-pleasant feeling (*SN* IV.208).

These two categories jointly represent "part of human nature". Cyclically reinforced over many lives, they have become embedded in an individual's psychological make-up (Hamilton 1996: 77). From this short reference made to Buddhist psychological explanation, it becomes clear that sensual desire has been understood as a deep-rooted psychological phenomenon.

Buddhist Cosmology and Sense-Desire

According to the *paṭiccasamuppāda* theory, the immediate cause that decides the place of rebirth is clinging (*upādāna*) which is of four types: clinging to sensual pleasure (*kāmupādāna*), clinging to views (*diṭṭhupādāna*), clinging to rules and observances (*sīlabbatūpādāna*) and clinging to a doctrine of self (*attavādupādāna*) (*MN* I.51). As Bhikkhu Bodhi points out, clinging in any of its varieties represents a strengthening of craving, its condition (*MLDB*, p. 1186 n. 125). Thus intensified desire decides the nature of the place of rebirth (*upādāna paccayā bhavo*). The early Buddhist discourses have included its cosmology into the link, becoming (*bhava*), which is a result of one's own mental tendencies. The *Mahānidānasutta* refers to the three realms of existence where birth (*jāti*) takes place.[30]

[30] *DN* II.57; *MN* I.50: *bhavo va hi ānando nābhavissa sabbena sabbaṃ sabbathā sabbaṃ kassaci kimhici, seyyathīdaṃ kāmābhavo rūpa-bhavo arūpa-bhavo vā* I

The Buddhist cosmos as given in the canonical sources is divided into three broad realms, the sense-sphere realm, the fine-material realm and non-material realm. Each of these comprises a range of subsidiary planes, rising to thirty-one places of existence. The realm of sensuous pleasure (*kāmāvacāra lokadhātu*) is formed out of eleven realms ranging from the realms of hell and "the hungry ghosts", through the realms of animals, jealous gods and human beings to the six realms of the lower gods; the common characteristic of beings in these realms is that they are all endowed with consciousness and five physical senses. These eleven can in turn be classified into as good destinations and bad destinations. The six divine abodes and the human world belong to the first category and the four hells (*apāya* — states of deprivation) to the second category. Beings in these eleven places are led by desire for pleasure of senses (*kāmanīta* — *J* II.214-15) and they are dependent upon it (*kāmanissita* — *Miln.* 11). An individual led by the desire for worldly pleasure seeks all possible ways and means to get what he wishes. Sometimes, he has no regard for morality or immorality involved in the act done in search of the enjoyment of senses. Such a person becomes blinded by passion (*kāmāndha*) (*Ud* 76).

Above the world of sense pleasure, there is "the world of pure form" (*rūpadhātu loka*) which consists of sixteen realms occupied by various higher gods collectively known as Brahmas; these refined beings have consciousness but only two senses — sight and hearing. Finally there are the four realms of "the formless world" (*arūpadhātu loka*) occupied by a further class of Brahmas who have only consciousness. Rupert Gethin (1998: 118) points out that these thirty-one realms, from bottom to top, reflect a basic movement from gross to subtle.

The term *loka*, which is associated with the different realms of existence, can be seen to have been used to refer to five internal sense faculties, five strands of sense pleasures and five aggregates subject to clinging (*pañcupādānakkhandha*). This implies that the subjective experience of individual in *saṁsāra* is recognized as the world in Buddhism. The elder Ānanda explains what is called "world" in the Noble One's discipline as follows:

> And what, friends, is that in the world by which one is a perceiver of the world, a conceiver of the world? The eye is that in the world by which one is a perceiver of the world, a conceiver of the world. The ear ... the nose ... the tongue ... the body ... the mind is that the world by which one is a perceiver of the world, a conceiver of the world. That in the world by which one is a perceiver of the world, a conceiver of the world — that is called in the Noble One's discipline.
>
> – *CDB*, p. 1190

As this passage implies, the world is identified with the six sense bases because they are the necessary internal condition for experience and thus for the presence of a world. As long as the six sense bases persist, a world will always be spread out as the objective range of perception and cognition (*CDB*, p. 394). The matter how the world originates is explained in terms of the process of sensory perception which involves the acquisition of psychological characteristics that cause one to be reborn thereby leading to suffering. The Buddha explains it thus:

> And what, *bhikkhus*, is the origin of the world? In dependence on the eye and forms, eye-consciousness arises. The meeting of the three is contact. With contact as condition, feeling [comes to be]; with feeling as condition,

> craving; with craving as condition, clinging; with clinging as condition, existence; with existence as condition, birth; with birth as condition, aging-and-death, sorrow, lamentation, pain, displeasure, and despair come to be. This, *bhikkhus*, is the world. – *CDB*, p. 581

Sense pleasure and sense faculties are inseparable. Sense faculties are conditioned by craving and ignorance. Consequently, they are inclined to perceive and conceive external objects as desirable. And they seek pleasure in them. That becomes the dominant characteristic in the individual's personality. This tendency to seek pleasure through senses exists until enlightenment. The world is understood in terms of sense pleasure. The Buddha, therefore, states: "It is these five types of sensual desire that are called the world in the discipline of the noble one."[31] Now we can understand that attachment to sensual pleasure is an inalienable psychological characteristic in the human psyche and that it functions as decider of rebirth (as *upādāna*) and the place for existence (*bhāva*) in the process of becoming.

Positive Aspects of Sensuality

It can be seen that in the early Buddhist literature sensuality and sexuality have been discussed in a negative tone, most of the time, with the purpose of strengthening the celibate's mind to remain in the spiritual pursuit of leaving the sāṁsāric cycle (*Vin* III.20). In spite of this emphasis upon the spiritual aspect and ill-effect of sensuality and sexuality, there are teachings pertaining to the way of leading a sensuous and sexual life in the proper manner. Buddhism is based on the middle path which rejects extreme attitudes and guides the world with a sense of realism. So, it never denies the

---

[31] *AN* IV.430: *pañcime brāhmaṇa kāmaguṇā ariyassa vinaye lokoti vuccati* ı

essential elements of the individual. Sensuality and sexuality are among those basic elements found in the individual. In the preceding section, we have discussed the Buddhist cosmological mapping and the place given to sensuality in it. The Buddhist *karma* theory is based on activities taking place within the realm of sensuality wherefore it is inevitable to have discussions on both negative and positive aspects of it, on a moral basis. In fact, a considerable number of discourses investigating various facets related to sensuality have been included in the canonical materials.

As for the lay community, they wish to lead their life smoothly and enjoying all the worldly pleasures as expected by any ordinary person. To have such wishes is not considered as wrong. In accordance with common worldling's needs and wishes, the Buddha preached the *dhamma* for the well-being of people who desired sensuality. Let us consider some of those discourses having a positive attitude to sensuality.

The *Kāmasutta* in the *Sutta Nipāta* states that the sentient being becomes happy by achieving what he or she wishes.[32] It is a universal truth that man longs for pleasure. The source of pleasure can be located in the psycho-physical make-up of an individual. As we have pointed out in the introductory chapter, pleasure is derived through the six senses. Frequent reference is made to the five senses: eye, ear, nose, tongue and body. These with the contact of external objects, form, sound, smell, taste and touch generate sensations which are of three kinds, happy, unhappy and neutral. In early Buddhist psychology, this is explained by the term *vedanā*.[33]

---

[32] SN 766: *kāmaṃ kāmayamānassa tassa ce taṃ samijjhati, addhā pīti mano hoti laddhā macco yadicchati* ।

[33] SN V.21: *tisso imā bhikkhave vedanā ... sukha vedanā dukkha vedanā* →

The *Visudhimagga* makes several definitions of the term *sukha*. One is "pleasure is embedded in the aggregate of feeling (*vedanākkhandhasaṅgahitaṃ sukhaṃ* – *Vism* 145)". Another definition is that "it is a kind of experiencing pleasant contacts (*iṭṭhapoṭṭhabbānubhavalakkhaṇam* – *Vism* 145, 461). What is pleasurable is desired by the individual more and more. In the *Aṅguttara Nikāya*, a list of dyads of pleasure is produced. As the first pair of pleasure, pleasures of lay persons and those who have renounced, is mentioned and following these two categories, the dyad of sensual and non-sensual pleasure (*kāmasukha* and *nekkhammasukha*) is given as the second (*AN* I.80). Sensuality aims at obtaining both physical and mental pleasures. In the *Aṅguttara Nikāya sukhavagga*, it is stated that *cetasikasukha* is superior to physical pleasure (*AN* I.80).

The Bodhisattva, Prince Siddhattha is represented to have led an extremely sensuous life before his renunciation.[34] Glory of his life is nicely depicted in the canonical accounts. The same is mentioned in the story of Yasa (*Vin* I.15). In the canon, it is recorded that the Buddha had a mass of lay followers from various castes and classes in his time. Kings like Seniya Bimbisāra and Pasenadi Kosala were his close supporters, who were leading a life of luxury.

According to the Buddhist *karma* theory, if somebody becomes rich of worldly pleasures, it is accepted as a result of merit that happened to be accumulated in his or her previous life. The *Cullakammavibhaṅgasutta* clearly states that

← *adukkhamasukha vedanā* ।

[34] *MN* I.504: *ahaṃ ... pubbe agāriyabhūto samāno pañcahi kāmaguṇehi samappito samangibhūto paricāresiṃ ... tassa mayhaṃ māgandiya tayo pāsādā ahesuṃ, ... so kho ahaṃ māgandiya vassike pāsāde vassike cattāro māse nipppurisehi turiyehi paricāriyamāno na heṭṭhāpāsādaṃ orohāmi* ।

the qualities of a happy life are the result of abstaining from unwholesome deeds and performing wholesome deeds (*MN* III.202-06). In the *Vimānavattthu*, this idea is further developed in terms of divine pleasure.

The story of Sunikkhitta's mansion is an example of the life of happiness that any sentient being wishes to enjoy. The elder Moggallāna in his *deva*-tour to the realm of the thirty-three, met Sunikkhitta and seeing his splendid life asked him thus:

> There do you bide and drink and eat while *deva*-like lutes make melody. Here are *deva*-like flavours, the five kinds of sense pleasures, and women decked in gold do dance. ... Because of what do you prosper here, and there arise whatever are those delights that are dear to your heart?
>
> – Horner 1974: 155

The *Vimānavatthu* is a collection of this type of narratives that have been composed with a positive view regarding sensual pleasure for it is a result of morally good actions. This description makes a beautiful picture in the readers' mind and is evocative of generating desire to have such an experience.

To obtain whatever is wished is a common psychological character in the earthly beings' mind. In contrast, most of such wishes become mere fantasies in the realistic world. But, in the concept of divine world, such ability too, seems to be enjoyed by certain gods. The category of goddesses called *manāpakāyika* (fairies of lovely form) declare to Ven. Anuruddha that they have power in the three domains of assuming any colour desired, producing any sound desired and obtaining any kind of happiness desired.[35]

---

[35] AN IV.263: *mayaṃ bhante anuruddha manāpakāyikā nāma devatā tīsu ṭhānesu issariyaṃ kārema vasaṃ vattema: ... yādisaṃ vaṇṇaṃ ākankhāma,* →

In the *Aṅguttara Nikāya*, the Buddha states that a woman can go to the union with *manāpakāyika devas* (fairies of lovely form) following eight virtuous qualities in the present life. The dance performed by these denizens in the presence of elder Anuruddha is given as a live concert in the scripture.[36] When we examine the three domains possessed by these fairies, colour (*vaṇṇa*), sound (*sara*) and pleasure are essential matters in pleasing one's mind and they are part of *pañcakāma-guṇa*. Enjoyment of such pleasures has been approved and even the avenues to achieve them are given in the discourse. This shows that in early Buddhism, while there is a soteriological blueprint in its major project for the world, transcending sensuality, it also leaves room for a kind of pleasure principle with certain forms of ethical control.

In the Buddhist literature, a lay devotee Visākhā is depicted as a commendable personality and set as an ideal woman in the lay Buddhist community. In addition to her virtues, her physical features and the glory she was fortunate to possess are colourfully described in the later Pali commentaries (in Malasekara's *DPPN*, pp. 900-04 *Dhammapadaṭṭhakathā* and *Aṅguttatanikāyaṭṭhakathā*, the account on Visākhā is given).[37] The commentator says that she herself kept all her life, the appearance of a girl of sixteen (*DPPN*, vol. II: 902). Nowhere

← *tādisaṃ vaṇṇaṃ ṭhānaso paṭilabhāma, yādisakaṃ saraṃ ... tādisakaṃ saraṃ ... yādiakaṃ sukhaṃ, tādisakaṃ sukhaṃ ṭhānaso patilabhāma* ।

36 Ibid.: *atha kho tā devatā ekā 'va gāyi, ekā 'va nacci, ekā 'va accharikaṃ vadesi* । *seyyathāpi naṃ pañcangikassa turiyassa suvinitasa suppatippatalitassa kusalehi susamannāhatassa saddo hoti vaggū ca rajanīyo ca kamanīyo ca pemanīyo ca madanīyo ca ...* ।

37 Even in the present Sri Lankan Buddhist society, at the houses *saṅghadānas* conducted for monks, her glories are mentioned suggesting that the similar results will be obtained by the donor.

in her story, we can find a gainsay to sensual pleasure.

Moreover, the approval and instructions given by the Buddha to a householder Dīghajānu Koliya is expressive of the Buddhist attitude towards the well-being connected with the sensuous life of the lay community. Dīghajānu describes the charms of the life led by him amidst the sensual objects. The life of householders is absorbed in pleasure; their time is spent among children and wives; they delight in the muslins from Benares and in sandalwood; they deck themselves with flowers, garlands and cosmetics; they enjoy the jewellery of both silver and gold.[38] Dīghajānu requests the Buddha to teach some *dhamma* for the benefit of both the present life and the next.

In response to the request of the householder, the Buddha preaches four conditions that lead to a clansman's advantage and happiness here on earth and four conditions for the betterment in the world to come (*AN* IV.281-85). In the *Veludvāreyyasutta*, it is reported that a group of brāhmaṇa householders came to visit the Buddha and said to him thus:

> Master Gotama, we are people of such desires, such wishes, such intentions as these: Oh we may live a crowded house encumbered with children! May we enjoy the use of Benares sandalwood! May we deck ourselves with garlands and unguents! May we handle gold and silver! When body breaks up, after death may we be reborn in the happy lot, the Heaven world. – *KS* V.308

[38] *AN* IV.281: *mayaṃ bhante gihī kāmabhogī puttasambādhasayanaṃ ajjhāvasāma kāsikacandanaṃ paccanubhoma mālāgandhavilepanaṃ dhārayāma jātarūparajataṃ sādiyāma, tesaṃ no bhante bhagavā amhākam tathā dhammaṃ desetu, ye amhākaṃ assa dhammā diṭṭhadhammahitāya diṭṭhadhammasukhāya samparāyahitāya samparāyasukhāyā 'ti*।

In these two contexts, the Buddha showing concern for the lay people's request, or the common aspirations in the worldlings, provides them with proper guidelines in order to satisfy their wishes and expectations (*SN* V.353-56). The Buddhist approach to the worldly matters is free from extremes, so, there is no denial of sensual enjoyment for the laity.

The ethical teachings expounded by the Buddha for the stability of the institute of the family validate the necessity of sensual life in the mundane world. The family is considered as the fundamental institution established in society to lead a legal sensual and sexual life in human civilization. The person who wishes to lead a religious life has to abandon his family as a symbol of renouncing the sensuality. Siddhatta did this prior to his spiritual investigation as reported in the Pali canon.[39] In contrast to this type of rare cases, the vast majority of people seek pleasure within the family itself. So, the Buddha had preached several discourses to maintain the well-being of it and in order to improve its quality. The *Sigālovādasutta* is an authentic example for such teachings in the Pali canon (*DN* III.180-93).

It is impossible for a person whose mind is immersed in sensuousness, at least, to think of a state without those pleasures for he perceives the five codes of sensual pleasure as his world (*AN* IV.430). A householder Tapussa expresses the general standpoint on sensual pleasures and the terror felt at the thought of giving them up. In his own words:

> We householders, reverend Ānanda, are pleasure-seekers, pleasure-fond, pleasure-doting, pleasure-mad and, being

[39] *Sn* verse 408: *sambādhoyaṃ gharāvāso rajassāyatanaṃ iti abbhokāso 'va pabbajjā iti disvāna pabbaji* ǀ

so, it seems a real precipice to us, this giving up of all.[40]

When this was put to the Buddha's inquiry, his answer was that it is natural to think so.[41] In the *Dvayatānupassanāsutta* too, it is cited that sensual pleasures are indeed thought of as happiness by the world including *devas*, but the fact that they stop is regarded as misery by them (Norman 1993: 88, v. 760). Until there arises full awakening to the knowledge of the peril of pleasures, this type of mental disposition is influential upon the individual.

It can be seen that the concept of divine sensual pleasure in the early scriptures of Pali literature has been fitted into cosmology. The idea that divine pleasures are superior to that of human is found at several places in canonical sources. In a discourse of the *Saṃyutta Nikāya*, the Buddha teaches how to chat with a patient who is about to die soon. Therein, it is advised to encourage the patient to achieve heavenly pleasures because they are more excellent than the five human pleasures of senses.

manussakehi kho āvuso kāmehi dibbakāmā abhikkantatarā ca paṇītatarā ca ।

sādhāyasmā manussakehi kāmehi cittaṃ vuṭṭhapetvā cātummahārājikesu devesu cittaṃ adhimocehi ।।

Finally, advice is given to fix the mind on "cessation from the person-pack" (*sakkāya nirodhe cittaṃ upasamharahi*) if the person gives up his thoughts to be born in the *Brahman* world *SN* V.410). The desire to enjoy divine pleasure is clearly

---

[40] *AN* IV.438: *mayaṃ bhante ānanda, gihī kāmabhogi kāmarāmā kāmaratā kāmasamudditā, tesaṃ no bhante ... kāmasamudditānam papāto viya khāyati yadidaṃ nekhammaṃ* ।

[41] Ibid. 439: *evaṃ etaṃ ānanda evaṃ etaṃ ānanda* ।

mentioned in the *Makhādevasutta*[42] and in the *Makhādevajātaka* (*J.* I.138).

Usually, the laity is encouraged to achieve the divine pleasures by means of right conduct (*DhA* I.129ff.). In the *Saṃkhāruppattisutta*, it is mentioned that if one is possessing *saddhā* (faith), *sīla* (moral purity), *suta* (learning), *cāga* (giving up) and *paññā* (wisdom), if he wishes to be reborn in a family of kings, *brāhmaṇa*, etc. he can do so. Further, if he wishes to get birth into the *tāvatiṁsa*, thinking they are enjoying a higher level of happiness (*cātummahārājikā devā dīghāyukā vaṇṇavanto sukhabahulāti*), he can get there too. And he can attain even *nibbana* (*MN* III.101-02).

The kings' life in ancient India was highly luxurious and full of sensual pleasure. In the *Pabbatūpamasutta* of the *Kosala Saṃyutta*, King Pasenadi explains his dealing with the activities of the kings who were politically established and leading a life given to sensuality. Kings were intoxicated with power, indulged in (*abhibhūtānaṃ*) their greed for sensuous pleasures (*SN* I.100).

This indicates that sensuality is an essential characteristic of a life of power and wealth. When, the person is intoxicated with power, he uses it to satisfy his carnal desire. The concept of *cakkavattīrāja* (wheel-rolling monarch) was an attempt to introduce ethical restrains in the life of sensuality in order to prevent harm to the country and its citizens due to the abuse of power by rulers as it was often in contemporary India. Within the concept of universal king, sensuality is accepted as an essential element and the discourses seem to deal with the concept with high esteem for worldly pleasures.

---

[42] *MN* II.75: *bhuttā kho pana me manusakā kāmā, samayo dibbe kāme pariyesituṃ* ।

It is useful to examine further reading into the concept of *cakkavattī* because of its relevance to an examination of the views on sensuality in early Buddhism. The wheel-rolling monarch and the Buddha are considered as having a very high status in the social hierarchy by the popular tradition. While the Buddha holds the highest position in the spiritual kingdom, the universal monarch is the greatest among ordinary human beings (*DN* III.142).

A wheel-rolling monarch possesses seven treasures and four kinds of success. Being endowed with these, he experiences pleasure and joy.[43] Depicting an ideal image of the woman-treasure (*itthiratana*), the canonical writer says that she surpasses human beauty without reaching divine beauty (*atikkanta mānusaṃ vaṇṇaṃ appatta dibbaṃ vaṇṇaṃ*). Apart from considering the *itthiratana* as an object of beauty possessing all desirable physical attributes,[44] it is of interest to note certain qualities enumerated in particular to emphasize sensual aspects of the *itthitratana*, thereby evaluating the *itthiratana* particularly as a sex object. Qualities found in her in respect of tactile sensation are described to the effect of highest sensuality. The touch possessed by her is such that it is like a tuft of *kapok* or a tuft of cotton-wool. When it is cool, her limbs are warm; when it is warm, her limbs are cool.[45] While her body permeates the scent of sandalwood, the

---

[43] *MN* III.172: *rājā cakkavatti sattahi ratanehi samannāgato catūhi ca iddhīhi, tato nidānaṃ sukhaṃ somanassaṃ paṭisamvedeti* ।

[44] Ibid. 174: *rañño cakkavattissa itthiratanaṃ ... abhirūpā dasanīyā pāsādikā paramāya vaṇṇapokkharatāya samannāgatā ...* ।

[45] *MN* III.175: *tassa kho pana bhikkhave itthiratanassa evarūpo kāyasamphasso hoti, seyyathāpi nāma thūla picuno vā kappāsa picuno vā ... itthiratanassa sīte uṇhāni gattāni honti, uṇhe sitāni gattāni honti* ।

mouth spreads the scent of lotuses.[46] Making an observation on this portrayal of the *itthiratana*, L.P.N. Perera (1993: 83f.) says that a significant characteristic of such descriptions is the emphasis given to the sensual aspect of a woman.

Here, in the *sutta* we can see the concept of heavenly pleasure being highlighted. The Buddha makes an analogy, by showing some sand or a few stones, questions the monks whether the handful of stones or the Himalaya mountain is larger. They answer that the Himalaya is the larger and when it is compared, stone in the hand is nothing. Then the Buddha states that divine pleasures are greater than the *cakkavattī* king's pleasures and it becomes nothing in comparison to the heavenly joys.[47]

It should be mentioned that the *Sotāpatti Saṃyutta* of the *Saṃyutta Nikāya* says that the wheel-rolling monarch after the life on the earth will be reborn in the *tāvatiṁsa* heaven (*SN* V.342). The interesting feature that can be seen in this context is the divine pleasures are considered as more excellent than the human sensual pleasures and the way to it is leading a morally good life. From the concept of *cakkavattī* and the related information given about him, a positive attitude towards sensual pleasures and it is clear that it is not a negative attitude towards them.

The *Mahāpadānasutta* can be considered as one of the most remarkable *suttas* concerning the Buddhological teachings in the Pali canon. In this *sutta*, enjoying five strands of sense-

---

[46] Ibid.: *tassa ... itthiratanassa kāyato candanagandho vāyati, mukhato uppalagandho vāyati*।

[47] *MN* III.177: *Evameva kho bhikkhave, yaṃ rājā cakkavatti sattahi ratanehi catūhi ca iddhīhi tatonidānaṃ sukhaṃ somanassaṃ paṭisamvedeti, taṃ dibbassa sukhassa upanidhāya sankhaṃ pi na upeti upanidhiṃ pi na upeti*।

pleasure after the entrance of *bodhisattva* into mother's womb has been elevated to the position of a law of nature related to *buddhas*.[48]

The concept of *taṇhā* is concerned with the idea of sensuality and it is a basic inclination in human life. So, the Buddhist teaching attempts to teach the follower how to have a happy sensual life within the limits of morally acceptable behaviour. As a fundamental characteristic in the person the desire to satisfy the senses is philosophically examined in the early Buddhist literature. In the preceding discussion, we have paid attention to this aspect of the sensuality and sexual desire.

We can conclude that there is a pleasure theory in the early Buddhist literature regarding sensuality and sexuality. Buddhism as a realistic approach to the human nature, accepts that sexual desire is a strong and one of the sweetest pleasures enjoyed by sentient beings. The *Aṅguttara Nikāya* mentions that the form, sound, taste, smell and touch of opposite sex are the sweetest sense objects for the correspondent senses (*AN* I.1). This shows a deep psychological and philosophical understanding in the subject of human sexuality. We can argue that the early Buddhism realistically had accepted the vitality of sexuality as a source of pleasure to the human being.

From the discussion carried out with regard to the positive aspect of sensuality or approval of it for the ordinary society, it is clear that Buddhism does not deny pleasure of sensuality and sexuality. On this, D.J. Kalupahana states that material

---

48 *DN* II.13: *dhammatā esā bhikkhave, yadā bodhisatto mātukucchiṃ okkanto hoti, lābhinī bodhisatta-mātā hoti pañcannaṃ kāma-guṇānaṃ, sā pañcahi kāmaguṇehi samappitā samangibhūtā parivāreti* ।

or physical comfort in itself is to be neither abandoned nor condemned. Physical deprivation, according to the Buddha, is as disruptive of moral and spiritual development as is indulgence in physical comfort (Kalupahana 1994: 96). The reason to admonish sense desire is that through that, there provides opportunity for the working of *lobha*, *dosa* and *moha* in the person's world. These three states of mind represent cognitive and emotional confusion resulting in falling into extreme forms of misconduct and immoral behaviour (*akusala*). That is a cause leading the person to suffering. What Buddhism denies is repercussions of the desire to gratify senses. In the *Saṃyutta Nikāya*, it is explained why one should give up sense pleasure because it is very easy to fall into wrong paths in seeking sensual pleasure (*mārapāsa*).[49] Otherwise, there is no problem about it.

And also, it should be mentioned that the Buddhist pleasure theory is characterized by the recognition of a gradual increase of the degree of happiness according to the level of one's mental cultivation and abiding in the moral life. The *Bahavedanīyasutta* represents the Buddha as saying that he denies the fact that the five strands of sense pleasure are the highest kind of pleasure. The reason for his denial is that the jhānic attainments call forth more excellent and sublime pleasure.[50] According to that *kāma* pleasure is the lowest. The

---

[49] SN IV.91: *santi bhikkhave cakkhuviññeyyā rupā iṭṭhā kantā manāpā piyarūpā kāmūpasamhitā rajanīyā। tañce bhikkhu abhinanadati abhivadati ajjhosāya tiṭṭhati। ayaṃ vuccati bhikkhave bhikkhu āvāsagato mārassa mārassa vasamgato। paṭimukhassa mārapāso baddho so mārabandhanena yathākāmakaraṇīyo pāpimato।*

[50] MN I.398f.; SN IV.225: *yaṃ kho ānanda ime pañcakāmaguṇe paṭicca uppajjati sukhaṃ somanassaṃ idaṃ vuccati kāmsukhaṃ। yo kho ānanda evam vadeyya: etaparamaṃ sattā sukhaṃ somanassaṃ paṭisamvedentīti,* →

Buddhist path is aimed at the highest level of happiness to which sensuality is an obstruction.

Problematic Nature of Sensuality

The Buddha recommends relinquishing attachment to sensuality, not because sensual pleasures are in any way evil, but because the attachment to them itself is dangerous both in terms of the pain experienced when a relished pleasure inevitably ends, and in terms of the detrimental influence such attachment can have on a person's actions and consequently thus on his or her well-being in the long run. Buddhism, being realistic about the nature of life of earthly being, presents its analysis in regard to sensuality focusing attention on the harmful consequences of it. Let us consider a few canonical references that focus attention on this aspect of seeing the danger of desire for sensual gratification.

A close examination of the harmful effects of sensuality reveals that they have equal repercussions on both physiological and psychological aspects of human beings. The *Mahādukkhakhandhasutta*[51] has given a detailed account of suffering which must be faced by the person who seeks sensual pleasures. The conflict of longing for gratification is presented on an empirical (*sandiṭṭhika*) basis using different kinds of issues in the contemporary society. The problems that cause man to suffer individually as well as social and international conflicts have, as their source, obsession with sensuality:

← *idam 'ssa nānujānāmi, taṃ kissa hetu: atthā' ānanda etamhā sukhā aññaṃ sukhaṃ abhikkantatarañca paṇītatarañca* ।

[51] *MN* I.83-90: As the *sutta* says only the Buddha and his disciples are able to offer a perfect and a realistic discourse on the subjects of sensuality, form and feeling (*kāma*, *rūpa* and *vedanā*).

> Again, with sensual pleasures as the cause, sensual pleasures as the source, sensual pleasures as the basis, the cause being simply sensual pleasures, kings quarrel with kings, nobles with nobles, brāhmaṇa with brahmaṇas ... mother quarrels with child, child with mother; And here in their quarrels, brawls, and disputes they attack each other with fists, clods ... whereby they incur death or deadly suffering ... men take swords and shields and buckle on bows and quivers, and they charge into battle massed in double array with arrows and spears flying and swords flashing; and there they are wounded by arrows and spears, and their heads are cut off by swords, whereby they incur death or deadly suffering. Now this too is a danger in the case of sensual pleasures, the cause being simply sensual pleasures. – *MLDB*, p. 181

The *Aṅguttara Nikāya* refers to five codes of sensual pleasures in relation to the two opposite sexes. The *rūpa* (material form) of the female is the highest pleasure among forms for the male and vice versa (*AN* I.1).

The *Mahādukkhandhasutta* has made an investigation into the change of a young girl's beauty in the course of time. A young beautiful damsel of ideal bodily qualities expected of a woman, and descending from a noble family calls forth pleasure for others at her age of fifteen or sixteen.[52] In contrast, after reaching old age, she loses all the beauties possessed earlier. This is the nature of material form. In this context, the simile that is used is of great power of appeal to the readers' mind because of its relevance to sensual and

---

[52] *MN* I.88: *ko ca bhikkhave rūpānaṃ assādo: seyyathāpi bhikkhave khattiyakaññā vā ... paṇṇarasā vā nātirassā nātikisā nātithūlā ... paramā sā bhikkhave tasmiṃ samaye subhā vaṇṇanibhā ... yaṃ kho bhikkhave subhaṃ vaṇṇanibhaṃ paṭicca uppajjati sukhaṃ somansassaṃ ayaṃ rupānaṃ assādo* ।

sexual life.

To what extent, the individual is psychologically affected can be seen in the phraseology used to indicate the after effects of seeking sense-pleasure:

> *so socati kilamati paridevati urattālim kandati sammohaṃ āpajjati.* – *MN* I.86

The frustration or anguish experienced leads the person to a state of psychological breakdown in which the ability to reason is lost as indicated by *sammohaṃ āpajjati.*[53]

With regard to adultery, its origin is placed in sensual lust (*MN* I.87). Adultery is a violation of an ethical norm accepted in Buddhism in the realm of sexuality. In the foregoing discussion, we have pointed out that sensual desire is a basic component of the human psyche. Therefore, it can be concluded that the root of deviation in sexual behaviour is to be found in one's consciousness.

Ven. Buddhaghoṣa examines the nature of behaviour of human beings in seeking sensually fascinating realms of rebirth. The uninstructed worldling is like a madman (*ummattako viya hi puthujjano*). Without considering good or bad, he is ready to do anything which is considered as a means to get sensual pleasures. For example, someone thinks in accordance with heresy or [false] view that sense desires come to be fulfilled in the human world among the great worrier (*khattiya*) families, etc., and in the six divine worlds of the sense sphere. Misled by listening to wrong doctrines, etc.,

[53] *PED* provides three meanings for the term *sammoha*: bewilderment, infatuation and delusion (p. 697). According to the etymology of the term, it seems "delusion" is more preferable. In psychiatry, delusion is a fixed false belief that is resistant to reason or confrontation with actual fact (*Random House Unabridged Dictionary*, p. 528).

and imagining that "by this *kamma* sense desires will come to be fulfilled", he performs for the purpose of attaining them acts of bodily misconduct, etc., through sense-desire clinging (Ñāṇamoli 1991: 595).

The assertion that sensual pleasure is of little satisfaction by nature is frequently mentioned in the canonical materials. The *Alagaddūpamasutta* says:

> *appassādā kāmā vuttā bhagavatā bahudukkhā bahupāyāsā ādinavo ettha bhiyyo*
>
> The Blessed One has stated how sensual pleasures provide little gratification, much suffering, and much despair, and how great is the danger in them.

The acute pain inflicted upon the individual in his attempt to satisfy the senses is revealed by the ten similes (ibid.: 130). Each simile puts forward one aspect of the problematic nature of sensuality as exposited in the commentary (*MA* II.10 (Devanāgarī)).

If we examine the terminology utilized, *bahudukkha* refers to the host of physical pains and *bahupāyāsa* refers to mental anguish and dejection. As Buddhaghoṣa defines *upāyāsa* (despair), it is the humour itself (*doso yeva*) which is produced by excessive mental suffering (*adhimattaceto-dukkhapabhavito*). It is characterized with burning of the mind and its function is to bemoan. It is manifested as dejection (*Vism* 504). Severity of after-effects that one has to undergo owing to chasing after sense gratification, becomes clear from this definition of the term *upāyāsa*.

The philosophical thesis of suffering in the first noble truth finds it cause in the second noble truth of *taṇhā*. Usually, *taṇhā* is defined in the scriptures in terms of six senses (in addition to *pañcakama-guṇa* definition) with rare reference to the other two aspects of it found in the truth of the origin of suffering. If it is reasoned out why man likes to be reborn, the very cause can be seen in the distorted thirst (due to ignorance) for sense pleasure. The truth of pain presents a list of existential suffering which are unavoidable as long as one is bound to the realm governed by what is produced by thirst produced through the contact of senses (*MN* III.250).

Contemporary Indian society was dominated by the two ideologies of rigorous asceticism and sensual indulgence (*SN* V.421). Certain religious groups were in a position to expound the virtues of enjoying five codes of sense pleasures as the way to attain liberation in this very life (*Diṭṭhadhammanibbāṇavāda* doctrine of *nibbana* in this life).[54] Five groups have been recognized among those who preached the liberation here and now. The first out of them was based on the view of gratifying the soul with sense pleasure as a mean to attain *nibbana*. The second companion of the view was against the view without denying the soul. The argument made against sensuality is identical with the phraseology used in the Buddhist sources in similar contexts:

> Because, good sir, sense pleasures are impermanent, suffering, subject to change, and through their change and transformation sorrow, lamentation, pain, grief and despair arise. – Bodhi 1992: 81

There has been no comment on the view from the Buddhist standpoint perhaps because the same idea is represented in

[54] *DN* I.36: *yato kho bho ayaṃ attā pañcahi kāmaguṇehi samappito samangībhūto paricāreti, ettāvatā kho bho ayaṃ attā paramadiṭṭhadhammanibbāna patto hoti*।

Buddhism.

The terminology selected to talk about the mental state of the individual who is assailed by the desire for sensual pleasure is associated with the images of fire, fever, sharp-weapons, etc. The idea of thirst (*pipāsā*) also frequently occurs. The term *kāma-pipāsā* is connected with the physical activity of seeking water. Thirst is an insatiable biological need in the body until it lasts with the consciousness attached to it. This imagery is very effective even on the simplest person in the world. And he feels its inherent effect within his mental and bodily life. This imagery is furthered in the imagery of rain of gold coins:

> *na kahāpana vassena titthi kāmesu vijjati*
> – *Dhammapada* 186

> Not for showers of coins is satisfaction to be found in pleasures.

After drinking a sort of beverage, one's thirst temporarily becomes satisfied and remains the feeling of satisfaction for a while. In contrast to physical satisfaction, mental thirst is unimaginably insatiable regarding objects of pleasure sources. Mental satisfaction is highly momentary because mind's very nature is evanescent. So the elder Samiddhi said, *kālikā hi āvuso kāmā* (sensual pleasures are time consuming — *SN* I.9). The imagery of fire is frequently mentioned in describing the general psychological make-up of the sentient being. The whole sensory perceptual process is recognized as a burning phenomenon.

The *Ādittasutta* recognizes three kinds of fire from which the individual's senses burn:

> The All is aflame. What All is aflame? The eye is aflame.

> Forms are aflame. Visual cognition is aflame. Visual contact is aflame. And whatever there is that arises in dependence on visual contact, experienced as pleasure, pain or neither pleasure nor pain, that too is aflame. Aflame with what? Aflame with the fire of passion, the fire of aversion, the fire of delusion.[55]

Shortly after the enlightenment, the Exalted One looks over the world and sees that beings in it are being tortured by diverse torments and burning with diverse burnings with the fires of lust, hatred and delusion.[56] Rhys Davids and W. Stede state that the term *pariḷāha* figuratively can be rendered as "fever of passion" (*PED*, 435). The *Udānapali* directly referring to the sphere of sensual attachment mentions that fire of passion burns a man excited with sensual desires (*rāgaggi dahati macce-ratte kāmesu mucchite — It* 92). The *Dhammapada* states that there is nothing to be compared with the fire of sensual desire (*natthi rāga samo aggi — Dhammapada* 148).

Here, we have cited three canonical quotations which have used the analogy of fire with attachment to sensuality. This shows that what a severe suffering is inflicted upon the person who seeks sensual and sexual pleasures. In addition to these abstract teachings on the feverish experience of lust, let us examine a more concrete presentation of the burning experience due to lust:

> I burn with desire for sensual pleasures, my mind is on

---

55 SN IV.19: *cakkhuṃ bhikkhave ādittaṃ rūpā। ādittā cakkhuviññāṇaṃ ādittaṃ। cakkhusamphasso āditto। yaṃ pidaṃ cakkhusamphassapaccayā uppajjati vedayitaṃ sukhaṃ vā dukkhaṃ vā adukkhamasukhaṃ vā taṃ pi ādittaṃ। kena ādittaṃ। rāgagginā dosagginā mohagginā।*

56 *Ud* 32: *addasā kho bhagavā buddhacakkhunā lokaṃ volokento satte anekehi santāpehi santappamāne anekehica parḷāhehi paridayhamāne rāgehi pi dosajehi pi mohajehi pī 'ti।*

> fire. Please, Gotama, from compassion, tell me how to put it out.[57]

In this self-expression, the inner pain caused by sensual attachment is reflected using the analogy of fire. In this case, the Buddha explains why this fire sensation comes to act upon the mind. It is due to distorted perception that the mind is on fire. To find release, one has to shun the sign of the beautiful, accompanied by lust (*Th* I, 1224).

The problematic nature of sensuality and its cause are well examined in the *Māgaṅdiyasutta*. The image of fire and the simile of a burning charcoal pit have extensively been elaborated in relation to sensual desire. As it was mentioned earlier, the Buddhist discourse on sensuality approaches the subject systematically. As a beginning to the discussion, the Buddha concedes that the internal sense faculties are attractive to external sense objects characterized by a pleasing quality (*piyarūpa*, etc.). For instance, the Buddha says that the eye delights in forms, takes delights in forms, rejoices in forms (*cakkhuṃ rūparamaṃ rūparataṃ rūpasamudditaṃ* । — *MN* I.503).

In this *sutta* a doctrinal view of sensual perception is presented by the recluse Māgaṅdiya, that is, the "growth" is determined by exposure to new sense objects as much as possible. As to this, the Buddha was not in agreement and therefore Māgaṅdiya called him "destroyer of growth" (*bhūnahuna*) (*MLDB*, p. 1278 n. 740). In answer to this accusation, the Buddha explains how sense perception leads to attachment to sensuality and the conflict-making nature of it.

The leper's simile is introduced to explain different

---

[57] *Th* I, 1223: *kāmarāgena dayhāmi, cittaṃ me paridayhati;*
sādhu nibbāpanaṃ brūhi anukampāya Gotama ।

aspects of sensual desire. Here, an account is given of the sensuous life led by the Buddha before leaving the worldly life and the inward happiness experienced after the abandonment of craving for sense pleasures. How he sees the sentient beings that are still indulged in sensual pleasures is explained by means of a comparison of the feeling of a leper recovered from his leprosy towards another leper in suffering. The recovered does not envy the unrecovered because the former has no delight in that pathetic condition (*MN* I.506). The description of the painful condition of a leper is portrayed in the *sutta* so as to generate a similar effect on the reader:

> Suppose, Māgaṅdiya, there was a leper with sores and blisters on his limbs, being devoured by worms, scratching the scabs off the openings of his wounds with his nails, cauterizing his body over a burning charcoal pit.[58]

This is the image continually referred to in order to portray the nature of suffering involved in craving for sensuality. The more one strives for gratification the more he is inflicted by pain. The reason to be steeped in lust is the satisfaction given by five codes of sense pleasures. So being attracted by little satisfaction, beings are subject to this type of fate:

> The more he scratches the scabs and cauterizes his body, the fouler, more evil-smelling and more infected the openings of his wounds would become, yet he would find a certain measure of satisfaction and enjoyment in scratching the openings of his wounds. So too, Māgaṅdiya, who are devoured by craving for sensual pleasures, who burn with fever for sensual pleasures, still indulge in sensual

---

[58] *MLDB*, p. 611; *MN* I.507: *seyyathāpi māgandiya kuṭṭhī puriso arugatto pakkagatto kimīhi khajjamāno nakhehi vaṇamukhāni vippatacchamāno aṅgārakāsuyā kāyaṃ paritāpeyya*।

> pleasures; the more their craving for sensual pleasures, still indulged in sensual pleasures; the more such beings indulge in sensual pleasures, the more their craving for sensual pleasures increases and the more they are burned by their fever for sensual pleasures, yet they find a certain measure of satisfaction and enjoyment in dependence on the five codes of sensual pleasures. – *MLDB*, p. 611

A leper being tormented by pain cauterizes his body over fire to find release whereby he gets a kind of pleasure. But in reality he does not find any release. He does this due to mistaken perception. After recovery, he sees the dreadfulness of fire. He never wishes to experience it again. Fire is now, in future as well as in the past painful to touch, hot and scorching. The Buddha says to Māgaṅdiya that sensual pleasures too, in all the three times, past, future and now, are painful touch, hot and scorching. But sentient beings who are not free from lust for sensual pleasures, devoured by craving for sensual pleasures, who burn with sensual pleasures, have faculties that are impaired; thus, though sensual pleasures are actually painful to touch, they acquire a mistaken perception of them as pleasant.[59]

The discussion based on this *sutta* reveals the burning sensation caused by craving for sensual pleasures and why it is found in the sentient beings. The final explanation given here is that it is due to mistaken perception in connection with sensual pleasures. Here, the force of ignorance is intended. It functions as a hindrance to seeing the truth as it is. It is clear that man is engaged in a project of seeking for something which is not really attainable. The more the thirst is felt, the

[59] *MN* I.507: *ime ca kho māgandiya sattā kāmesu avītarāgā kāmataṇhāhi khajjamānā kāmapariḷāhena paridayhamānā upahatindriyā dukkha-samphasses 'va kāmesu sukham-iti viparītasaññaṃ paccalatthum* ।

more striving for it is intensified. Buddhism being realistic recognizes that there is temporary satisfaction provided by pleasure derived from desired objects.

According to the Buddha, (Freud too) man's behaviour and his outlook on life are determined by several instincts such as "desire to live", desire to avoid death, longing for happiness and aversion to pain (*SN* IV.172ff). Obviously, he gains satisfaction from what is desired. Being confused by this short-lived excitement, beings are propelled to achieve an eternal gratification. Philosophical justification of the inner tendency to find pleasure has been sought after by man since ancient times. As we already have referred to the Upaniṣadic doctrine of an eternal and immortal "self", it was introduced with the intention of satisfying the deep-seated craving of man for permanent happiness (Kalupahana 1977: 38). In contrast, the whole phenomenon, mental and physical, is devoid of such an entity (*sabbe saṅkhārā aniccā*).

As we discussed in the section of *āsava* and *anusaya*, beings have been conditioned by inclinations such as lust for an incalculable time. In consequence, human being is unable to realize the transient nature of conditioned existence. Therefore, he is prepared to find pleasure from any sort of activity. The *Sallattenasutta* (The Dart) describes the fact that how an uninstructed person seeks for sensual happiness and the reason why he behaves in such a manner:

> Being touched by painful feeling, he seeks delight in sensual pleasure. What is the reason? Because the uninstructed worldling does not know of any escape from painful feeling other than sensual pleasure.[60]

---

[60] *SN* IV.208: *so dukkhāya vedanāya puṭṭho samāno kāmasukhaṃ abhinandati* I *taṃ kissa hetu? na hi bhikkhave pajānāti assutavā puthujjano aññatra*

This idea in the canon is provocative of seeking reasons how certain sexual deviant acts like sadomasochism come into existence. If someone is happy in pain within his own body, it is not something strange to have persons looking for pleasure by inflicting pain on others. In the context of sexual deviance, it can be seen how man attempts to find pleasure in various ways through certain acts like rape.[61]

The assertion made in the *Māgaṅdiyasutta* is that the distorted perception is the origin of craving for sensual pleasure (*viparītasaññaṃ paccalatthati*). In the *Vaṅgīsa Theragāthā*, it is mentioned that in one's mind fire is lit by misconceived perception (*MN* I.39). Previously, it was mentioned that Ven. Buddhaghoṣa compares the ordinary person to a madman whose life is governed by confusion. On account of clinging to basis (either emotional or intellectual), one is psychologically intoxicated and consequently his faculty of cognition is barred from seeing the reality (causality) in the world.[62] Man's attempt to find earthly pleasure is to be understood in this ground in Buddhism. This is fully indicative of an obsessed state of mentality. It is really the mentality of seeking sensual and sexual pleasure.

In the *Mahādukkhakkhandhasutta*, it is clearly accepted that the deterioration of morality is due to sensuality. So, we can have the conclusion regarding the origin of sexual deviant behaviour that, in the deepest level, ignorance (mistaken perception – *avijja*) and thirst for pleasure (*taṇhā* or *kāma-*

---

kāmasukhā dukkhāya vadanāya nissaraṇaṃ ।

[61] It is interesting to see that a rapist is considered as one needs mental treatment.

[62] *DN* II.37: *ālaya-rāmāya kho pana pajāya ālaya-ratāya ālaya samudditāya duddasaṃ idaṃ ṭhānaṃ yadidaṃ idappaccayatā paṭiccasamuppādo* ।

taṇhā) are nothing but the manifestation of ignorance.

In the canon, the alluring nature of sensual objects is readily accepted. The *Khaggavisāṇasutta* in the *Sutta Nipāta* states:

> *kāmā hi citrā madhurā manoramā-virūparūpena mathenti cittam, ādīnavam kāmaguṇesu disvā eko care kaggavisāṇakappo*
>
> – *SN* 50
>
> For sensual pleasures, variegated, sweet (and) delightful, disturb the mind with their manifold form. Seeing peril in the strands of sensual pleasure, one should wander as a rhinoceros horn. – Norman 1993: 6 v 50

Here, it is explicit that there is no end to sensual objects and eventually to the desire to obtain them. By this unimaginable diversity, human mind is enticed and tempt to seek more and more. In the unending search for them, he becomes exhausted (physically and mentally), yet desire is not fulfilled and fatefully reaches to the end of life as a man without inner fulfilment (*ūṇāva hutvāna jahanti dehaṃ*).

If we attempt to connect the concept of diversity of sensual objects with the origin of sexual deviance, it is natural to have a variety of behavioural patterns to achieve sexual pleasure on the very ground that there exists an infinite variety of objects. According to the Buddhist idea, man is misled or confused by this diversity and consequently loses the power of reason (*sammohaṃ āpajjati*) whereupon he himself becomes exposed to practise any kind of activity supposed to be a way to pleasure.

Sex and Psychological Obsession

As we have made a sufficient examination of how sensual desire leads the individual to become psychologically obsessed, a brief reference is made regarding sexuality. Among the sensual pleasures, sex can be considered as the highest. In sexual performance, all the sense faculties come to activate and a strong feeling of desire is gratified. The *pañcakāma-guṇa* (five strands of sense pleasure) is defined in the context of sexuality in the *Aṅguttara Nikāya*. Female's form, sound, smell and touch are of the greatest pleasure for male and vice versa (*AN* I.1f.).

When a person is assailed by desire for sex, his inward conflict is visible to others from his change in outward appearance. The compilers of the Pali canon seem to have had an understanding of the change in general mentality of members of the community. This can be seen in the portrayal of the elder Seyyasaka's episode. The stock phrase used to describe his appearance is of psychological importance:

> ... venerable Seyyasaka led the Brahma life, dissatisfied. Because of this he was thin wretched, his colour bad, yellowish, and his veins showing all over his body.[63]

This change occurred to him as a result of being in an unsettled state of mind, burning with a fever of passion and sense desire, but not wishing to give up the recluse life.[64] The nature of intense feeling for sex (in this context *rāga* refers to sexual desire) is explained in the phrase *rāgo cittam anuddhamseti* (passion assails the heart). When the person is affected by lust, there occurs an excessive heartburn and he becomes confused and withered (*kāmarāgo cittam dhamseti*

---

[63] *BD* I.192; *Vin* III.110: *āyasmā Seyyasako anabhirato brahmacariyaṃ carati, so tena kiso hoti luko dubbaṇṇo uppaṇḍuppaṇḍukajāto dhamani-santhatagatto* ।

[64] *VinA* 517: *vikkhittacitto kāmarāgapariḷāhena pariḍayhamāno na pana gihībhāvaṃ patthayamāno* ।

padhamseti vikkhipati ce'va milāpeti ca — *VA* 518). This effect on the person after being assailed by sexual desire is well understood from the description given of Seyyasaka. What would happen to the individual of such mentality is evident from Seyyasaka's being tempted to seek sexual satisfaction through masturbation, a practice prohibited for the Buddhist clergy (*Vin* III.100).

The strength of sexual desire more than the other aspects of sensuality has been observed in the canon as well as in the commentarial literature. For instance, the *Aṅguttara Nikāya* mentions that even one who is over 100 years old never loses his sexual desire (Gamage 1998: 31 fn. 65). Once, the Buddha stated that women die with incomplete desire which is that of having sex and giving birth to children (ibid.: 31 fn. 66). The *Asātamantajātaka* (Dolour Text) evidently expresses the view that the sex drive is active till the end of one's life. In this story, a young student attends his teacher's old-aged mother. Being recuperated by his service, the old lady falls in love with him and decides to kill her own son to live together with the young man. The mother was of 120 years old by this time (*J.* I.285-89). It is obvious that sexual desire so strong that one can become a murderer and lead to various kinds of unskilful and deviational activities. On this ground, it can be concluded that the origin of deviant sexual behaviour, in Buddhist psychology, lies in one's mentality subjugated by lust which is the manifestation of ignorance regarding the true nature of sensual happiness.

3

Buddhist Attitude to Human Body

Introduction

In the attempt to understand the position held by Pali Theravada Buddhism about deviant sexual behaviour, it is useful to look into the concept of the human body because sexual desire, deviant sex acts and human body are three closely connected factors. It is interesting to see that Pali Theravada Buddhism has formed a negative attitude towards the human body because of several reasons. The Buddhist view on the body can be said to be ambivalent; in some ways it is negative and in other ways positive. In this chapter, I discuss the concept of the human body in relation to terms used to designate human body and the constitution of human body, the use of it as a meditation object, negativism expressed towards it and, finally point out, why such negativism is expressed.

In the initial discourse of the Buddha to his disciples he recognized the human individuality formed out of five aggregates and the clinging to them as suffering. Those five aggregates are known as the aggregates of material form, feeling, perception, volitional formations and consciousness. While the aggregate of material form (*rūpa*) represents the physical body of the human being, the other four represent the psyche of the individual. In addition to the term *rūpa*, the terms '*kāya*',[1] *deha, sarīra*[2] and *sandeha*[3] have been used to refer to the body. The term *kāya* has definitely and frequently been used in the canonical and later Pali literature to indicate the human body. The use of the term *rūpa* in a few contexts to denote the physical body needs a close examination. In the five-aggregates formula, the first item is *rūpa* (*SN* III.7). In the *paṭiccasamuppāda* formula, it occurs in combination with *nāma*, as *nāma-rūpa*.[4] This literally means "name and form", but has also been interpreted as "mind and body" (Hamilton 1996: 3). Rhys Davids and W. Stede state that in the *nāma-rūpa*, *rūpa* resembles *kāya*:

> in the making up of the individuality as such (*nāma-rūpa*), where in contrast with *nāma* (as abstract, logical, invisible or mind-factor) *rūpa* represents the visible (material) factor, resembling *kāya* (cp. phrase *nāma-kāya* in same sense).
>
> – *PED*, p. 575

Rūpa is found in another context, in the list of external objects of internal sense organs, as *rūpayatana* (*ND* II.238). As the object of the eye, the aggregate of material form is more concerned with "colour" (*vaṇṇanibha*) or appearance and shape than the human body (Hamilton 1996: 3). The aspect of colour of material aggregate is not much concerned with the human body (ibid.). The definition of the aggregate of material as found in the *Sutta Piṭaka* refers to four elements, element of

---

1 *SN* III.120: *kāya* in combination with the term *pūti* — *kim te vakkali iminā pūtikāyena*; *MN* II.65: *añjanī 'va navā cittā pūtikāyo alankato-alaṃ bālassa mohāya no ca pāragavesino* ।

2 *Abhi* 151: *sarīraṃ, vapu gattaṃ, (ca)* ... ।

3 *Dh* 148: *bhijjati pūtisandeho* ... ।

4 *DN* II.56: *iti kho ānanda nāmarūpa-paccayā viññāṇaṃ, viññāṇapaccayā nāmarūpaṃ* ।

earth, element of water, element of fire and element of wind, and what is derived from them. The term *kāya* is defined in the context of human body with details in the *Sutta Piṭaka* itself. In the *Dīgha Nikāya*, we find the definition of the human body as follows:

> This body of mine, made of material form, consisting of the four great elements, procreated by a mother and a father, and built up out of boiled rice and porridge, is subject to impermanence, to being worn and rubbed away, to dissolution and disintegration, and this consciousness of mine is supported by it and bound up with it.[5]

This definition is comprehensive enough because it has covered many aspects of the body including its main characteristic (*rūpī* — material), properties in it (*cātummahābhūtika* — four elements), origin (*mātāpettika sambhava* — born of parent), dependence (*odanakummāsa paccaya* — built up out of boiled rice and porridge) and more important its function as the basis for consciousness. Elder Ānanda defines the *kāya* as dependent on four factors:

i. originated from sexual intercourse (*methunasambhūta*),
ii. dependent on edible food (*āhārasambhūta*),
iii. origin and dependence on desire (*taṇhāsambhūta*), and
iv. origin and dependence on conceit (*mānasambhūta*) (*AN* II.145).

Bhikkhu Bodhi who is a modern Buddhist scholar defines the body as:

---

[5] *MN* II.17: *ayaṃ kho me kāyo rūpi cātummahābhūtiko mātāpettikasambhavo odanakummāsapaccayo anicc-ucchādana-parimaddana-bhedana-viddhansanadhammo, idañ ca pana me viññāṇaṃ ettha sitaṃ ettha paṭibaddhaṃ*।; *MLDB*, p. 642.

> The aggregate of material form (*rūpa*) includes the physical body with its sense faculties as well as external material objects. – *MLDB*, p. 26

Both the terms *rūpa* and *kāya* have been used to refer to the human body. The term *rūpa* is used in the contexts of more philosophical explanation concerned with deconstructive attempt of early Buddhism, which was implemented against the contemporary view on the eternal self (*atta* or *ātman*).[6] *Rupa* in relation to the colour and shape (which generally constitute the physical beauty) in the human body has been referred to in the *Mahādukkhakkhandhasutta* (*MN* I.88). A comprehensive account of the human body under *rūpā* is included inside the *sutta* and the description begins referring to colour and the other bodily parts. The passage shows what is loved for its beauty lacks permanence (*MN* I.88). In the *sutta*, this explanation is preceded by an analysis of five strands of sensual pleasures and in that a logical connection between sensual desire and influence of physical beauty in generating attachment is shown.

The *kāya* is also the same in its physical aspect as *rūpa* aggregate. As for the physical aspect of the *kāya*, Rhys Davids states:

> *Kāya* under the physical aspect is an aggregate of a multiplicity of elements which finally can be reduced to the four "great" elements, viz. earth, water, fire and air (*cātummahābhūtiko ayam puriso* — *D* I.55). This "heap", in the valuation of the Wise (*muni*) shares with all other

---

6 *PED*, p. 574: There are various groups of psychological and metaphysical systematizations, in which *rūpa* functions as the material, gross factor. In all these representations of *rūpa* we find that an element of moral psychology overshadows the purely philosophical and speculative aspect.

objects the qualities of such elements, and is therefore regarded as contemptible, as something which one has to get rid of, as a source of impurity. It is subject to time and change, it is built up and kept alive by cravings, and with death it is disintegrated into the elements. But the *kamma* which determined the appearance of this physical body has naturally been renewed and assumes a new form. *Kāya,* under psychological aspect, is the seat of sensation, and represents the fundamental organ of touch which underlies all other sensation. – *PED*, p. 207

The Constitution of the Human Body

In Theravada Buddhist literature, there are two kinds of definition of the human body. One is the definition of material aggregate (*rūpakkhandha*) which explains the body according to four (rarely five) elements and the other the standard list of thirty-two bodily parts mentioned in the definition of *kāya.* Let us first deal with the explanations that come under *rūpa.*

The doctrine of five aggregates is a core Buddhist teaching in its discourse on the problem of human suffering. The five aggregates have been the subject in the *Khandha Saṃyutta* of the *Saṃyutta Nikāya* as well as in other canonical material. The *Khandha Saṃyutta* continues its discussion on the basis that human being is composed of the five aggregates.

According to *pañcakkhandha* analysis, the things that constitute the human being can be explained as follows: The material aggregate consists of four great elements and their derivatives. The feeling aggregate is of six classes: feeling born of eye contact, feeling born of ear contact, feeling born of nose contact, feeling born of tongue contact, feeling born of body contact and feeling born of mind contact. The third aggregate, perception, is also of six classes: perception of forms, sounds, odours, tastes, tactile objects and mental phenomena. The aggregate of volitional formations has six classes: volition regarding forms, sounds, odours, tastes, tactile objects and mental phenomena. The last one, the aggregate of consciousness is of six classes: eye consciousness, ear consciousness, nose consciousness, tongue consciousness, body consciousness and mind consciousness (*SN* III.59f.). Within the ordinary mind these come to be grasped as things belonging to oneself and the person identifies himself with them. Thus the aggregates grasped with craving are called in Pali *pañcupādānakkhandha*, aggregates subject to clinging (*SN* III.47). Ven. Ñāṇavīra says that *pañcakkhandha* is found in the *arahant* as well but in the case of the ordinary individual they have become *pañcupādānakkhandhas* (Ñāṇavīra 1987: 26; also Gethin 1986: 37ff.).

In the *Khandha Saṃyutta*, *rūpa* is examined under the material aggregate in the sense of visible object and a person's own body. Regarding these five constituents, the Buddha teaches that none of these constitutes a permanent, unchanging self: one is to become detached from each of them (*SN* III.59ff.). The analysis made with regard to the body of a human being is presented in the form of an abstract account of elements. Here, we find only an abstract view of human being formed of four elements and their derivatives.[7] In the canon itself, the categorizing of bodily parts according to elements recognizing them in terms of time and according to their location (internal and external) occurs. In the

---

[7] *SN* III.59: "And what is the *bhikkhu* body (*rūpa*)? It is the four great elements and whatever physical thing is derived from the great elements: This *bhikkhus* is called the body." (*katamañ ca bhikkhave rūpaṃ? cattāro ca mahābhūtā catunnaṃ ca mahābhūtānaṃ upādāya rūpaṃ idaṃ vuccati bhikkhave rūpaṃ*)

Mahāhatthipadopamasutta, elder Sāriputta makes an explicit description under material aggregate (in relation to human body) in terms of four elements, earth, water, fire and wind. He defines material aggregate as consisting of these four and their derivatives.[8] The description of the earth element is thus:

> What, friends, is the earth element? The earth element may be internal or external. What is the internal earth element? Whatever internally, belonging to oneself, is solid, solidified, and clung-to; that is head-hairs, nails, teeth, skin, flesh, sinews, bones and so on (nineteen bodily parts are mentioned by name) ... faeces or whatever else[9] internally, belonging to oneself, is solid, solidified, and clung to; this is called the internal earth element. Now both the internal earth element and the external earth element are simply earth element. And that should be seen as it actually is with proper wisdom thus: "This is not mine, this I am not, this is not my self" (*MN* I.186).

The other three aggregates are also explained in relation to bodily parts and things taken into body like food and drinks, whatever internally connected to the human body (*MN* I.185-91). Even though the canonical sources frequently refer to the derivative forms of the material aggregate, we cannot find a place where they have been defined. Buddhaghoṣa in his seminal work, the *Visuddhimagga*, has defined those secondary forms (*upādāya rūpa*) in the discussion on material aggregate (*Vism*, p. 444).

---

8 *MN* I.185: *katamo c 'āvuso rūpupādānakkhandho: cattāri ca mahābhūtāni catunnan ca upādāya mahābhūtānaṃ upādāya rūpaṃ* ।

9 *MLDB*, p. 1220, n. 329: "whatever else" is intended to include the earth element comprised in those parts of the body, not included in this enumeration.

An account of the body as material aggregate explained in terms of elements is included in the *Mahārāhulovādasutta*. The Buddha explaining the material form to the elder Rāhula states that any kind of material form whatever, whether past, future, or present, internal or external, gross or subtle, inferior or superior, far or near, all material forms should be seen as it actually is with proper wisdom thus: "This is not mine, this I am not, this is not myself" (*MN* I.421). Following this definition, each element is examined connecting to the bodily parts and with related characteristics. The description is the same with the *Mahāhatthipadopamasutta* (*MN* I.185ff.).

In the *Mahārāhulovādasutta*, space element is also included in the material aggregate and the passage indicates the places and the things in the body where the space element exists.[10] This understanding on body leads to the exclusion of the concept of "self" and a consequence of this is that the mind becomes disenchanted with each element and it develops detachment towards the elements.

In view of the descriptions included in these *sutta*s on the body, S. Hamilton says that though they include actual parts of the body, it can be suggested that the point intended to make is to establish that the body includes things that are characterized either by hardness/solidity or liquidity/fluidity. In neither case are the literal meanings of the elements, earth and water, directly applicable. These descriptions produce characteristics of the body rather than

---

[10] *MN* I.423: *ākāsadhātu siyā ajjhattikā siyā bāhirā ... yaṃ ajjhattaṃ paccattaṃ ākāsaṃ ākāsagataṃ upādinnaṃ, seyyathīdaṃ kaṇṇacchiddaṃ nāsacchiddaṃ mukhadvāraṃ ... yaṃ vā pan 'aññam-pi kiñci ajjhattaṃ paccattaṃ ākāsaṃ ākāsagataṃ upādinnaṃ, ayaṃ vuccati rāhula ajjhatikā ākāsadhātu। yā c 'eva kho pana ajjahttikā ākāsadhātu yā ca bāhira ākāsadhātu ākāsadhatur-'ev'esā।*

real bodily parts (Hamilton 1996: 10).

The intention of promoting an analytical approach to the physical body of the human being by breaking it down to elements and their various characteristics is to encourage a detached attitude to the body. Even though the mind factor is more crucial in producing desire for sensual objects, the involvement of body as a whole with its physical parts including physical sense organs cannot also be ignored. The whole physical body functions as an agent of enticing persons to seek sensual pleasures. At the end of the description of each element, the insight gained from the contemplation is presented thus:

> "This is not mine, this I am not, this is not myself." When one sees it thus as it actually is with proper wisdom, one becomes disenchanted with the earth element (the same with regard to the other elements) and the mind becomes dispassionate towards the earth element.[11]

Actually, being enchanted by elements does not imply the abstract sense of elements. They are embodied in various bodily parts and the individual in the first instance forms the concept of "I"-ness and "my"-ness regarding them and consequently he or she is compelled to find pleasure in them. So, he or she becomes enchanted by body (as a whole and each part as a single object for desire) and becomes passionate about it. This emotional attachment occurs due to materiality being of pleasing quality to the human mind.

If we consider the general tendency in persons to have interests in material objects, there is a variety of interests. One may show a preference for roughness of objects and

[11] MN III.240: *n'etaṃ mama, n'eso 'ham asmi, na me so attā ti, evaṃ etaṃ yathābhūtaṃ sammappaññāya daṭṭhabbaṃ* ।

another may show a preference for their softness. Both these attitudes can be in relation to the element of earth which represents solidity (*paṭhavī*). The body (*kāya āyatana*) is the sense faculty which experiences the touch (*phoṭṭhabba*) of such qualities (roughness, flexibility, etc.) found in the elements. *Kāya* sensation is the underlying internal sense which pervades over the whole body (*PED*, p. 207).

To go by the sexological understanding of the nature of bodily parts and productions, almost every bodily part and bodily production is sexually attractive to the person. For example, urine and faeces are used in sadomasochistic sexual unions.[12] Such modern scientific findings reveal the nature of the human being's attachment to infatuation with bodily parts. So, even though, the body is not a direct agent that creates desire, its contribution in stimulating the desire in the mind is crucial. Seeing this possibility of obsession with the body, early Buddhism has attempted to point out that solidity or mobility is not in the body but merely in the parts.

In addition to the descriptions made on the basis of elements and the analysis of material aggregate (*rūpa*), a list of bodily parts is presented in a stock passage describing *kāya*. This list is presented in contexts where the human body is recommended for use as an object for meditation. In the *Kāyagatāsatisutta*, human body (*kāya*) is defined as follows:

> Again, *bhikkhus*, a *bhikkhu* reviews this same body up from the soles of the feet and down from the top of the hair, bounded by skin, as full of many kinds of impurity thus: "In this body there are head hairs, body hairs, nails, teeth, skin, flesh, sinews, bones, bone marrow, kidneys, heart, liver,

---

[12] Navid, Rathus and Rathus 1995: 569: refer to golden showers (urination) in sadomasochistic practices.

> diaphragm, spleen, lungs, large intestine, small intestine, contents of the stomach, faeces, bile, phlegm, pus, blood, sweat, fat, tears, grease, spittle, snot, oil of the joints, and urine.
> – *MLDB*, p. 951

The same list of bodily parts is mentioned in the *Mahāsatipaṭṭhānasutta* in its explanation of mindfulness of body (*kāyānupassanā*).[13] It is repeated in the *Satipaṭṭhānasutta* of the *Majjhima Nikāya* too (*MN* I.57). In these canonical lists, the brain is missed as a body part and the *Visuddhimagga* has added it to the list.[14]

The anatomical description on the body is purely analytical and is a direct division of the body. We can point out the difference between the descriptions given with regard to the body under the two concepts *rūpa* (material aggregate) and *kāya* (human body) in the canon. *Rūpa* is explained on the basis of elements whereas the analysis of *kāya* is not on such a basis. However, both are equally useful to have a comprehensive understanding about the constituents of the human body.

The Body as a Meditation Object

The main discussion on the human body in the Pali canon deals with the body as an object for the practice of meditation. In this part of the chapter, let us discuss how the human body is utilized as a meditation object and the importance of it in

---

[13] *DN* II.293: *puna ca paraṃ bhikkhave bhikkhu imaṃ eva kāyaṃ uddhaṃ pādatalā adho kesa-matthakā taca-pariyantaṃ pūraṃ nānappakārassa asucino paccavekkhati: 'atthi imasmiṃ kāye kesā lomā nakhā dantā taco maṁsaṃ nahāru aṭṭhi aṭṭhi-miñjā vakkaṃ hadayaṃ yakanaṃ kilomakaṃ pihakaṃ papphāsaṃ antaṃ anta-guṇaṃ udariyaṃ karīsaṃ pittaṃ semhaṃ pubbo lohitaṃ sedo medo assu vasā khelo singhāṇikā lasikā muttan ti'* ।

[14] *Vism* 240; Ñāṇamoli 1991: 236: brain is included in the bone marrow.

the way to detachment from worldly life. Negativism found in the Theravada Buddhism with respect to the human body cannot be seen in its application in meditation. We can see that a wider investigation has been done in the Buddhist literature with regard to the human body in relation to the practical aspect of mind cultivation.

From the canonical as well as post-canonical references, we can learn that the purpose of utilizing the human body for meditation is to verify the doctrinal teaching of non-self. The human body is, as the canon itself has accepted, relatively more permanent than the mind. The Buddha himself acknowledged the apparently greater permanence of the body. It is mentioned in the *Nidāna Saṃyutta* of the *Saṃyutta Nikāya* that the Buddha stated that anyone looking for something permanent and lasting would do better to attribute such a nature to the body, which lasts up to hundred years, than to attribute it to the mind, which changes every moment.[15] At the same time, the change of the body can be perceived even by an uninstructed worldling, and experience revulsion towards it. One can see the growth and decline in the body composed of the four great elements, it is seen being taken up and laid aside.[16] Because of the visibility of the change of body, it makes easier for the practitioner to cultivate insight into impermanence by contemplating on

---

[15] *SN* II.94f.: *varaṃ bhikkhave assutavā puthujjano imam cātummahābhūtikaṃ kāyaṃ attato upagaccheyya na tveva cittaṃ*। *taṃ kissa hetu: dissatāyaṃ bhikkhave ayaṃ cātummahābhūtiko kāyo ekampi vassaṃ tiṭṭhamāno ... vassa sataṃ pi tiṭṭhamāno, bhiyyo pi tiṭṭhamāno*। *yaṃ ca kho etaṃ bhikkhave vuccati cittaṃ iti pi mano iti pi viññāṇaṃ iti pi*। *taṃ rattiyā ca divasassa ca aññadeva uppajjati aññaṃ nirujjhati*।

[16] Ibid. 94: *dissati bhikkhava imassa cātummahābhūtikassa kāyassa ācayo pi apacayo pi ādānaṃ pi nikkhepanaṃ pi*।

it. Seeing this usefulness of the human body as a means to acquire an understanding of worldly phenomena, in the main discourse on mind cultivation, in the *Mahāsatipaṭṭhānasutta*, as well as in some other *suttas*, the body has been selected as the first object to develop mindfulness.

As for the development of mindfulness (*sati*), four grounds have been prescribed and their helpfulness to achieve the final goal of *nibbana* is described in the *Mahāsatipaṭṭhānasutta* of the *Dīgha Nikāya*, the *Satipaṭṭhānasutta* of the *Majjhima Nikāya* and in the *Satipaṭṭhāna Saṃyutta* of the *Saṃyutta Nikāya* as follows:

> There is, *bhikkhus*, this one way for the purification of beings, for the overcoming of sorrow and distress, for the disappearance of pain and sadness, for the gaining of the right path, for the realization of the right path, for the realization of *nibbana*: — that is to say the four foundations of mindfulness. "What are the four? Here, monks, a monk abides contemplating body (*kāya*) as body, ardent, clearly aware and mindful, having put aside hankering and fretting for the world; he abides contemplating feelings as feelings (*vedanā*) ... mind as mind (*citta*) ... and mind objects as mind objects (*dhamma*) ardent, clearly aware and mindful, having put aside hankering and fretting for the world.[17]

According to this view, all the four grounds of mindfulness are equally important in order to achieve liberation. However, there are indications that the contemplation pertaining

[17] *DN* II.290, 315; *MN* I.55f., 63: *ekāyano ayaṃ bhikkhave maggo sattānaṃ visuddhiyā sokapariddavānaṃ samatikkamāya dukkhadomanassānaṃ atthagamāya ñāyassa adhigamāya nibbānassa saccikiriyāya; yadidam cattāro satipaṭṭhānā। katame cattāro? idha bhikkhave bhikkhu kāye kāyānupassī viharati ātāpi sampajāno satimā, vineyya loke abhijjhādomanassaṃ, vedanāsu ... citte ... dhammesu ...*।

to the body itself is enough to attain enlightenment. For example, a passage in the *Aṅguttara Nikāya* mentions that the cultivation of mindfulness developed on the human body is in itself sufficient to remove cankers. The *Kāyagatāsatisutta*, a discourse solely describing meditation on the body states the benefits of mindfulness of the body thus:

> By realizing for oneself with direct knowledge, one here and now enters upon and abides in the deliverance of mind and deliverance by wisdom that are taintless with the destruction of the taints.[18]

In the *Mahāgopālakasutta*, the Buddha emphasizes that if a monk lacks insight regarding material form, he is incapable of understanding the *dhamma* and see it (*MN* I.220). If we consider the value of such statements concerned with the body as meditation object, in early Buddhism, it becomes evident that a great significance has been given to the human body as facilitating insight into the four noble truths. It is perhaps for this reason that the Buddha refers to the human body in the following terms:

> Nay, your reverence, in this fathom-long body, along with its perceptions and thoughts, I proclaim the world to be, likewise the origin of the world and making the world to end likewise the practice going to the ending of the world.[19]

The phenomena of the empirical world to which the *tathāgata* (thus gone one) was awakened were the five aggregates. How the Buddha tried to explain the reality of them and the method

---

[18] *MN* III.99: *āsavānaṃ khayā anāsavaṃ cetovimuttiṃ paññāvimuttiṃ diṭṭhe va dhamme sayaṃ abhiññā sacchikatvā upasampajja viharati* ।

[19] *GS* II.58; *AN* II.48: *api cāhaṃ āvuso imasmiṃ yeva bhyāmamatte kalebare saññimhi samanake lokañca paññapemi, loka samudayañca loka nirodhaṃ ca lokanirodhagāminiṃ paṭipadanti* ।

used for that is mentioned in the *Pupphasutta* as follows:

> ... Form, *bhikkhus*, is a world phenomenon in the world to which the *tathāgata* has awakened and broken through. Having done so, he explains it, teaches it, proclaims it, establishes it, discloses it, analyses it and elucidates it.[20]

Further, the *sutta* says that even when it is clearly explained thus by the *tathāgata*, if someone does not know and see, there is nothing to do with such an ignorant worldling, blind and sightless (*SN* I.40).

The examination of the human constitution has been done in a very comprehensive manner, in the canonical literature. Here, we are dealing only with the physical aspect of the individual and so are limited to the descriptions on the material aggregate and to the *kāya* concept. The techniques introduced in the *Mahāsatipaṭṭhānasutta* to use the body as an object for meditation, occur in several other places in the canon. The techniques used to realize the true nature of the human physical body, are:

1. *Mindfulness of breathing* — In this practice, the monk's principal meditation object is his body and he selects breathing as one way to produce concentration on it. During this exercise, the monk mindfully breathes in and mindfully breathes out. In the progress of the practice, he becomes conscious of the whole body. In persistently breathing with full awareness of the body, the practitioner receives the ability to calm the whole bodily process. Contemplation leads the meditator to

---

[20] *SN* III.139: *rūpaṃ bhikkhave loke lokadhammo taṃ tathāgato abhisambujjhati abhsameti* ׀ *abhisambujjhitvā abhisametvā ācikkhati deseti paññāpeti paṭṭhapeti vivarati vibhajeti uttānīkaroti* ׀

have insight into bodies of others too.[21] On seeing the breathing process both internally and externally, the *bhikkhu* contemplates arising, vanishing and arising-vanishing phenomena in the body. Finally, he becomes free from clinging to the world (*DN* II.291f.; *MN* I.56; III.89).

2. *Contemplation on four postures* — Here, mindfulness is developed in regard to the four postures of walking, standing, sitting and lying down. All the four are performed in mindfulness and abiding in constant contemplation on them. And the meditator overcomes the cling to the world.
3. *Clear awareness* — At this stage, the monk trains one-pointedness in the mind concerned with all the activities including postures and wearing garments, etc.
4. *Reflection on the parts of body as impure* — In this step, the body is divided into its constituent parts and one reflects on them. An analogy is used to show the way how the *bhikkhu* analyses the body:

> Just as if there were a bag, open at the both ends, full of various kinds of grain such as hull-rice, paddy, green gram, kidney beans, sesame, husked rice and a man with good eyesight were to open the bag and examine them, saying: "This is hull-rice, this is paddy, this is green gram, these are kidney beans, this is sesame, this is husked rice", so too, a monk reviews this very body: "There is head hairs, body hairs ... urine". — *DN* II. 294

---

[21] *MLDB*, p. 1190: According to the *Majjhima Nikāya* commentary "internally" (*ajjhattatikā vā kāye*) means contemplating the breathing in his own body. "Externally" (*bahiddhā vā kāye*) means contemplating the breathing occurring in the body of another.

The meditator realizes that this body is a collection of various parts and that it is the same in the case of the bodies of others too. This practice of mindfulness is not aimed at repulsion over the body but developing a mind that does not respond in terms of an emotional repulsion or attraction. As Ven. Nyanaponika points out one will be able to achieve, in this course of practice, a growing detachment from the body and an effortless detachment from sensuality (Nayanaponika 1992: 65). Though this contemplation of the parts of the body is sometimes called "meditation on loathsomeness", the "mood" produced by its correct practice is not one of violent revulsion or of gloom, but of unruffled calm or even of exhilaration resulting from sobre, analytical observation (ibid.: 66).

Sexual pleasures are generally known by the phrase "the pleasures of the flesh" and it means pleasure derived from the body. A major part of sexuality is concerned with the human body whether it is heterosexual, homosexual or bisexual in orientation. The pleasing quality of the physical body is invariably operative in bodily attachments. One purpose of analysing the body is to avoid attachment to physical beauty.

In the *Saṃpasādaniyasutta* (Serene Faith), the realization of body in terms of its parts is described as the first attainment of vision. And furthering the practice, the monk contemplates the bones covered with skin, flesh and blood. It is the second attainment of vision (*DN* III.104). It should be noted that in this *sutta*, four steps of attainment of vision are given and two of them are produced by contemplating the body and the other two attainments are concerned with contemplating the unbroken stream of human consciousness (*DN* III.105).

5. *Mindfulness on the four elements* — here, the monk develops mindfulness based on the four elements from which the body is derived:

> Again, a monk reviews this body; however it may be placed or disposed, in terms of the elements: "there are in this body the earth element, the water element, the fire element, the air element". Just as if a skilled butcher or his assistant, having slaughtered a cow, were to sit at a crossroad with the carcass divided into portions, so a monk reviews this very body ... in terms of elements. – *DN* II.294

The discussion continued up to this is concerned with a live body of human being. The first three steps are more related to the process and characteristics rather than to the body itself. By these techniques, it is taught to see the day-to-day life and the body's relation to it. In the fourth and fifth, one aspect of the early Buddhist attitude to the body is reflected: that it is analytical. These two steps serve to establish the early Buddhist doctrinal thesis that there is no particular essence in the body and thereby to falsify the notion of "self" (*atta*).

In view of examining early Buddhist position concerning the human body, the analysis made in terms of elements and thirty-two bodily parts is very useful. This analytical method was used in Buddhism with the purpose of falsifying the concept of eternal "self" (*atta* or *ātman*). The methodology used by the Buddha was called "*Vibhajjavāda*" (analytical method) to explain the truth. As Kalupahana (1994: 68f.) points out, the Buddha utilized this method to disprove wrong philosophical views but not to postulate any theory though there was a possibility for him to do so.

By applying this philosophical method of going into details to show the reality of the human body, Buddhism points out that in the body, there is no part at all that can be considered as "self" and the body is only a collection of various parts. To a question as to what is being (*satta*), Vajirā *bhikkhuṇī* gave the following answer which clearly expresses the Buddhist standpoint regarding human individuality:

Just as, with an assemblage of parts,
The word "chariot" is used,
So when the aggregates exist,
There is the convection "a being".[22]

The body is the manifestation of life and until the body exists as a well-functioning system, the psychic factor of individual too functions. It can be proven from a simple example. Any serious damage in someone's body due to external or internal conditions and irregularity of vital bodily processes results in death. Without a physical body one cannot experience life. Therefore, in modern philosophy, Merleau Ponty (1962: 82) mentioned the body as a vehicle carrying life.

In the *Mahānidānasutta* it is said that if there is no complex of psycho-physicality (*nāma-rūpa*), the psychic component of an individual (*viññāṇa*) does not find a support (*DN* II.63). As we earlier referred to, in the combination of *nāma-rūpa*, *rūpa* represents the physical body of a human being (*PED*, p. 575). In the *Cullamāluṅkyasutta*, man's formation of the concept of self on the basis of the psychological aspect of

---

[22] *SN* I.135: *yathā hi anga sambhārā hoti saddo ratho iti-evaṃ khandhesu santesu, hoti satto ti sammuti* ।

personality (*viññāṇa*) has been mentioned (*MN* I.430). The analysis of the five aggregates, the division of the body into constituent parts and the meditation on the body (*kāyagatāsati* or *kāyānupassanā*) are intended to avoid the possibility of forming a self concept on a physical basis.

6. The last method mentioned in the *Satipaṭṭhānasutta* and the sixth one in the *Kāyagatāsatisutta* is the mindfulness on the dead body thrown away in the charnel ground. Contemplation on the dead body is developed in nine stages (*navasīvathika*). The contemplation on the dead body results in the insight that in the same way as other people die oneself is also subject to death. As it is mentioned:

> Again, a monk, as if he were to see a corpse thrown aside in a charnel ground, one, two or three days dead, bloated, discoloured, festering, compares this body with that, thinking: "This body is of the same nature, it will become like that, it is not exempt from that fate."
>
> – *DN* II.295; *MN* III.92

At the end of each stage, the practising monk compares the other's fate of dying with oneself. This understanding leads him to contemplate body as body internally, externally and both internally and externally. And he abides independent, not clinging to anything in the world.

If we try to see the practical purpose behind contemplating on the dead body, it is clear that it is connected with the doctrinal view that all the conditioned things are impermanent (*sabbe saṅkhārā aniccā*). A body thrown out in the cemetery is not at all a pleasing thing. No one loves to have a look at it. The vast difference between a living body and a dead body was explained by the Buddha in the episode of the prostitute Sirimā. Her body was given a great price while she was living but after she was dead, nobody was willing to give a value of a single penny to the same body. The Buddha arranged to put the Sirimā's dead body for auction with the intention of bringing back to his good senses a monk who had fallen madly in love with Sirimā (*DhA* III.104f.; *VvA* 74ff.). Here, disenchantment with love for the body is pointed out as something natural and it is the fate of every physical body when it loses vitality (*āyu*), heat (*usmā*) and consciousness (*viññāṇa*).

The reason why early Buddhism utilized such a disgusting object like dead body as a meditation object requires clarification. The attachment to a person and the human body in certain situations is not limited only to the live body in contrast to the story of Sirimā. Once, a monk fell in love with a woman shortly before she died. Her body was left in the charnel ground and the monk had sex with her festering body.[23] There are several events mentioned in the *Suttavibhaṅga* similar to this. In the selection of the dead human body as a meditation object, this kind of events too, might have been considered by the early Buddhists.

The contemplation on impurity (*asubha*) is also similar to the technique of nine-stage contemplation on the dead body (*navasīvathika*). The contemplation on impurity as a meditation technique has culminated in the *Visuddhimagga* of Ven. Buddhaghoṣa. The ten stages of a dead body from decomposition to the stage of being reduced to a skeleton, on which an ascetic meditates with careful observation, are as follows:

i. disgusting swelling of the dead body (*uddhumātika*),

---

23 *Vin* III.37: According to sexological classification, having sex with a dead body is called "necrophilia". *ESB*, p. 810; Laws and O'Donohue 1997: 406.

ii. the flesh turning blue (*vinīlaka*),
iii. pus flowing out of the broken parts of the body (*vipubbaka*),
iv. the body cut into two at the middle (*vicchiddaka*),
v. the body bitten and eaten by animals (*vikkhāyitaka*),
vi. hands, legs and head dispersed here and there (*vikkittaka*),
vii. all body and limbs mutilated and scattered in fragments (*hatavikkittaka*),
viii. blood shed around the body (*lohitaka*),
ix. worms wriggling on the body (*puḷavaka*), and
x. the skeleton (*aṭṭhika*). (*Vism*, p. 178)

Both the charnel-ground meditation and contemplation on impurity aim at detachment to the human body and the practice brings about an understanding of the final fate of an object which has been once passionately loved. This understanding on body stabilizes one's state of mindfulness and is considered to be conducive to progress in the path.

In Buddhism, it is clearly recognized that bodily pleasures are enjoyable by sentient beings and at the same time it is pointed out that there are different levels of experience of happiness according to the development in one's mind. In the *Bahuvedanīyasutta*, the Buddha discusses the real pleasure as gained from meditation experience and they are superior to that gained from the gratification of the desires of the senses (bodily pleasures) (*MN* I.398). In the *Kāyagatāsatisutta*, we are shown how to experience higher pleasures having withdrawn one's mind from sense pleasures (*vivicceva kāmehi*) and contemplating on body. The jhānic experience and bodily pleasure is inseparable. The internal tranquillization is necessarily experienced by the physical body. As for the monk dwelling upon the first *jhāna*, it is said:

> He makes the rapture and pleasure born of seclusion drench, seep into, fill and pervade this body, so that there is no part of his whole body unpervaded by the rapture and pleasure born of seclusion. - *MN* III.92f.

In explaining the spiritual progress of contemplation on the body, it is said that if someone has developed mindfulness on the body, the Māra cannot find an opportunity to have access to him (*MN* III.95). A list of benefits of meditation on the body has been presented and it is assured that one can attain final liberation destroying subtle mental tendencies (*āsavas*) by means of such meditation:

> By realizing for oneself with direct knowledge, one here and now enters upon and abides in the deliverance of mind and deliverance by wisdom that are taintless with the destruction of the taints.[24]

In early Buddhism, the five aggregates and six senses are discussed in different contexts and particularly the senses have not been discussed as to which aggregate they belong (Hamilton 1996: 14). In the *Abhidhamma* literature, the senses are included in the material aggregate (ibid.). In our examination of the early Buddhist understanding of body, we have in the first step, tried to see its utility as a meditation object in which the analytical attitude is developed and falsify the idea of an eternal self.

The connection between the body and sensual pleasure is another important aspect that is required to be understood.

---

[24] *MN* III.99: *āsavānaṃ khayā anāsavaṃ cetovimuttiṃ paññāvimuttiṃ diṭṭhe va dhamme sayaṃ abhiññā sacchikatvā upasampajja viharati* ।

In the *Saṃyutta Nikāya*, the simile of six animals tethered to a pillar explains how the degree of insight into the nature of the body is relevant to the growth or the reduction of sensual desire. If the monk is not well established in the mindfulness of the body, the six senses draw the mind to their six different domains and to the external sense objects either pleasing or repellent. When there is no mindfulness, the influence of the senses becomes strong and mind is drawn to sense objects. But, when the mindfulness of the body is developed, the senses cannot draw the mind to different directions:

> ... Here having seen a form with the eye, a *bhikkhu* is not intent upon a pleasing form and not repelled by a displeasing form. He dwells having set up mindfulness of the body, with a measureless mind, and he understands as it really is that liberation of mind, liberation by wisdom, wherein those evil unwholesome states cease without remainder. – *SN* IV.200

When he reaches to this state of liberation he is free from the vacillation of mind by sense objects:

> ... *bhikkhus*, when a *bhikkhu* has developed and cultivated mindfulness directed to the body, the eye does not pull in the direction of agreeable forms nor are disagreeable forms repulsive; the ear ... (sounds) ... nose ... (odours) ... tongue ... (tastes) ... body ... (tactile objects); the mind does not pull in the direction of agreeable mental phenomena nor in that of the disagreeable. – Ibid.

The implication of this statement concerning the mindfulness of body and the vacillation of mind in relation to the six sense objects can be seen in terms of restraint of the senses (*indriya saṁvara*). The ordinary mind is focused on pleasing the body through the six senses without knowing that the body is subject to change. The contact between the six senses is the way through which the body is fed both psychologically and physiologically. Sensuality is a result of this process. Sense experience can produce perverted perception regarding it as good or bad due to mental tendencies lying within the deepest layer of consciousness.

All the psychological modes of thinking that affirm a fixed person of individual can be included under ignorance and desire. Until one realizes it, the psychological process of interpreting sense objects as pleasant and unpleasant continues. To eliminate ignorance and desire, according to Buddhism, one must cultivate one's own mind. In selecting objects to develop mindfulness, it can be said that in early Buddhism, such objects that are most conducive to the realization of the four noble truths have been given priority.

On the other hand, there is a philosophical significance in choosing the human body as meditation object. In the *Dhammacakkappavattanasutta*, it is said that in brief the five aggregates are suffering. Body is the first aggregate and one of the two necessarycomponents (psycho and physical) of human existence. The manifestation of a human being is due to these two and the affirmation of a conception of self is based on these two. Having the concept and the associated attachment and conceit of a "self" leads to please a self supposed to be eternal (Kalupahana 1976: 38). The activity of sensation is inseparable from the body. As Rhys Davids points out, the sense faculty of touch is the underlying sense faculty (*PED*, p. 208). So, the relation between human body (*kāya* precisely and also the concept of *rūpa*) and attachment can thus be clarified. This can be confirmed from the commentarial view given in relation to the female human body.

The commentarial passage states that five codes of sense pleasure are found in the female human body (for man).[25] The realization of the real nature of the body is conducive to become free from attachment to sensual gratification (including sexual pleasure, the major aspect of sensuality). Thus, we can understand the relation of meditation on body with regard to the Buddhist goal and the issues of sensual attachment (*kāmarāga*). The purpose of the *Kāyagatāsati* is to be understood from this perspective of Buddhism regarding the nature of the body rather than as an attempt to produce a negative attitude towards it.

Negativism on the Human Body

In addition to this analytical approach adopted with regard to the human body in connection with meditational experience, in the Theravada Pali canon as well as in the commentaries, the body sometimes has been seen as a problematic and impure object. Before, we try to reason out why both early Buddhist as well as later interpreters like Buddhaghoṣa adopted this type of attitude to the physical body of the human being, we need to discuss as to what kind of impurity has been perceived as causing the body impure. In other words, we have to find answers to the questions, what constitutes this impurity and the problem relating to the body or why is the body seen from this point of view and what are the reasons denigrating the body as foul? This needs to be clarified in order to understand one aspect of early and later Theravada negativism with regard to the human body. I will refer to some canonical references and Buddhaghoṣa's views on the body where its impurity and problematic nature are emphasized.

---

[25] *Theragāthā Aṭṭhakathā*, II, pp. 104f. (Devanāgarī).

The problem of the body has been discussed in two contexts in the canon. One is in the five aggregates formula and the other under the concept of *kāya*. The material aggregate is described without any special negative connotation and its relation to desire, non-self, impermanence and essencelessness of any aggregate is mentioned. But, when there is a direct reference to the body (*kāya*, *deha* and *sarīra*) negativity is added to the context.

The body under the material aggregate has been examined in the *Devadahasutta* of the *Khandha Saṃyutta*. In this discourse, without talking about any ill effect of the materiality, advice is given to get rid of desire and lust for form (and also for feeling, perception, volitional formations and consciousness). The reason to abandon desire and lust for the body is that unless one is not devoid of the attachment to it, sorrow, lamentation and pain will be the consequence when material form changes and alters. This is the disadvantage of desire and lust for the body (*SN* III.7).

The doctrine of self is based on the view that within the individual, there is an essence which is everlasting and imperishable. Buddhism contradicted such a substantialist view on the nature of the human individual. To counter this eternalist theory, Buddhism presented the doctrine of five aggregates. In the *Phenamsutta* (*A Lump of Foam*), the real nature of the five aggregates is explained by means of similes. As to the material aggregate, it is compared to a lump of foam in the Ganges River:

> *Bhikkhus*, suppose that this River Ganges was carrying along a great lump of foam. A man with good sight would inspect it, ponder it and carefully investigate it, and it would appear to him to be void, hollow and insubstantial.

> For what substance could there be in a lump of foam? So too, *bhikkhus*, whatever kind of foam there is, whether past, future, or present, internal or external, gross or subtle, inferior or superior, far or near: a *bhikkhu* inspects it, ponders it and carefully investigates it, and it would appear to him to be void (*rittakam*), hollow (*tucchakam*), insubstantial (*asārakam*). – *SN* III.141; *CDB*, pp. 951-53

> *Material Form is like a lump of form,*
> *Feeling like a water bubble,*
> *Perception is like a plantain trunk,*
> *And consciousness like an illusion,*
> *So explained the Kinsman of the Sun.* — *SN* III.142

The terminology and metaphors used to reveal the reality of aggregates do not connote any negativism but emphasize only their insubstantiality and impossibility to find any essence in them. Realization of this emptiness of aggregates gives rise to the cultivation of an attitude of disenchantment (*nibbindati*) towards all five aggregates.

As to the translation of the term *nibbindati* as "revulsion", Sue Hamilton points out that translating the word *nibbindati* either as "revulsion" or "disgust" can cause misunderstanding, particularly in contexts where the body is discussed. Bhikkhu Bodhi also has translated it as "revulsion" in his English translation of this *sutta*.[26] Based on etymological and contextual meaning of the term *nibbindati* we can agree with Hamilton's suggestion that it is used to mean "indifference" or "disenchantment" (Hamilton 1996: 184). From this *sutta*, it is clear that there is no need to produce a negative (emotional)

---

26 *SN* III.142: *evaṃ passaṃ bhikkhave sutavā ariyasāvako rūpasmiṃ pi nibbindati*। B. Bodhi translates as: "seeing thus, *bhikkhus*, the instructed noble disciple, experiences revulsion towards form ... "

attitude to the aggregates but to have insight into their insubstantiality and consequently to see them without being enchanted by them.

Negativism regarding the human body is presented in the canonical as well as post-canonical works in relation to the concepts of fear, death, ageing, disease, impurity, etc. This line of ideas can be seen as the second context in which the body is explained in Buddhism. In this respect, the body appears as a worthless object. In the *Abhayasutta* of the *Aṅguttara Nikāya*, two conditions are mentioned from which a human being experiences death, fear and terror of death. One is attachment to the sensuality and the other is the attachment to the body. It is mentioned thus:

> Then there is the case of the person who has not abandoned passion, desire, fondness, thirst, fever and craving for the body. Then he comes down with a serious disease. As he comes down with a serious disease, the thought occurs to him, "Oh, my beloved body will be taken from me, and I will be taken from my body!" He grieves and is tormented, weeps, beats his breast and grows delirious. This, too, is a person who, subject to death, is afraid and in terror of death.
>
> – *AN* II.173

A passage in the *Aṅguttara Nikāya* describes the body as a boil (*gaṇḍo*) which has been gathering for several years. The description is as follows:

> A boil — that is the name for the body, monks, made up as it is of four elements, begotten of mother and father, lump of gruel and sour milk, impermanent, subject to erosion, abrasion, dissolution and disruption, with nine gaping wounds (*nava vaṇa mukhāni*), nine natural openings (*nava abhedana mukhāni*). And from it, whatever oozes

> out, foulness certainly oozes out (*asuci*); stench certainly oozes out (*duggandhaṃ*); loathsomeness certainly oozes out (*jegucchiyaṃ*); whatever be discharged, foulness is certainly discharged; stench is certainly discharged; loathsomeness is certainly discharged.[27]

The reference to the body as a boil has occurred in the *Dīghanakhasutta* of the *Majjhima Nikāya* and it is advised to see as a thing that gives pain. As it is put in the *sutta*:

> It should be regarded as impermanent, as suffering, as a tumour, as a dart, as a calamity, as an affliction, as alien, as disintegrating, as void, as not self. When one regards the body in this way, he abandons desire, affection and subservience to the body.[28]

Particularly the passage extracted from the *Aṅguttara Nikāya* is marked by negativism towards the human body. It is seen as a boil having nine doors from which foulness, stench and loathsomeness ooze out. The picture created by this description with regard to the body is utterly repulsive. The second passage extracted from the *Dīghnakhasutta* is also marked with negativism and explains several aspects of the body as subjected to a variety of pains.

One of the drawbacks of the physical body frequently referred to in the scriptures is that it is subject to different kinds of diseases. The first noble truth recognizes getting sick as one major aspect of suffering (*vyādhi pi dukkho*).

---

[27] AN IV.386: *tato yaṃ kiñci pagghareyya, asuci yeva pagghareyya, duggandhaṃ yeva pagghareyya, jegucchiyaṃ yeva paggnareyya*; *GS* IV.258; *M* I.500, II.17: *Mahāsakuludāyi sutta* also describes the nature of body.

[28] MN I.500: *ayaṃ kāyo aniccato dukkhato rogato gaṇḍato sallato aghato ābadhato parato palokato suññato anattato samanupassitabbo* । *yo kāyasmiṃ kāyacchando kāyasneho kāyanvayatā sā pahīyati* ।

According to the *Dhammapada*, the body is a nest for diseases (*roganiḍḍhaṃ*).[29] In the *Girimānandasutta*, vulnerability of body is understood to be the vulnerability to sickness from a number of diseases in bodily parts and organs. A list of diseases is mentioned and it is presented as the perception of drawbacks (*ādīnavasaññā*). It is noteworthy that drawbacks are perceived in terms of bodily ones. The monk engaged in meditating on the perception of drawbacks reflects thus:

> "This body has many pains, many drawbacks. In this body many kinds of diseases arise, such as: eye diseases, ear diseases, nose diseases, tongue diseases, body diseases, head diseases, mouth diseases, teeth diseases, cough, asthma, catarrh, fever, ageing, stomach ache, fainting, dysentery, grippe, cholera, leprosy, boils, ringworm, tuberculosis, epilepsy, skin diseases, itch, scab, psoriasis, scabies, jaundice, diabetes, hemorrhoids, fistulas, ulcers; diseases arising from bile, from phlegm, from the wind, from combinations of bodily humours, from changes in the weather, from uneven care of the body, from attacks, from the result of *kamma*; cold, heat, hunger, thirst, defecation, urination." Thus he remains focused on drawbacks with regard to this body. This is called the perception of drawbacks.[30]

Another problematic characteristic inherent in the body is its easily breakability (*pabhaṅgura*). A verse in the *Dhammapada* states:

> Thoroughly is worn out this body, a nest of diseases,

---

[29] *Dh* 148: *parijinnamidaṃ rūpaṃ, roganiḍḍaṃ (nilaṃ) pabhanguraṃ, bhijjhati pūtisandeho, maraṇaṃ taṃ hi jīvitaṃ* ।

[30] *AN* V.109f.: *bahudukkho kho ayaṃ kāyo bahu ādinavoti* । *iti imasmiṃ kāye vividhā ābādhā uppajjanti, seyyathīdaṃ cakkhurogo sotarogo ghānarogo jivhārogo kāyarogo ... jigacchā pipāsā uccāro passāvoti* ।

perishable. This putrid mass breaks up. Truly, life ends in death. – *Dh*, p. 148

The same text compares the body to a pot (*kumbhūpamaṃ kāyaṃ imaṃ viditvā*) to indicate that bodily nature is of subject to easily breaking. The body is as fragile as a water pot. A notable characteristic in discussions on various defects of body is not to generate antipathy to the body but to guard mind against the influx of defilements, which are the cause of suffering. This *Dhammapada* verse is presented to the practitioner to destroy the opportunity for the access of Māra, the symbol of all suffering.[31]

According to the *Sutta Nipāta*, the body appears in a disguise and its real nature is covered with the skin.[32] Impurity always flows from its nine openings.[33] Even though the body is desired by an ignorant person, when it lies dead, swollen up and discoloured, cast away in a cemetery, relatives have no regard for it.[34] The thrown out body is devoured by various animals and worms (*Sn* 200-201). Negativism shown in relation to the human body is culminated in the statement that only a completely deluded fool would think of the body as beautiful (*subhato nam maññati bālo avijjāya purakkhato*) (*Sn* 199).

---

[31] *Dh*, p. 40: *kumbhūpamaṃ kāyaṃ imaṃ viditvā, nagarūpamaṃ cittaṃ idaṃ ṭhapetvā yodheta māraṃ paññāvudhena jitaṃ ca rakkhe aniveasano siyā* ।

[32] *Sn* 194: *aṭṭhinahārusaññutto tacamamsāvalepano — chaviyā kāyo paṭicchanno yathābhūtaṃ na dissati* ।

[33] Ibid. 197: *ath'assa navahi sotehi asuci savati sabbadā* ।

[34] Nyanaponika 1992: 67f. points out that in ancient India, dead bodies were thrown away in cemetery grounds without any care, especially of poor people and of executed criminals. Those bodies were exposed to the elements and to the beasts of sky and earth. This condition might have facilitated the monks to take the dead body as a meditation object.

One of the facts that people wish to enjoy in the body is its long-lasting healthiness. In several places in the canon, this has been discussed and it has pointed out that one cannot get a lasting healthy condition in the body. At the Buddha's time, certain ascetic groups considered the healthy body as *nibbana*. When the Buddha questioned the wanderer Māgaṅdiya as to what is *nibbana* and as to what is health, he rubbed his limbs and said:

> this is that health, Master Gotama, this is that *nibbana*; for I am now healthy and happy and nothing afflicts me.[35]

The Buddha states that it is a mistaken belief to take the health (in body) as *nibbana* and the reality of the body is that it is a disease, a tumour, a dart and an affliction.[36] In the *Nakulapitāsutta* of the *Khandha Saṃyutta*, the Buddha states that if anyone says that the body is healthy even for a moment, it is due to foolishness.[37] Even though, this statement appears to be negative, it comes to be seen that it is not so. Ven. Sāriputta explaining this brief statement advises to train oneself to keep the mind unafflicted despite the body being afflicted. The ordinary person clings to the view that he is form and form is his and subsequently he becomes obsessed by these views. His life is led in this obsessed mentality wherefore he cannot see the change and alteration of form. As a result of that there arise in him, sorrow, lamentation, pain, displeasure and despair (*SN* III.3). What is taught is to give up the view of

---

[35] *MN* I.509: ... *idaṃ taṃ gotama taṃ ārogyaṃ, idaṃ taṃ nibbānaṃ* । *ahaṃ hi bho gotama etarahi arogo sukhī, na maṃ kiñci ābādhatīti* ।

[36] Ibid. 510: *ayaṃ kho pana māgandiya kāyo rogabhūto gaṇḍabhūto sallabhūto aghabhūto ābādhabhūto ...* ।

[37] *SN* III.1: *yo hi gahapati imaṃ kāyaṃ pariharanto muhuttaṃ pi ārogyaṃ paṭijāneyya kiṃ aññatra bālyā* ।

"I" and "mine" through which path one gains the ability to remain mentally unaffected. This implies that bodily pain is not strong enough to generate volitional formations which result in the continuity of existence. So, one should train the mind, not the body. The body engages in performing volitional acts when the mind arises as the forerunner.[38]

A passage in the *Aṅguttara Nikāya* classifies diseases into two as physical and mental. One can be free from bodily diseases for one year or even for hundred years but it is very difficult to remain unafflicted by mental diseases even for a moment. Only those who have destroyed their deep-rooted cankers (*āsava*) are saved from psychological afflictions (*GS* II.146). In accordance with this idea, it is not implied, however, that we should completely deny the value of physical health. It is evident from the praise offered to Ven. Bakkula for his bodily health (*AN* I.25).

In the *Saṃyutta Nikāya*, the body is compared to a cart. It consists of four great elements, originating from mother and father, built up out of rice and gruel, subject to impermanence, to being worn out and rubbed away, and to breaking apart and dispersal (*SN* IV.292). In the *Vammikasutta*, the body is symbolized by an anthill (*MN* I.144).

The utterances made by elder monks and nuns sometimes have been marked with a negative attitude to the human body. For example, the elder Moggallāna presents an account of the female body consisting of the element of utter negativism. The elder Moggallāna is reported to have entered the order at an early age and was a close disciple of the Buddha. The similes mentioned in his utterance to describe the female body are excessively negative and loathsome. As it is given:

[38] *Dh*, p.1: *manopubbangamā dhammā, manoseṭṭhā , manomayā ...* |

> You little hut made of a chain of bones, sewn together with flesh and sinew. Fie upon the evil-smelling body.
>
> You cherish those who have another's limbs.
>
> You bag of dung, tied up with skin, you demoness with lumps on your breast. There are nine streams in your body which flow all the time.
>
> Your body with its nine streams makes an evil smell and is obstructed by dung. A *bhikkhu* desiring purity avoids it as one avoids excrement.
>
> If any person knew you as I know you, he would avoid you, keeping far away, as one avoids a cess-pit in the rainy season.
>
> This is so, great hero, as you say, ascetic; and here some sink down as an old bull in the mud. – *Th* I, pp. 1150-60

When we have a look at this dialogue taking place between the elder and a woman, it can be considered as a statement carrying utterly disgusting impression about the human, and particularly towards the female body.[39] In the commentarial literature, we can find the developed negativism assumed by the Theravada tradition towards the human body and the initial phase of this trend can be traced to the canonical material as evident from the above-mentioned references to the human body. It is important to note the statement made by the elder Moggallāna regarding the female body. It can be assumed this type of canonical view might have influenced the later commentators.

As Sue Hamilton in her study on the concept of human individuality points out, negativism regarding the human body was an aspect of the Buddhist teaching developed

---

[39] *Theragāthā Aṭṭhakathā* II.412 (Devanāgarī): These verses were told to a prostitute who came to seduce the elder.

by the commentators, particularly by Buddhaghoṣa in his commentaries. As she states:

> Theravada Buddhism is often, one might say commonly, understood to have a negative attitude towards the human body. Though there are what appear to be negative statements about the body in canonical material, as we shall see in this chapter that this negative attitude has largely been promulgated by Buddhaghoṣa, both in his *Visuddhimagga* and in the commentaries on the Pali canon.
>
> – Hamilton 1996: 170

Even though, for the most part we can agree with Hamilton with regard to Buddhaghoṣa, the statements like that of Moggallāna prove that the beginning of excessive negativism was in formation during the canonical era itself. At the same time, it is obvious that the culmination of negativism is found in the Pali commentarial literature. How far Buddhaghoṣa has expanded the early Buddhist view towards an intensified negativism can be seen from his exposition made on the nature of the body.

In explaining the standard list of the thirty-two constituent parts of the body, Ven. Buddhaghoṣa adds some details which are not found in the canon. The standard list of thirty-two bodily parts as mentioned in many places in the canon:

> There are in this body head hairs, body hairs, nails, teeth, skin, flesh, sinews, bones, bone marrow, kidneys, heart, liver, membranes, spleen, lungs, intestines, mesentery, stomach, excrement, bile, phlegm, pus, blood, sweat, fat, tears, serum, saliva, mucus, synovic fluid, urine, (brain).
>
> – Quoted in Hamilton 1996: 185

The same list is used in the *Satipaṭṭhānasutta* and in the

Kāyagatāsatisutta to concentrate on the body and it is done completely on an analytical basis. Each bodily part is to be regarded as a complete neutral object. In the commentary on this list, however, qualitative descriptions are added and the body and its parts are described as "vile" (*kucchita*), "impure" (*asubha* and *asuci*) and "loathsome" (*jeguccha*) (*Paramatthajotikā*, pp. 38f.).

In the *Visuddhimagga*, in the section on the meditation on body, Ven. Buddhaghoṣa makes a substantial description of each of the parts of the body to be meditated upon and also he introduces many negative adjectives which are not found in the canonical text. Thus just mere head hairs are subject to a "fivefold repulsiveness" (*pañcadhā paṭikūlato*), as to colour (*vaṇṇa*), shape (*sanṭhāna*), odour (*gandha*), habitat (*āsaya*) and location (*okāsa*) (*Vism*, p. 249).

In addition to this fivefold analysis, he compares the body to a sewage village (*gāmanissanda*), a dunghill (*gūtharāsi*) and to a charnel ground (*susāna*) (*Vism*, p. 250). Buddhaghoṣa sums up his exposition on the body as follows in which his negativism for the human body is well reflected:

This filthy body stinks outright
Like ordure, like a privy's site;
This bodymen that have insight
Condemn, is object of a fool's delight.
A tumour where nine holes abide
Wrapped in a caught of clammy hide
And trickling filth on every side
Polluting the air with stenches far and wide
If it perchance should come about
That what is inside came out,
Surely a man would need a knout

> *With which to put the crows and dogs to rout.*
> – *Vism*, p. 196; Ñāṇamoli 1991: 207f.

The passage concludes:

> So a capable *bhikkhu* should apprehend the sign wherever the aspect of foulness is manifest, whether in a living body or in a dead one, and he should make the meditation subject reach absorption. – Ibid.: 203

These views produced by Buddhaghoṣa makes the reader feel that he is a major contributor to the culmination of negativism towards the human body in Theravada Buddhism. In the following section of this chapter, I discuss what kinds of reasons have led Buddhaghoṣa to propagate a negativism drawing its implications on the Buddhist attitude towards sexuality.

If we leave the discussion only with the negative statements on the human body as found in the Pali scriptures, it is only a half truth. In the first place, Buddhism perceives the birth in the human world as a worthy attainment entailing the possession of a human body.[40] In the *Aṅguttara Nikāya*, it is said that attaining a human birth is rare.[41] A perfect human body is praised as a reward of one's merit. The body of the Buddha and of the wheel-rolling monarch are said to be characterized by thirty-two physical characteristics and it is the greatest form of physical body that a human being can achieve (*DN* III.142).

And in the case of female body, its beauty is highly praised

---

[40] *Dh*, p. 182: *kiccho manussa paṭilābho*
kiccaṃ maccāna jīvitaṃ
kicchaṃ saddhamma savaṇaṃ
kiccho buddhānamuppādo ।

[41] *AN* I.35: *evaṃ eva kho bhikkhave appakā te sattā ye manussesu paccajayanti* ।

in the context of the treasure of woman (*itthiratana*) (*MN* III.174f.). Having a beautiful body is a wealth for one's life (*rūpasampatti* – *SnA*, p. 397 and *J* III.187). The concept of *vaṇṇa* is connected with physical beauty (*vaṇṇanibha*) and it is advised that a person should keep oneself clean without letting oneself be dirty due to laziness (*malaṃ vaṇṇassa kosajjaṃ*).

In the morality laid down for monks, one of the four grave moral offences is taking the life of a human being and doing any kind of act resulting in harm one's life (*Vin* III.73). As for abortion, it is completely prohibited for monks and nuns and it calls forth defeat in the holy life (*Vin* III.83). In Buddhism, there is no room for taking anyone's life and even that of an animal. The first of the five precepts is abstaining from destroying life (*pāṇātipātā veramaṇi sikkhāpadaṃ samādiyāmi*).So, it is clear that in Buddhism, there is a set of teachings established promoting a positive attitude towards the physical body.

Reasons for Negativism

In the last part of this chapter, an attempt is made to examine the reason why there is a negativism concerning the human body in the scriptures. As Sue Hamilton points out, one of the reasons is the influence of Brāhmanism and contemporary ascetic traditions. Brāhmanism considers the body as a barrier to liberation because of its secretions. She contends that Ven. Buddhaghoṣa on the one hand commits a doctrinal distortion regarding the human body by propagating a negativism of the body. As she points out, the early Buddhist approach to body is purely analytical and indifferent (Hamilton 1996: 187). Further, she states that through the process of developing an antipathy to the body, Buddhaghoṣa engages in the act of Brāhmanization of Buddhism as an apology for challenging the caste system on a ground of spiritual purity against the Brāhamanic conception of purity as bodily one (ibid.).

Regarding instances which reflect aversion towards the body, we have to look into the internal factors in addition to the external ones. In finding internal reasons, it is clear that there was a trend towards asceticism among the monastic community during the Buddha's time itself. Ven. Mahākassapa showed a preference to practices more severe than the normal ones (*AN* I.23; *SN* II.155f.). And he is considered as the founder of the special set of ascetic practices called *dhutaṅga*, which increased up to thirteen in the *Visudhimagga* where the concept is comprehensively described (Ñāṇamoli 1991: 58). Devadatta *thera* made an attempt to gain special status among the Buddha's *saṅgha* community by canvassing for the ascetic practices which were not much appreciated by the Buddha (*Vin* II.197). It shows that there had been a considerable degree of acceptance for such observances in the Buddhist monastic community. Even though these trends do not appear to have a direct relation in generating aversion towards the body, the inclination to asceticism might have prepared the background for the development of an antipathetic view towards it.

As regards the personal position of the Buddha relating to rigorous practices, he was flexible and followed a democratic principle in establishing certain practices. The meditation on foulness of the body was happened to be questioned at the Buddha's time itself. Once the Buddha spoke in praise of development of contemplation on foulness and went into seclusion for a fortnight leaving the monks to practise by themselves.

They dwelt intent upon the practice of contemplating what is impure in different ways. They were troubled by their own body, ashamed of it, loathing it (*SN* V.320f. (*Vesālīsutta*)).

The result of becoming disgusted with one's own body (*Vin* III.68) was disastrous and some monks committed suicide while some were killed by others at their request. After two week's time the Buddha rose from his meditation and saw the *saṅgha* community diminished. After being aware of what has happened in his absence, the Buddha instructed to practise the breathing meditation (*SN* V.320f.). Regardless of such problems of this meditation practice, the Theravada tradition was willing to continue with it.

Another reason that is noteworthy here is the inclination of the *saṅgha* society towards luxury (*J* I.126f.). Even though the majority of monastic members were strivers for liberation, there were some others who were fond of worldly pleasures. For instance, the Chabbaggiya, Vajjiputtaka and Sattarasa monks and nuns were notorious for their sensualistic behaviour. For the most part, sensualistic pleasures are recognized as bodily pleasures. The elders with a sense of responsibility in the community attempted to find ways and means to curb the sensualist trend that became evident within the monk community. The First Buddhist Council is reported to have been held to get rid of the growth of anti-doctrinal and anti-disciplinary groups (*Adhammavāda-Avinayavāda*) in the Buddhist order (*Vin* II.285). In such attempts, it is possible to include into the canon certain views deemed to be salutary to the well-being of the order.

In the initial discourse of the Buddha, the two extremes of self-indulgence (*kāmasukhallikānu-yoga*) and self-mortification (*attakilamathānu-yoga*) were rejected (*SN* V.421). It is natural that the common mentality tends to fall into one or the other extreme. Popularity of the Buddha's dispensation attracted many followers and some of them sought membership in the monastic community. The popularity naturally resulted in earning a lot of material benefits from the lay society (the construction of permanent monasteries, etc.) and the monastic life became luxurious. In the absence of rigorous asceticism, it became easy to fall into sensuality. So, it can be assumed that the attempt made to formulate a negativism on the body was intended to maintain the spirit of recluse-life among the monastic community and to avoid falling into attachment to sensuality and infatuation with the body (*kāmasukhallikānu-yoga*).

The last factor that may have been contributory to negativism regarding the human body is connected with facts about the sexual instinct. For a celibate person, the most difficult instinct to deal with is the sexual instinct. The mastery of sexual desire is of paramount importance to the Buddhist who renounces mundane pleasures (Wilson 1996: 25 fn. 37). Celibacy looms large among the strategies for social disengagement because it safeguards the recluse from entering into bonds of matrimony, reproduction and patrimony. There is a clear negative language used to describe the female body in the texts. This can be considered as a resistance to sexual attachment which entails all those personal and social bonds. The issue of the attachment to body and subsequent worldly pursuits might have been still haunting the minds of monks who had left their lay life. For example, Ven. Nandaka, according to the *Theragāthā* commentary, was going for alms and met his former wife who tried to seduce him. And then he said:

> A curse upon bodies, evil-smelling, on Māra's side, oozing;
> there are nine streams in your body which flow all the time.
>
> – *Th* I.279-80

The expression of such insulting to one's own former wife may reasonably be explained as an attempt to bring forth to his memory all the encumbrances of the lay life with which he was fed up. The main cause which tethered him to the life was attachment to his wife and her physical charms. Being a victim to her seduction is a returning to the secular world and embracing all the problems. So, it is reasonable to consider that the negativism emerged in this context is a resistance to sexual seduction.

Attraction to the physical beauty of woman was a fatal obstacle to the male practitioner. In the *Theragāthā* commentary, it is reported that once, Ven. Abhaya saw an attractively dressed woman while making an alms round in a village. His composure was shaken, and he returned to the monastery thinking about how the sight of this woman had disrupted his mindfulness. Censuring his own mind, he developed insight and he became an *arhat* right then and there (*Paramattadīpanī*, 1, p. 213; quoted in Wilson 1996: 236).

In the verse he uttered upon attaining arhatship, Abhaya reviewed what happens if one allows the mind to fix on the beauty of a woman:

> With the mind fixed on what is pleasing, one sees beauty and suddenly mindfulness is destroyed. One experiences passion in the mind and heart, and becomes addicted to this. In such a person grow the influxes (*āsava*) that bring new existence in their wake. – Wilson 1996: 236

Abhaya attains enlightenment by overcoming the attraction to beguiling appearance of a beautiful woman and considering the harmful consequences of such obsessions. It can be assumed that Abhaya might have striven to suppress the desire arising in him by reflection on the impure constituents of the alluring body he had seen. The nature of such impure constituents found in a female body can be known from the story of Ven. Nāgasamāla, which is very similar to Abhaya's story. One day while Nāgasamāla was going for alms, he saw a female dancer who was well adorned and ornamented. Seeing her, elder Nāgasamāla came to the understanding that this body is impermanent. The commentary describes how he reflected on the body:

> That this body displays such deformations as: that it is (comparable to) a baggage of bones joined with sinews, smeared with flesh, covered with skin; (that it is) impure, smelly, disgusting, and repulsive; (and that it) is subject to impermanence (subject to), cleaning and rubbing away (subject to), dissolution and disintegration – there occurred to me this proper reflection.[42]

We can understand the element of negativism appearing as a device to guard the mind against infatuation with the physical beauty of opposite sex. According to the *Aṅguttara Nikāya*, the *rūpa* (physical body) of opposite sex is the highest bodily pleasure for either sex (*AN* I.1).

Five strands of sensual pleasures are available in one single object, i.e. in the physical body. One aspect of desire (*taṇhā*) is attachment to sensual pleasures (*kāmarāga*). For the male practitioner, embodiment of sensual desire was found in the female body and vice versa. So, the monks are reported to have seen this as a threat to their holy life coming from

---

[42] *Theragāthā Aṭṭhakathā* II, p. 3 (Devanāgarī).

ayam aṭṭhisaṅghāto nahārusaṁbandho maṁsena anupalitto chaviyā paṭicchanno asuciduggandhajegucchapaṭikkūlo aniccuc-chādanapar imaddanabhedanaviddhansanadhammo īdise vikāre dassetī 'ti etaṃ yoniso manasikāro uppajji.

womenfolk. The story of the elder Sabbakāma discusses the relation between sensuality and female human body:

> This two legged, impure, evil-smelling (body), full of various corpses, oozing here and there, is cherished. As lurking deer with a snare, as fish with a hook, as a monkey with pitch, so they trap an ordinary individual. (Namely) pleasant sights, sounds, tastes, smells, and things to touch; these five strands of sensual pleasure are seen in a woman's form. Those ordinary individuals, who with impassioned minds pursue them (i.e. women), fill up the terrible cemetery. They heap up renewed existence.
>
> – Norman, *Elder's Verses*, I, p. 47

The commentator explains that the five sense pleasures are especially associated with opposite objects (contextually opposite sex members) due to wrong reflection caused by perverted perception. The confused conception causes the blind and unintelligent person to be attached to the figure of a woman as a desirable object for his mind. Therefore, it is said that five sense pleasures are found in the female body and eventually it becomes a source for cankers. Persons, who are obsessed with lustful thoughts about the female body, become subject to fearful suffering including rebirth and death.[43] As the Pali texts are a production by male authorship, there are frequent references to the female body in the discussions of problematic matters like sensuality and sexuality. The reality is that sensuality and sexual attachments are a danger to the practitioner irrespective of gender difference.

The culmination of negativism regarding human body is seen in the texts of Buddhaghoṣa. In the *Visuddhimagga*, after producing a comprehensive account of the human

---

[43] *Theragāthā Aṭṭhakata*, II, pp. 104f.

body marked with typical antipathy, he gives his rational for providing such an exposition as follows:

> So, men delight in women and women in men without perceiving the true nature of (the body's) characteristic foulness, masked by adventitious adornment. But in the ultimate sense there is no place here even the size of an atom fit to lust for.[44]

It is clear that this statement is a warning against being a victim to sexual attraction. It implies that the body of opposite sex can cause deep attachment to sensual pleasures and culminate in seeking gratification through sexual union misled by external appearance due to lack of correct understanding of the nature of the body. This statement has to be seen in the context of Buddhist meditation practice because the *Visuddhimagga* is a guide book for meditation practice in the Theravada tradition. Buddhaghoṣa, seeing the biggest challenge to the practitioner as coming from sexual desire, has attempted to intensify the antipathy towards body with the intent of avoiding allurement to body of others as well as oneself. Liz Wilson has been able to understand the purpose for which Buddhaghoṣa as well as other commentators emphasized a negativism towards the body. Wilson (1996: 43) says that this attempt was for the benefit of religious practice.

We cannot completely ignore these very subtle teachings concerned with bodily attachment and sexuality. Even though generating aversion to body may seem philosophically contradictory, the attempt to deconstruct the concept of

---

[44] *Vism* 195: *tato iminā āgantukena alankārena paṭicchannattā tad assa yathāvasarasaṃ asubhalakkhaṇaṃ asañjānatā purisā itthīsu, itthiyo ca purisesu ratiṃ karonti* । *paramatthato pan 'ettha rañjitabbakayuttaṭṭhānaṃ nāma aṇumattaṃ pi natthi* ।

body appears to have served an important practical purpose. Attachment to the body is recognized as a deep-seated tendency in individual psyche. According to *Saññogasutta*, a person first becomes attached to his or her maleness or femininity and appreciates one's physical beauty and seeks the pleasure in the body of opposite sex (*AN* IV.57).

To sum up this chapter on the Buddhist attitude towards human body, attention was drawn to the teachings on the body under the concept of five aggregates and its first aggregate *rūpa*. The other set of teachings comes as teachings on *kāya*, *deha* and *sarīra*. Body is mainly used as an object for meditation which is sufficient to gain liberation. As connected with *satī* (contemplation), body has been subject to a comprehensive study in Theravada Buddhism and its approach to it in meditation is analytical. However, Theravada Buddhism contains a negativism on the body due to various reasons. And the early as well as later Buddhist texts have understood the body as having an inseparable relation to sensuality and particularly to sexual desire.

4

Celibacy, Chastity and Normal Deviant Sexual Behaviour

Introduction

In order to realize the Buddhist attitude towards deviant sexual behaviour, it is necessary to understand what decides conformity and deviance in sexual behaviour according to Buddhist scriptures. The norm for sexual behaviour in Buddhism has been established in the form of precepts. The norm is presented in two forms as there exist two different communities within the order, viz. ecclesiastical (monks and nuns) and the laity; celibacy is established as the norm for the former group and chastity[1] for the latter. In the first section of this chapter, I pay attention to each different norm established for these two categories of the Buddhist community. In the second half, the place given to marriage, the Buddhist attitude to adultery and data on monogamy and polygamy are discussed. In the last section, premarital sex and masturbation, which are recognized as normal sexual deviations, are discussed based on the two norms and ethical criteria in Buddhism.

There are two objectives to be achieved in this chapter:

---

[1] *Oxford Advanced Learner's Dictionary* (p. 198) gives two definitions: I. the state of not having sex with any one. II. Only having sex with the person one is married to. In the present chapter, the term is employed in its second sense.

one is to recognize the doctrinal and ethical importance given in early Buddhism to the two norms, the norm of complete sexual abstinence and the norm of sexual purity within marriage. The other is to recognize a tenable position from the Buddhist point of view, on normal sexual deviation in terms of moral implications.

The criteria used in Buddhism regarding normality and deviance of sexual conduct, as we mentioned, is twofold: celibacy and chastity. Celibacy means complete abstinence from sexual behaviour, especially for religious purposes,[2] and chastity means to confine sexual relationship to one's spouse. In the Buddhist order, a person, who receives membership of the *saṅgha* community, has to renounce his household life which is based on sensual gratification and heterosexual relationship.

In ancient India, the majority of religious seekers gave up the family lives (that they were already leading) while others abandoned the hope of future marriage and observed sexual abstinence on entrance to doctrines and disciplines of their teachers. The Buddha conformed to this tradition and persuaded his followers also to do so. At the early stage of his Order, observance of sexual restraint took place as a virtue (*sīla*) and later on it evolved into a rule (*sikkhāpada*). The first *pārājikā* rule in the *Suttavibhaṅga* deals with heterosexual and other forms of sexual relations which bring about defeat in the career of holy life under the teaching of the Buddha. The concept of celibacy is rendered by the Pali term *brahmacariya* which advocates complete denial of sex of whatever kind, hetero, homo or bisexual. It is necessary to understand the doctrinal as well as other factors involved in enforcing this

---

[2] *Random House Unabridged Dictionary*, p. 333.

norm for the clergy.

The norm concerned with the laity is expressed in the third precept of the *pañcasīla* which requires one to confine sexual relationship only to one's own spouse or sex life within the institution of marriage and prohibits sex outside it. The observance of the third precept is known as chastity and its violation comes to be known as adultery (primarily, extramarital sex) and the term also embraces other forms of illegal sexual acts such as fornication, rape and incest. However, the precepts in Buddhism are not commandments but voluntary observances to purify one's moral behaviour.

Like the celibacy norm, chastity was perceived by Buddhism on a doctrinal and ethical basis rather than a blind following of social customs of sexuality in the contemporary society. Ethical and doctrinal reasons given in relation to the third precept in the canonical and post-canonical works are explained in order to recognize what decides normative sex in Pali Theravada Buddhism. Further, I explain the moral theory of early Buddhism in relation to adultery and ethical teachings provided for the well-being of marriage.

The universal standard of normalcy regarding sexual behaviour is that of having heterosexual penal–vaginal sexual contact between adult opposite members of the opposite sexes with their mutual consent. In view of this standard, Buddhism puts the frame of marriage as a condition for proper sex. The liberal attitude towards marriage is a special characteristic seen in Buddhism. And also there can be seen a range of deviant sex acts within the heterosexual behaviour like fornication, premarital sex and adultery.

Early Buddhist sources speak about adultery as a moral issue because it brings about the kammic consequence of rebirth in a bad realm of the cosmos. So, it is a serious moral violation ranked with other offences such as killing, theft, telling lies and taking intoxicants in relation to lay precepts and as to the ecclesiastical society, completely prohibited. Standards which are used to judge a sex act as normal or unacceptable are different from society to society, from time to time and are dependent on a variety of other conditions. It is interesting to see that in the same Buddhist community, two different norms are used to judge acceptability and deviance in sexual behaviour.

Celibacy

In this section, I intend to examine the relation of celibacy to the spiritual path and the reasons for enforcing a strong law against sex life of the monks and nuns who are ardent followers of the Order. In early Buddhism, the term *brahmacariya* is usually applied to signify the life of a religious seeker who withdraws from sensuality and observes complete abstinence from sexual life. The meaning of the term *brahmacariya* depends on the context in which it is used, and in some contexts, both celibacy and chastity are signified (*DA* I.177). As for the meanings of the term *brahmacariya*, Tachibana states that one definite sense of the term is complete sexual abstinence by monks and nuns for their whole life and the lay person on *uposatha* days by observing eight precepts (Tachibana 1986: 142). The first precept in the *Suttavibhanga* prohibits sexual intercourse with opposite sex by a monk and breach of the rule results in expulsion from the Order and loses the membership of the community.

To make definite the concept *brahmacariya* (noble faring) in the sense of sexual restraint, we can refer to the story of Sudinna who is reported as the first to violate the norm of celibacy in the Buddha's *saṅgha* community. Sudinna after having sex with his former wife, repents for being unable to maintain his holy life unblemished. The context carries the meaning of leading a life devoid of sexual engagement by the term *brahmacariya*. So, it is clear that *brahmacariya* connotes a life involving abstention from sexual pleasures.[3]

Why one should restrain from sexual pleasures in order to lead a perfect religious life is to be understood in terms of the second meaning (wider) of the concept *brahmacariya*. That is a perfect life of holiness or purity. To lead such a life, it is required to have a proper training of physical and verbal restraint. *Sīla* (observance of precepts) provides with this need which is the beginning of higher spiritual attainment. Celibacy, consisting primarily of avoiding sex and sensuality, helps the person to become free from bondages and obligations which are an inseparable part of leading a sexual life. The sensual life is centred on the family which is the basic institution that binds the person to personal and social obligations and emotional attachments. One who prepares to become free from all sort of attachment (which is the basic root of suffering) is kept away from the physical engagement of sex by giving up family life.

Sexual relationship is a major part of the family life. On the other hand, man becomes a slave to issues arising from the family environment. So, the first condition for the spiritual seeker was refusing sexual life. In Buddhism, for a person who receives the membership of monastic community, which is set to follow an intensified spiritual career, abstention from sex is compulsory and also it requires observing abstention

---

[3] Vin III.19: *yvāhaṃ evaṃ svākkhāte dhammavinaye pabbajitvā nāsakkhiṃ yāvajīvaṃ parisuddhaṃ paripuṇṇaṃ brahmacariyan carituṃ* ।

from stealing, killing and lying. The *Sīlakkhandhavagga* of the *Dīgha Nikāya* has produced a long list of such restraints for the person ready to undergo mental development aimed at liberation (*DN* I.3). This basic observance, in a later stage, evolves into precepts entailing punishment depending on the degree of severity of the offence. According to the canonical texts, the observance of these precepts is the basic stage of *brahmacariya*. Based on bodily and verbal restrain (*saṁvara*), the monk cultivates concentration (*samādhi*) and thereby wisdom (*paññā*), the understanding of the four noble truths and the relationship between cause and effect.

The culminating attainment of leading a holy life is the eradication of cankers and purification of the mind from all defilements and attainment of perfect enlightenment. *Brahmacariya*, in this sense, covers the entire religious life of a Buddhist monk beginning with the observance of the precepts and ending with the attainment of *nibbana*. The entire path of training consisting of the three stages of morality, concentration and wisdom is called the eightfold path. The destruction of the three roots of unskilfulness (*akusalamūla*) is the perfection of *brahmacariya* because the complete uprooting of these three roots brings about the perfect purification of the person (*SN* V.7f., 16). As Tachibana points out, this is the goal, *summum bonum* of the Buddhist culture. The practitioner of *brahmacariya* keeps always this single objective before him and it is not followed for the purpose of being reborn in the heavenly world, or for obtaining celestial long life, handsome appearance, pleasure, reputation or celestial authority. None of them is concerned with the fulfilment of *brahmacariya* (*AN* I.115). In the canonical material, the object of this undertaking is stated as the destruction of five avarices (*AN* III.272), of seven bonds (*AN* IV.7) or of suffering and pain

(*SN* II.24f.). In brief, the goal of *brahmacariya* is to realize four noble truths (*SN* IV.51) or simply the noble truth concerning suffering (*SN* IV.138, 253). All these references to *brahmacariya* can be reduced to the sense of destructing mental evil and attainment of enlightenment.

Despite the fact that leading a celibate life was a common characteristic in the Indian religious traditions, certain religious groups that existed during the time of the Buddha had not conformed to this norm. As A.L. Basham (1951: 124) points out, many ancient ascetics such as earlier Jainas who were the followers of Pārśva, had not observed the vow of celibacy.

The seers (*ṛsis*) and ascetics (*tapasvīs*) reported in certain legends, shared the spiritual career with their wives; it is not known what was the nature of their conjugal relationships while they practised asceticism (Wijayatanta 1990: 92). There is a story about a Brāhmanic wanderer who tried to lead religious life in the company of his pregnant wife (*Ud* 13). The commentaries to the *Dhammapada* (*DhA* I.270 quoted in ibid. 92) and to the *Udāna* (*UdA* 241 quoted in ibid: 92) refer to some categories of ascetics who had a wife and children; their asceticism consisted in living outside society, but with the families. In the *Mahāvagga*, it is mentioned of an ascetic called Keniya, a brāhmaṇa, who became an ascetic to protect his wealth and also kept several families (*Vin* I.244). During the daytime, he behaved as an ascetic and during nighttime enjoyed sensual pleasures (*VinA* 270; *DPPN*, vol. II: 663). As these data indicate, there had been in the Buddha's time some ascetics who lived their life with families. However, the usual characteristic of such groups was to give up family life, to avoid sexual intercourse and sexual relationship with the opposite sex.

On renouncing the worldly life, one is supposed to be rid of sex life. Entering the order of the Buddha means to undertake the life of celibacy (*brahmacariya*). Sex belongs to the realm of *abrahmacariya* (non-*brahmacariya*). As an ardent spiritual seeker, one has to give up the thoughts and desires related to sensual life of the household. In the *Kakacūpamasutta*, the Buddha asks *bhikkhu* Phagguna to be free from such thoughts as he was unnecessarily attached to nuns (*MN* I.123). The consideration here was the element of attachment to opposite sex. There are four kinds of blemishes (*cattāroupakkiḷesā*) which destroy the glitter of life of religious people such as recluses and brāhmaṇas. Among them sex is recognized as the second item.[4]

If we turn to the first precept in the *Suttavibhaṅga*, it completely prohibits sexual intercourse for monks with opposite sex, even with a female animal. This precept deals with heterosexual relationship covering major sexual outlets such as anal and oral. However, in this section, I am confined only to heterosexual penile–vaginal intercourse and views pertaining to the texts. The first rule was promulgated after Ven. Sudinna committed sexual intercourse with his former wife. What compelled him to engage in this false act was his parent's insistence on receiving a heir to their property. Sudinna left his wife and family in his youth after realizing that the perfect holy life expounded by the Buddha cannot be fully undertaken without leaving the household life (*Vin* III.12).

But, subsequently, his parents were worried about future loss of their wealth owing to not having a progeny

---

[4] *Vin* II.295f: *santi bhikkhave eke samaṇabrāhmaṇā methunaṃ dhammaṃ paṭisevanti methunasmā dhammā appaṭiviratā* । *ayaṃ bhikkhave dutiyo samaṇabrāhmaṇānaṃ upakkileso yena upakkilesena upakkiliṭṭhā eke samaṇabrāhmaṇā na tapanti na bhāsanti na virocanti* ।

to inherit the family wealth. After ordination, he arrives in his hometown and was led to his parental house. His mother urged him to disrobe and enjoy the pleasures in lay life while performing merits. He did not consent and then the mother suggested him to give at least a seed to have an offspring for the family heritage. He felt it quite agreeable. On the arrangement by his mother, he had sexual intercourse with his former wife three times for the sole purpose of making her pregnant. After coming to the temple, Sudinna felt guilty of what he did because such an act was not supposed to be performed by a disciple of the Buddha. The text describes the psychological pain he consequently suffered by showing the change that occurred in his outward appearance (*Vin* III.19).

On inquiry by fellow monks, Sudinna revealed what had happened and it was reported to the teacher. After a severe reprimand,[5] the Buddha establishes the following rule prohibiting sexual intercourse for monks:

> If a monk who has accepted the Discipline, who has not rejected the discipline and has not, pronounced himself unable to continue with the religious life, has sexual intercourse even with an animal, he commits an offence entailing defeat.[6] That monk is defeated; he is not in communion. – *Vin* III.23

---

[5] *BD* III.19: "It is not fit, foolish man, it is not becoming ... it is unworthy of a recluse, it is not lawful, it ought not to be done." Whoever engages in sexual intercourse is neither a monk nor a true brāhmaṇa. Gombrich 2002: 104: A central idea related to monasticism was sexual abstinence, so, sexual desire and sexual activity were subject to be condemnation of the Buddha.

[6] *Vin* I.96-97: To describe four major grave offences, the similes used are four different. For sex: "as a beheaded man can not live with the body alone, so monk who has had sexual intercourse is not a monk any more, he is not a disciple, a son of the Śākyan. From this offence you must try to abstain, for the rest of your life."

Since the earlier stage of the Buddha's order, sexual intercourse had been considered morally wrong. There are several injunctions in the canon demanding sexual abstinence. In the primary stage, according to the history of Buddhism, there was only observance of virtues (*sīla*) instead of disciplinary rules. In the *suttas* of the *Dīgha Nikāya Sīlakkhandhavagga*, sexual abstinence has been included in the list of minor virtues (*cūla-sīla*).[7] The *Brahmajālasutta* describes:

> Putting away unchastity, Gautama the recluse is chaste. He holds himself aloof, far off, from the vulgar practice, from the sexual act.[8]

Several sermons of the *Aṅguttara Nikāya* deal with prohibitions relating to sexual intercourse (*AN* I.265-73; II.141-48). According to the *Tevijjasutta*, whoever engages in sexual intercourse is neither a monk nor a true brāhmaṇa (*DN* I.246-47, 250). The *Sutta Nipāta* has included many exhortations to the ascetic ideal, frequently extolling sexual abstinence (*Sn* 400, 609, 814, 835). The *Sammāparibbājanīyasutta* and the *Dhammikasutta* are considered as representing the closest form to the later developed *Vinaya Piṭaka* (*Sn* 359-404). The indications to the rejection of sexual intercourse in these materials prove that there had been a clear awareness of the norm of sexual abstinence among the Buddhist clergy. In the case of Sudinna, it is impossible that he was unaware of the vow of celibacy. In spite of his knowledge, the strong persuasion by his mother and his inner urge to keep his

---

[7] *DN* I.4: *abrahmacariyaṃ pahāya brahmacārī samaṇo gotamo arā-cārī virato methunā gāma-dhammā* ।

[8] Dialogues I.4: The commentary to this statement, says that *brahmacarīya* involves refraining from other forms of erotic behaviour besides intercourse. — *DA* I.67 (Devanāgarī)

own obligation to produce a heir, might have momentarily made him forget about the norm. The knowledge and conscientiousness later made him repent.

As in the case of monks, sexual intercourse was prohibited for nuns too. The rules established for them are found in the *Bhikkhuṇīvibhaṅga*. The first *pārājikā* rule forbids having sexual intercourse for nuns; this is quite similar to the rule laid down for monks. The second *pārājikā* rule (the fifth in *Bhikkhuṇīpātimokkha*) was enforced after a *bhikkhuṇī* named Sundarīnandā had sexual intercourse with the grandson of Migara, the millionaire. As a result of this incident, it was proscribed for nuns to have any physical contact with a man:

> If a nun, filled with desire, willingly hold herself against, embraces, touches, or presses (any part of) the body of a man who is also filled with desire, in between the collar-bone and the knees, then she becomes one who is defeated; she is not in communion. – *Vin* IV.213

The third, *pārājikā* rule (number eight) is more definite:

> If a nun, filled with desire, willingly takes the hand of a man who is also filled with desire, or the edge of his robe, or if she stands close to him, or talks to him, or goes to a rendezvous with him, or if she waits for him to visit, or enters a concealed place (with him), or prepare herself physically (for such acts and meetings), then she becomes one who is defeated, she is not in communion.
>
> — *Vin* IV.220f.

The second reason is that the sexual act does not mean a mere violation of norm because it is concerned with the goal of the path:

> How can you strive, foolish man, while *dhamma* is taught

> by me in various ways for the sake of passionlessness ... is not *dhamma* taught by me in various ways for the waning of passion ... the destruction of pleasures of the senses ... the allaying of the fever of the pleasures of the senses have been declared? – *BD* III.36

The unavoidable consequence of transgressing sexual restraint, and theft, killing, and lying (regarding supramundane matters) is expulsion from the *saṅgha* community. Therefore, they are called *pārājikā*, literally meaning defeat. There is no way of restoring the purity of a person after transgression of these rules. Anyone who commits this kind of offence is thereby regarded as one who leaves the community for ever. There is no possibility of ever being reordained in the community.

The beginner entering the Order is called *sāmaṇera* (or *sāmaṇerī*). There is a code of ten precepts to be observed by the beginner. Even very young children (above age seven) have to follow these ten precepts. The third item of these ten precepts is complete abstinence from sexual intercourse (*abrahmacariyā veramaṇī sikkhāpadaṃ*). The *Khuddakapāṭha Aṭṭhakathā* has dealt with them in detail (*KhA* 26-27).

During the Buddha's time, even certain lay people had been leading a celibate life while they were still laymen. They were called "the white-clad men, the celibate" (*gihī odātavasanā brahmacārino* — *DN* III.125; *MN* I.490f.). Normally, lay Buddhists spend the *uposatha* day as celibates and that is mentioned as living similar to *arahanta* (*... ahaṃ p'ajja imañca rattiṃ imañca divasaṃ ... iminā 'pi aṅgena arahattaṃ anukaromi* — *AN* I.211).

If we try to see the rationale of establishing the rule of restraining heterosexual intercourse, it may be understood in terms of twofold reasons: one is concerned with the social attitude which consists of two aspects: intrasocietal and extrasocietal. In the first case, a religious person gives up family or marriage life, of which sexuality is a dominant part.

On renouncing family life, the person observes lifelong celibacy on his own accord. A uniform principle adhered to by all members who enter the Buddhist order is this self-affirmed vow. A breach of one's own promise, subsequently leads to the loss of identity and oneness within the society. This becomes evident from the strict injunction laid down in the Pali Vinaya texts which do not offer a chance to re-enter the community for a person who enjoys sexual intercourse or commits any of the other three grave offences. One point at which all the members become identical is virtuous purity. Once, the Buddha refused to perform *pātimokkha* because of the immorality of one monk within the pure gathering (*AN* IV.204ff.). *Abrahmacariya* is a stain for the monk. All are supposed to have strictly undertaken the vow of *brahmacariya* (celibacy).

Falling into non-celibacy is a violation of the uniformity of commitment to the principles of the Buddhist *saṅgha*. Such an act is a threat to the image of the community and it could influence fellow monks and nuns who are in a battle against sexual instinct which is the most powerful impediment in the life of the practitioner. Possible harm and destruction of identity by engaging in sexual intercourse might have led the Vinaya authority to impose a non-returnability condition against the transgressors of celibacy. We may understand the norm of sexual abstinence in relation to internal unity of the *saṅgha* community in the above sense.

Throughout the Pali *Vinaya Piṭaka*, consideration of the factor of external society has been a crucial one. In the episode of Sudinna, much prominence is given to the element of public opinion. The Buddha says to Sudinna that such an act is conducive neither to win the favour of unbelievers, nor win the increased favour of the believers, but it is to the detriment of both. In addition, it affects the faith of some (*BD* I.37). This shows evidently the Buddha's awareness of the importance of the response of the general public and the possible reactions from them towards the *saṅgha* society. It is clear that in the establishment of the norm of sexual abstinence, public opinion was taken into consideration.

The second reason for complete denial of sex is doctrinal. Sexuality is the most intensified form of sensual desire. The highest sensual pleasure for man is found in relation to woman and vice versa. Sensual desire leads to sāṁsāric continuity and thereby to suffering. From the doctrinal point of view, sexuality is not restricted to sexual intercourse. Any contact leading to sensual desire between a man and a woman is described as a "sexual fetter". A passage in the *Aṅguttara Nikāya* addressed to Jānussoni brāhmaṇa, explains sevenfold breaches of the vow of celibacy:

> Brāhmaṇa, there are ascetics and brāhmaṇas who pretend to practise chastity (celibacy), and to this end they do not have sexual intercourse with women. But they consent to be massaged, rubbed, bathed and shampooed by women. They derive pleasure from it, they enjoy and desire it. I think Brahmin, that their chastity is torn, distorted, stained and blemished. These impure men cannot be freed from birth, old age, illness and from death. They cannot escape from *dukkha* because they are fettered by sexuality.
>
> ... there are ascetics and brāhmaṇas who pretend to practise chastity, and to this end they avoid sexual intercourse and also being massaged (etc.) by women. But they enjoy

themselves with women, they play with them, they laugh with them. They derive pleasure from it, they enjoy and desire it ... their chastity is torn. ...

... there are ascetics and brāhmaṇas, who pretend to practise chastity, and to this end they avoid sexual intercourse and also being massaged (etc.) by women, and also enjoying themselves with women. But they look at women with desire. They derive pleasure from it, they enjoy and desire it ... their chastity is torn. ...

... there are ascetics and brāhmaṇas, who pretend to practise chastity, and to this end they avoid ... (as above) and they also avoid looking at women. But they remember their smiles, the talks and games that they had with women.[9] They derive pleasure from it, they enjoy and desire it ... their chastity is torn. ...

... there are ascetics and brāhmaṇas, who pretend to practise chastity, and to this end they avoid sexual intercourse ... (as above) and they also avoid remembering women. But they look with envy at householders or at their wealthy sons.[10] They derive pleasure from it, they enjoy and desire it ... their chastity is torn. ...

Brāhmaṇa, there are ascetics and brāhmaṇas who pretend to practise chastity, and to this end they avoid sexual intercourse, they avoid being massaged, rubbed, bathed and shampooed by women, they avoid playing with women and looking at them; they do not remember their smiles ... they do not look at householders or their wealthy sons with

[9] Nevid, Rathus, and Rathus 1995: 139: This is connected with the idea of sexual fantasies which are actually not different from actual sex acts. In modern sexological studies, it is accepted that one can derive sexual stimulation through memories, imaginations or fantasies that originated in the brain.

[10] This hints at sexual jealousy.

> envy either. But they practise chastity with the thought that it is a virtue, a ritual and ascetic practice which will make them reborn as gods in a future life. I think brāhmaṇa, that their chastity is torn, etc. (as above). – *AN* IV.54f.

As we have discussed in the second chapter, desire for sensual gratification is deposited in the deepest layer of the human psyche. Tendency to sensual desire (*kāmāsava*) is explained as a very subtle form of thirst. Any act, performed to satiate the thirst for sensual gratification, is conducive to the strengthening of the bondage to *saṁsāra*. Therefore, even a single thought concerned with sensual desire is counted to be problematic. From the above quotation, it becomes clear that for a true undertaking of celibacy in Buddhism, a mere abstention from sexual intercourse does not suffice because involvement in any kind of sensual pleasure becomes a sexual binding. On this ground, it can be concluded that sexual intercourse constitutes only one aspect of "the desire for sensual pleasures". In establishing the norm of sexual celibacy, major consideration has been given to obstruction arising from attachment to sensuality whose eradication is the purpose of the religious practice proposed by the Buddha. In the episode of Sudinna, the fellow monks remind him of the goal of the teaching:

> Is it not true brother, that the Doctrine is taught in various ways by the Master in order to eliminate passion, not to stimulate it? Is it not true, brother that the Doctrine is taught in order to remove fetters, not to create them? Is it not true, brother that the doctrine is taught to prevent grasping, not to further it? Brother, the Master teaches the Doctrine in many different ways to uproot the passion?
>
> – *Vin* III.19f.

In this statement, there is no reference to sexuality but sense desire. Sexual intercourse is the final expression (*vītikkama*) of a long psychological process. So, blame is not put on it. What is emphasized here is the purpose of a spiritual career free from sexuality, which is intended at the eradication of all kinds of attachment, desires and grasping in relation to sensuality. Leading a life devoid of attachment tends towards liberation. One's falling into the realm of desire means getting caught up in the circle of re-becoming, which is suffering. Sexual desire is one of the easiest channels to drag the person down to sensuality. Therefore, abstinence from it is emphasized strongly in Buddhist texts. It is a norm which has spiritual and doctrinal consequences. Any sexual act that violates this norm can be recognized as a sexual deviation within the community of *bhikkhus*.

In the lay society, heterosexuality is a universal value of sexual conformity, but as far as members of the Buddhist monastic order is concerned, it is the gravest offence or deviation in sexual behaviour. The concept of celibacy in Buddhism has been defined including mental, verbal and physical restraint in sexual desire. And the norm of sexual abstinence is linked with the crucial issue of continuity of existence. This is evident in the Buddha's statement made to Sudinna that the breach of the vow of celibacy (*brahmacariya*) leads to rebirth in hell.[11] On such grounds, we can conclude that the norm of sexual abstinence, according to Buddhist doctrinal understanding, is linked to rebirth, *kamma* and the final goal of liberation (*nibbana*). A recluse, who has left the world in pursuit of self-realization, must overcome all the

[11] *Vin* III.20f.: *ito nidānañca kho moghapurisa kāyassabhedā paraṃ maraṇā apāyaṃ duggatiṃ vinipātaṃ nirayaṃ uppajjeyya*।

passions controlling this carnal desire (sex):

> As long as the desire, however small, of man for woman is not destroyed, so long is his mind attached (to existence) as sucking calf is to its mother.
>
> – Radhakrishnan, *Dhammapada*, p. 284, quoted in Misra 1995: 91

Chastity

Parallel to the norm of celibacy for the ecclesiastical community, Buddhism prescribes chastity for worldly people. Enjoyment of sensual pleasures including sexual pleasure is obviously permissible and the lifestyle of the laity is understood in terms of sensuality (*gihī odātavasanā kāmabhogino*). Sexual behaviour is an integral part of human behaviour; many social institutions have attempted since ancient times to regulate this so that it would not cause personal and social problems.[12] In the measures adopted to maintain the sexual life of the laity within an ethical frame, Buddhism establishes the precept of abstinence from sexual misconduct, which is generally understood as avoiding adultery. Many places in the canon as well as commentaries have discussed the issue of adultery. Other religions such as Judaism, Christianity, Hinduism and Islam prohibit adultery for their followers.

The universal acceptance regarding desirable sexual behaviour is that heterosexual intercourse between a married man and a woman is permissible. It is an established bond that such couples limit their sexual relationships only within

---

[12] Misra 1995: 90: The Buddha recognized that "of all the lust and desires, there is none so powerful as sexual inclination"; Humphreys 1972: 112.

the confines of that bond. A violation of this sexual bond is known as adultery. If one spouse seeks sexual pleasure from a person other than one's own spouse, he or she becomes adulterous. Buddhist morality is often formulated in terms of its doctrine of *kamma*. In this section, it is intended to discuss how Buddhist moral teachings, particularly related to *kamma* and rebirth, are connected with sexual misconduct.

Criteria which determine a sex act as acceptable or deviant are largely dependent on place, time, nature of act and some other factors. The Buddhist criterion is presented under the precept of abstinence from sexual misconduct (*kāmesu-micchācārā veramaṇī*). In certain places of the Sutta and Vinaya sources, abstention from sensual misconduct is defined in terms of sexual behaviour. The *Sāleyyakasutta* produces a list of ten unwholesome deeds leading to rebirth in unhappy destinations, in perdition or in the hell. Three of these actions, which are not in accordance with the *dhamma*, occur through the body: killing of living beings, theft and sensual misconduct. In this context, sensual misconduct is defined as the effect of sexual misconduct:

> He misconducts himself in sensual pleasures; he has intercourse with women who are protected by their mother, father, mother and father, brother, sister, or relatives, who have husbands, who are protected by law, and even with those who are garlanded in token of betrothal. – *MLDB*, pp. 380, 914

The scope of the third precept has been widened in the commentaries by adding ten kinds of other women in addition to the above-mentioned ones. Ven. Buddhaghoṣa in the *Papañcasūdanī*, the commentary to the *Majjhima Nikāya*, gives a comprehensive account of how an act constitutes an offence of sexual misconduct. In accordance with the canonical definition, the commentary says that "sensual misconduct" (*kāmesu micchācārā*) means sexual misconduct.

The term "misconduct" is defined as extremely blameworthy bad behaviour. "Sensuous misconduct" is the will to transgress against those whom one should not go into, and the carrying out of this intention by unlawful physical action. By "those one should not go into" first of all men are meant.[13] Next, the twenty kinds of women are included. The first ten are taken from the above-quoted list. The other ten kinds are:

1. women bought with money,
2. concubines for the fun of it,
3. kept women,
4. women bought by the gift of garment,
5. concubines who have been acquired by the ceremony which consists in dipping their hands into water,
6. concubines who once carried burdens on their heads,
7. slave girls who are also concubines,
8. servants who are also concubines,
9. girls captured in war, and
10. temporary wives (*MA* I.207).

These can be categorized into three groups:

i. A girl who is under the care of the family.
ii. A woman who is prohibited by convention, that is, close relatives forbidden under family tradition, nuns and other women vowed to observe celibacy as a spiritual

[13] This refers to homosexuality.

discipline, and those forbidden under the law of the land.

iii. A woman who is married or engaged to another man, even one bound to another man only by a temporary agreement.

As for the violation of the precept on the part of men, the given list of twenty women does not permit sexual relationship with any other than one's own wife. According to the Sanskrit Buddhist text, *Abhidharma-Koṣa-Bhāṣya*, the third precept can be transgressed by a man in the following ways:

1. intercourse with a forbidden woman that is the wife of another, one's mother, one's daughter, or one's paternal or maternal relations;
2. intercourse with one's own wife through a forbidden orifice;
3. in an unsuitable place: an uncovered spot, shrine or forest;
4. at an unsuitable time: when the wife is pregnant, when she is nursing, or when she has taken a vow. Some say, when she has taken a vow only with the consent of her husband.

On item two, Nāgārjuna says that it is "repugnant to the spirit of woman", so that "to be coerced into this unseemliness" breaks the precept (Lamotte 1949: 801).[14]

---

[14] Harvey 2000: 73: A Tibetan text called *Jewel Ornament of Liberation* (1079–1153) concurs with and expands on the *Abhidharmakoṣa-Bhāṣya*. According to it, one should not have intercourse:

i. in an improper part of the body, i.e. "by way of the mouth or anus";
ii. in an improper place, i.e. "near the retinue of the *guru*, a monastery, a funeral monument (*stūpa*), or where many people have gathered";
iii. at an improper time, i.e. "with a woman who has taken a vow, is pregnant or nursing a child, or in daylight";

→

In the case of married women, any person other than the husband is an illicit partner. For all women a man banned by tradition or under religious rules is prohibited as a partner. For both men and women, any violent, forced, or coercive union, whether by physical compulsion or psychological pressure, can be considered as a violation of the norm even when the partner is not otherwise illicit.

When the person in relation to whom the transgression is committed is a person who possesses a higher degree of morality and virtue, the offence becomes more serious for the transgressor.[15] An offence of sexual misconduct to occur, four factors are required to be completed:

1. Someone who should not be gone into (*agamanīyavatthu*),
2. the thought of cohabiting with that one (*tasmiṃ sevana cittaṃ*),
3. the actions which lead to such cohabitation (*sevana payogo*), and
4. actual performance (*maggenamaggappaṭipattiadhivāsanaṃ*) (*MA* I.207).

The primary element of carrying out of such action is involvement of one's own body (*MA* I.207). The condition indicated here is involved in the object. The women given in the above list or a male used for sexual gratification are considered as improper objects or ones involving deviant acts. The second condition is of primary importance in determining an act as immoral. How the role of intention becomes crucial

← iv. too often, i.e. "more than five successive times";
v. in a generally improper way, i.e. "by coercion, or with a man".

[15] *DhA* II.49f. (Devanāgarī); *MA* I, p. 207 (Devanāgarī): *so panesa micchācāro sīlādiguṇarahite agamaniyaṭṭhāne appasāvajjo, sīlādiguṇasampanne mahāsāvajjo*।

in sexual misconduct can be known from the complete description provided to elucidate the first defeat offence.

In certain cases, monks are reported to have been unknowingly or forcefully used to derive sexual pleasure by some ladies and certain men. For instance, one monk slept during day-time in his residence leaving the doors and windows open. The women who came to visit the temple, seeing his private parts, had sex with him as they liked. After waking up, the monk saw what had happened and reported to the Buddha.[16] In one case, the monk was *arahanta* so it was impossible to derive sexual pleasure (*Vin* III.37f.). And in many other similar cases, monks who were not involved mentally in the act, were declared free of guilt (*Vin* III.38f.). In many cases reported in the *Suttavibhaṅga* (both *bhikkhu* and *bhikkhuṇī*) intention has been taken as a criterion to decide any case involving a controversy. This criterion is certainly connected with the Buddhist *kamma* theory in which one's volition (*cetanā*) is considered to play a crucial role.

The third item can be clarified from the third *pārājikā* given to *bhikkhuṇī saṅgha*. Any action that a nun does with the purpose of having sexual union with a man causes breach of the rule of *pārājikā* (*Vin* IV.213, 220f.). With regard to lay persons' sexual activities, the deficiency of data hinders the possibility of reaching a definite judgement. However, as it was clear from the Vinaya, the principle used to determine the act of sexual misconduct by laity is similar to that of the monks.

The canon frequently mentions of extramarital relationships as improper and therefore admonishes to

---

[16] *Vin* III.38f.: The monk was declared to be free of charge as there was no intention to enjoy sexual pleasure.

refrain from it. The major admonition to followers is to observe celibacy. But as it is impractical, they are advised not to indulge in adultery. The *Sutta Nipāta* advises that the wise man should avoid the non-celibate life (*abrahmacariyam*) like a pit of burning coals. But if he is incapable of living a celibate life, he should not transgress against another's wife (*Sn* 396).

The third precept relates primarily to the avoidance of causing suffering by one's sexual behaviour. Adultery — "going with the wife of another" (*AN* I.189) — is the most straightforward breach of this precept. The wrongness of this is seen partly in terms of its being an expression of greed and partly in terms of its harm to others. The *Sutta Nipāta* explains the first of this twofold harm resulting from adultery:

> Not to be contended with one's wife but to be seen with prostitutes or the wives of others — this is the cause of one's downfall. — *Sn* 108

Buddhism teaches that self-comparison could be a criterion for determining the moral value of an action. The *Dhammapada* advises to compare others with oneself and not to inflict any harm upon others (*attānam upamam katvā na haneyya na ghātaye* — *Dh* 129, Narada edn). The rationale as to why one should abstain from adultery is made clear in terms of such comparison with oneself in a passage found in the *Saṃyutta Nikāya*:

> You would not like someone to commit adultery with your wife, so do not commit adultery with someone else's wife.
> — *SN* V.354

For this reason, one should not "seek sexual company 'with others' women', who are as dear to them as life". As Nāgārjuna points out:

> The pleasure of husband and wife is to be two bodies but one flesh; to take away one who another loves and destroy this deep sentiment is a crime.
>
> – Lamotte 1949: 801, quoted in Harvey 2000: 71

Peter Harvey explaining the scope of adultery says:

> What count as "adultery" varies according to the marriage patterns of different societies, though, and Buddhism has been flexible in adapting to these. Adultery with a woman without her husband's knowledge, or with his compliance, still breaks the precepts on account of the malicious nature of the act (Lamotte 1949: 801). Moreover, the precept is extended to intercourse with any woman who is, in modern parlance, "in a relationship" with another man (*Aṭṭhasālinī* 98).
>
> – Harvey 2000: 71

Adultery is always seen in the texts as an undesirable characteristic found in men and women. The *Mātugāma Saṃyutta* of the *Saṃyutta Nikāya* talks about five factors which cause the downfall of a woman. Among them, adultery is given as one. Those five are:

1. being devoid of faith (*assaddho*),
2. being shameless of evil (*ahiriko*),
3. being fearless of evil (*anottāpi*),
4. being adulterous (*aticāri*), and
5. being devoid of wisdom (*duppañño*) (*SN* IV.242).

When the person lacks the belief in the theory of cause and effect (*assaddho*) related to one's actions, he becomes fearless to perform any act harmful to himself and to others. In Buddhism, shame of evil and fear of evil (*hiriottappa*) are considered as principles governing the world (*lokapālaka dhammā*) and their absence would make the world chaotic.

By referring to adultery after *ahirika* and *anottāpi* in the list, adultery is understood as a result of the two previous bad traits. The text further reads that such a woman after death, is to be reborn in a state of misery (*SN* IV.242).

In the context of five precepts, abstaining from taking life, taking what is not given, sexual misconduct, lying and taking intoxicants are not single items but are interconnected. Sexual misconduct, specifically, adultery, can be interpreted as using an object belonging to another for one's pleasure in an immoral way. It is involved in the act of theft, taking what does not belong to oneself. One reason to consider adultery as immoral is that it is a breaking of a promise. On entrance to a marriage relationship, the two spouses make the promise to have exclusive sexual relationship and not to have sexual relationship with a third party (Wasserstrom 1994: 94f.). Committing adultery leads to break the promise and breaking a promise is immoral.[17] Wasserstrom says that more than any other promise, breach of this is more hurting and painful (Wasserstrom 1994: 97).

A strong moral argument against adultery is that it can be conceived as deception. If one spouse transgresses the bond of exclusive sexual relationship between the two, he or she deceives the other. Here, lying is inevitable. Lying is characterized by the intention of deceiving a person. In the light of modern standpoint on adultery, it is argued that committing adultery involves lying, cheating and infidelity on the part of one marriage partner or another, and that these actions are morally reprehensible in most ethical systems (Thiroux 1995: 355).

[17] Wasserstrom 1994: 102. One of the four essential characteristics of marriage is willingness to have sexual intercourse only with each other.

In the case of adultery, one can avoid active deception in the non-participating spouse's absence of knowledge on the matter. A basic moral assumption that condones adultery is "what they don't know won't hurt them"; bad results only occur when adultery is discovered (ibid.). The moral theory advocated by Buddhism allows no room for committing evil (*pāpa*) in secret. The position held regarding this is stated in the *Petavatthu* (II.7.17): *mākattha pāpakaṃ kammaṃ āvi vā yadi vā raho* — do not commit unwholesome deeds either in public or in secret. One becomes a worthy person by not doing wrong even in the absence of others'awareness (*na raho karoti pāpāni: arahan tena vuccati* — *Vism*, p. 201).

According to Buddhist understanding, whether one commits an evil deed in public or in secret makes no difference to the seriousness of the offence. Even though adultery is committed in secret and without the spouse's knowledge, it is counted as intentional deceiving. Deception is involved in the realm of misinterpreting truth, which is a serious breach of the fourth precept of abstaining from concealing the truth and reality from others. Thus, sexual misconduct can be understood as not only a single offence, but involving a range of moral violations such as theft and lying.

To provide people with ideal moral personalities, the concept of *bodhisattva* has been used in the Buddhist literature both in Theravada Buddhism and in Mahāyāna Buddhism. In the *Jātakas*, *bodhisatta* is portrayed as a morally worthy character. We can see the position held by *bodhisatta* regarding others' wives in the *Ummadanti Jātaka*. A king fell in love with a woman called Ummadanti who was of splendid beauty. Yet, she was already married. Her husband knowing the king's serious (that he could die of love), proposed to the king to make her his queen. Even though, the king's attachment to the woman was overwhelming, still he could discriminate between vice and virtue and so refused the unusual offer of his officer and explained why he refused it:

> How can happiness be expected for him who commits a wicked action, though unwitnessed? ... I should dare throw myself on a sharp sword or into a fire with blazing flames, but I shall not be able to offend against righteousness, which I have always observed, and to which I owe my royal bliss. ... The virtuous do not like for themselves a pleasure procured at the expense of others whom they have distressed by bringing them into disrepute and the like. ... If I should lack the power of ruling my own self, say, into what condition would I bring this people who long for protection from my side? Thus considering and regardful of the good of my subjects, my own righteousness, and my spotless fame, I do not allow myself to submit to my passion.
>
> –Tachibana 1986: 154

Finally, the king refused to accept his wife. The respect for another's chastity and the respect for righteousness made the king, who was sick with love, rightly deny accepting another's wife. A Mahāyāna text describing the *bodhisattva's* conduct in sexual life states that he is contended with his own wife and does not cast longing eyes on the wives of other men. He does not harbour even a lustful thought with regard to women married to others (Rahder 1926: 23). Adultery is like poison that mars and destroys human life, even if it is committed in secret.

An inquiry into the Buddhist philosophical standpoint regarding sexual misconduct becomes necessary to get a correct understanding of the norm of chastity as the measure for deciding conformity or deviation in sexual behaviour of the Buddhist laity. There are direct references in the canon describing the consequences of sexual misconduct. Any volitional act characterized by unwholesome roots (*akusala mūla*) and wholesome roots (*kusala mūla*) generates bad and good consequences respectively. The breach of precepts is an unwholesome act which is a product of unwholesome roots (greed, anger and ignorance). In the canonical sources, the violation of the third precept and corresponding ill effects are presented in two contexts. In the first context, adultery is considered as one of many other evil deeds and harmful consequences of such acts are discussed. The second type of references is concerning only sexual misconduct. However, both of them explain the *kamma* theory in relation to adultery.

Buddhism speaks of the applicability of extrasensory perception to verify the consequences produced by volitional actions. In earlier Buddhist doctrine, the Buddha's knowledge is described as constituting threefold higher cognition, namely, the knowledge of previous lives, the knowledge of passing away and reappearance of beings, and the knowledge of destruction of cankers (*MN* I.22f.). By means of the second superhuman knowledge, the Buddha is believed to verify the *kamma* theory of his doctrinal system. It assures that bad deeds performed through the doors of body, speech and mind result in harmful effects whereas good deeds bring about pleasant results (*MLDB*, p. 23). The *Sevitabbāsevitabbasutta* (*To Be Cultivated and Not To Be Cultivated*) of the *Majjhima Nikāya* explains three evil deeds done through body: killing, theft and sensual misconduct; sensual misconduct causes unwholesome states to increase and wholesome states to diminish in one who cultivates it (ibid., p. 914). Regarding tenfold bodily, verbal and mental unwholesome deeds, the *Bahudhātukasutta* says that it is impossible for a person who commits these, to be reborn in a happy destination after death. What is possible for such a person is to reappear in a state of deprivation ... even in hell (after death) (ibid., p. 930).

Adultery is recognized as an evil (*akusala*) expressed through body. There are three bodily misdeeds, viz. killing, animals, theft and sexual misconduct. The Buddhist texts explain the consequences of each of these actions in various places in the canon. In modern thinking on sex, some argue that sex is personal and if there is mutual consent, they can enjoy it. Accordingly, premarital sex and extramarital sex are condoned and sexual liberals state that they are not morally wrong. According to Buddhism, adultery or other forms of sexual misconduct are invariably connected with retribution. In general, it is stated that those who commit bad *kammas* through body, word and mind are sure to be reborn in hell after death (*MN* III.165, 179).

The *Mahākammavibhaṅgasutta* mentions four kinds of persons. The first group of them is described as follows:

> here some person kills living beings, takes what is not given, misconducts himself in sensual pleasures, speaks falsehood, speaks maliciously, speaks harshly, gossips; he is covetous, has a mind of ill will, and holds wrong view. On the dissolution of the body, after death, he reappears in a state of deprivation, in an unhappy destination, in perdition, even in hell. – *MN* III.209

The references made to adultery in the enumeration of ten evil deeds show that the kammic consequences of adultery is rebirth in unhappy states after death. Buddhism does not limit the result of *kamma* to the other world but certain *kammas* come into fruition in this very life. If one performs an evil act, its result can fall on him here and now (*diṭṭha-*

dhammavedanīya). The *Bālapaṇḍitasutta* of the *Majjhima Nikāya* explains how a person suffers in this very life because of sensual misconduct and other evil deeds. This is due to one's own conscience. One can engage in immoral deeds without public knowledge. Yet, such a behaviour makes one recollect his or her evil deed and cause him/her repent or feel guilty. It is mentioned as follows:

> If a foolish person is seated in an assembly or along a street or in a square and people there are discussing certain pertinent and relevant matters, then if the fool is one who kills living beings, takes what is not given, misconducts himself in sensual pleasures, speaks falsehood and indulges in wine, liquor and intoxicants, which are the basis of negligence, he thinks: "These people are discussing certain pertinent and relevant matters; these things are found in me, and I am seen engaging in those things". This is the first kind of pain and grief that fool feels here and now.
>
> – *MN* III.163

In the canonical material, there is information on the adultery as a single moral breach sufficient to cause a lot of pain and suffering in this life and more severely in the afterlife. If we cite a story from the Jātaka literature, the *Lohakumbhī-Jātaka* is pertinent to understand the *kamma* and rebirth theory in relation to adultery. This Jātaka story is characterized by a horrific sense of after effects undergone in hells due to sexual misconduct. In the present story, the King Pasendi listens at night to the four syllables, *du*, *sa*, *na* and *so* uttered by four inhabitants of hell. After this was reported to the Buddha, he related that in a previous existence, those four hell beings had been in Sāvatthi, and had been guilty of adultery. They had led a life given to adultery by seducing their neighbours' wives, however carefully they be guarded against misconduct.

After death, they came to life again in Four Iron Cauldrons.[18] After being tortured for 60,000 years, they came up to the top, and on seeing the edge of the Cauldron's mouth, thought to themselves, "When shall we escape from this misery?" (Francis 1981: 29). This story is well illustrative of the kammic results of committing sexual misconduct. However, many Jātakas are devoid of the concept of severe retribution in purgatory retribution for adultery.

A similar story is found in the *Petavatthu*. The king of Kosala had two amiable sons in the prime of youth. In their unrestrained youthful passion they committed adultery, and after death were reborn as *peta*s who were being crushed in a trench (Gehman 1984: 99). In this story, there is a meaningful discussion of morality; one can be a lord in the human world, but if he were to be born in the world of *peta*s for his evil deeds, he has to undergo suffering as any other low person (ibid.: 100). And also, the Buddha advises rulers in his contemporary society to give up their wantonness seeing the danger of after effects of such a life (ibid.).

The story of Kaṇṇamuṇḍā *peti* describes the moral theory related to adultery followed by deception. A woman of good character was seduced to commit sexual misconduct by a rogue. When her husband questioned, she denied the fault. In seeing that he did not trust her, she pointed to a dog which was standing nearby, and took an oath:

> If such a wicked deed was done by me, may this crop-eared black dog devour me, when I am reborn here or there!
>
> – Ibid.: 58

[18] Francis 1981, III: 31. The nature of suffering in cauldron is explained in the past story thus: "Where ... in thick corrosive liquid heated to boiling point, they would at one time sink till they struck the bottom of the cauldron, and at another time rise top the top like a foam bubble."

In consequence of adultery and deception, she was seen as a mansion *peti*. Since she had done a lot of merit, in the day-time she experienced divine pleasure. But, at every midnight, she was devoured by a dog for her oath in the previous life (ibid.: 59). The references in Buddhism to moral retribution for the breach of the third precept show clearly the gravity of the norm of chastity to which the Buddhist lay persons should conform in their sex life. The discussion carried out with regard to moral theory in Buddhism established for the breach of the third precept is well showing the gravity of the norm of chastity to which the laity of Buddhism should conform in their sex life. Any violation of this norm could result in ill effects in the immediate life (*diṭṭhadhammavedanīya*) and retribution in undesirable states after death.

Marriage

As many other world religions, Buddhism accepts the value of marriage as a social institution. In spite of teachings pertaining to the adverse consequences of sexual desire, Buddhism approves of sexual relationships within marriage. The Buddhist view regarding married life is a liberal one because there is no commandment for people to marry. Buddhism is silent about the general expectation of society that the objective of marriage should be reproduction. One is free to marry or remain unmarried. Also one may or may not have children. Married people can exercise all their family rights as they wish. What Buddhism has tried to do is to found the institution of marriage on a moral basis and show how the respective roles of wife and husband ought to be performed in such a way as to preserve mutual harmony and respect.

The Buddhist view on marriage is ambivalent. In the path to spiritual liberation, leading a family life is considered a barrier to perfection (*MN* I.179). On the other hand, there is a clear positive attitude towards maintaining a family. The Buddha once said:

> Waiting on mother and father, protecting child and wife, and being engaged in a quiet calling, this is the highest blessing. – *Sn* 262

In the *Cakkavattisīhanādasutta*, the king grants subsidies to people in order to enable them to procure their material needs, support mother and father, and to maintain wife and children (*DN* III.65). The need of marital union of man and woman is accepted to be essential for the betterment, particularly of women:

> for a husband is a woman's real covering, and she that lacks a husband — even though she be clad in garments costing a thousand pieces — goes bare and naked indeed. Like kingless kingdoms, like streams run dry, so bare and naked is a woman seen, who, having brothers ten, yet lacks a mate. – Chalmers 1981, vol. I: 165

It is well known that Prince Siddhattha lived a wedded life with Princess Yaśodharā (generally "Rāhulamātā") and fathered a son, Rāhula before his renunciation (Thomas 1993: 49). In the tradition, the great human beings such as the Buddha and wheel-rolling monarch, are married persons. It is evident that Buddhism adopted a positive attitude to marriage. The relationship between wife and husband has been raised to an ideal position transcending carnal desires. As indicated in many Jātakas, in the case of the Buddha and Yaśodharā, they lived together as husband and wife in numerous previous births. This was so in the last birth as well. The tradition says that just before Prince Siddhattha left home he took a last look at his wife from the door of her room, not daring to go nearer, lest he should awake her (*DPPN*, vol. II, p. 742).

As Liz Wilson (1996: 29) points out, the Buddha had a Great Renunciation and a Great Return. He renounced the home life not because of the burden of family or conjugal problems, but with the purpose of bringing liberation for all. On his Great Return home, he paid special visit to his former wife Yaśodharā and praised her for love and intimacy shown to him throughout *saṁsāra* (*J*. IV.282ff.). For a man to have a wife of morality is considered as a great fortune. According to the Jātakas, the Buddha's mother and father had been in conjugal bond just as Nakulamātā and Nakulapitā (*AN* III.295). A special characteristic seen in the Buddhist concept of marriage is that it is of a transcendental nature regarding time and the ideal marriage is characterized as involving the highest degree of virtue and fidelity.

In order to make a marriage successful, it requires five qualities from both man and woman. The Buddha states that when a woman possesses five factors, she is extremely agreeable to man. She is beautiful, wealthy and virtuous; she is clever and industrious and she begets children (*SN* IV.238). In the same place, it is mentioned that a woman expects five factors from a man: handsomeness, wealth, virtue, being clever and industrious and begetting children (*SN* IV.239).

The qualities given in this list are the same for both parties. The first factor that helps the development of mutual attachment is physical attraction. The second item is an essential factor to lead a successful married life. Unless one is economically strong, his married life becomes full of hardships. The significance of economic stability for successful married life has been recognized since ancient times up to the present day. The third factor is concerned with one's purity in behaviour. In this context, it can be applied to sexual fidelity or observance of chastity as well as all the other virtues cultivated through eradicating evils by the observance of precepts. As a person in society, to maintain a well established family, it is essential to be clever and industrious. Without this a happy wedded life would not be possible. The last factor, begetting children is in many societies, a personal as well as a societal expectation from a married couple. Especially, in the Indian society, it was an obligation to produce male children in order to maintain the family name. And it was the duty of a son to perform religious rites for his father (Harvey 2000: 354). A man or a woman, lacking at least one of these qualities, would not be contributing to a successful and perfect relationship.

The Buddhist marriage is an institution which involves several aspects of life. One's personal beauty, economic power, morality, abilities and being fertile are qualities conducive to a happy wedded life. According to the view expressed here, it becomes clear that the Buddhist concept of marriage is founded on a broader system of mutual relationships and not limited only to sexuality.

The most influential *sutta* preached for the well-being of married life is the *Sigālovādasutta*. It establishes a well-balanced social system centred on the householder. The relationship between wife and husband is the foundation in the marriage relationship. It is obvious that the mutual need of gratifying sexual desire is highly conducive to maintain a lasting marriage bond. At the same time, intimacy, love and respect for each other are also necessary to lead a better wedded life. The texts in the canon have not provided detailed advices regarding how to lead one's sexual life. Such a subject is obviously too secular to be discussed in the Buddhist scriptures. Only explicit advice relates to living a virtuous life is given.

The basic requirements to be fulfilled to have a successful relationship between the married couple have been explained in the above-mentioned *sutta*. As a husband, one has to perform five duties towards his wife:

1. honour her,
2. respect her,
3. be faithful to her,
4. hand over authority to her to manage household wealth and other affairs, and
5. provide her with all the necessities.

There are five duties to be performed by a wife to the husband:

1. arrange his business well,
2. treat his attendants with kindness,
3. be faithful to him,
4. protect what he earns, and
5. be skilful and diligent in all her duties (*DN* III.190).

Man and woman have been positioned in equal ground regarding their responsibility enhancing the pragmatic value of these mutual duties. Due to the opportunity granted to both partners to develop one's personality as an important figure in the family, there is no room left for any superiority or inferiority complex to grow within the family. Both wife and husband are equals.

The later texts such as Jātaka have dealt with many aspects of conjugal relationships. Tachibana (1986: 152) says that the Buddha did not talk about the love between wife and husband as it was deemed to be natural. This contention, even though is valid with regard to the canonical material, it is not relevant to the commentarial works. Yaśodharā, the wife of Gautama Buddha during his career as a householder, is reported to have retained her great love for him even after he left home. On the great return to his home after enlightenment, the Buddha was informed of the great love Yaśodharā had for him. Then the Buddha said that it was not a wonder that her love for him in this last life was such because even when she was an animal in a previous life, her love for him was strong. In order to illustrate their conjugal love continuing since unfathomable time in sāṁsāric existence, the Buddha related, the *Candakinnara Jātaka*, which mentioned the great love of *kinnara* Candā (this life Yaśodharā) for her mate *kinnara* Canda (present life Buddha) (*J* IV.282ff.).

Mutual love between two partners in marriage is appreciated in the Buddhist literature and it is considered as an obligation. The past story of the *Puṭabhatta Jātaka* recounts a king who neglected his chief queen. A king being afraid of his son, sends him away. The prince with his wife left the palace and lived in a remote place. On hearing the father's death, the prince and his wife left for the kingdom. On the way, they receive food but the husband does not share with the wife. After the husband was appointed the king, the wife was promoted to the chief queen but without honour. Then, the king's adviser recognizing the goodness of the queen and her pathetic condition in the palace, points out the king his wrong:

> Why dwell here with the king after he has become unkindly? In the world, union without love is painful.[19]

---

[19] *J* II.202f.; the *Godha Jātaka* (*J* III.106f.), is similar to this story. A similar version of the *Godha Jātaka* is included in the Chinese version of the

This story is illustrative of the harmony and mutual love that should be found between a wife and a husband.

All these duties from either party are aimed at maintaining pleasant environment within the family. It is general understanding that frequent experience of unpleasant psychological relationship between a wife and a husband could cause damage even to their sexual life. Sensual life is liable to turn into divine joy as well as hellish fire. According to the Buddhist point of view, marriage is for the most part to gratify senses. In this process, love and hatred both are working in equal degree. Love can easily become hatred. A slight mistake could bring about eternal separation of the partners. Sexual jealousy is predominant within the wedded life. Therefore, the Buddha has advised against undesirable situations between wife and husband by introducing ethical values.

Adultery

Regarding the normative sexual behaviour of wives and husbands, the Buddha frequently emphasizes the necessity to limit one's sexual life only to one's own spouse. In the *Aṅguttara Nikāya*, it is mentioned that "Going after another's wife the wise commend not" (*GS* II.80). In brief, regarding a man's sexual behaviour, the ethical principle to be adhered to is *sadārasantuṭṭhī* (*sehi dārehi santuṭṭho-paradārañca nārame*) being satisfied only with one's wife.[20] In addition to the emotional harm for others caused by adultery, the *Parābhavasutta* is concerned with one's economical and social

Abhiniṣkramaṇasūtra. The English translation of the text is *The Romantic Legend of Sākya Buddha* by Samuel Beal. The story revolves around the *bodhisattva* and Yaśodharā in a previous life. — pp. 81f.

20 *Aṅguttaranikāya*, BJTS, vol. 20, pt. 3, p. 345 in Gamage 1998: 120.

downfall. The discourse states:

> If one is addicted to women, liquor and gambling, he destroys all what is earned and falls into decline.[21]

According to the Vinaya, leading a promiscuous life is a barrier to one's spiritual development. Promulgating a disciplinary rule for the monks, the Buddha declared that a person who has sexual intimacies with prostitutes, widows, people who are deformed in their genders or with the nuns should not be given ordination in the Buddhist Order.[22] Here, it seems that such a person has been counted as mentally polluted to the extent that he cannot undertake a higher spiritual career.

In Buddhist literature, an ideal example of a wife is found in the character of Nakulamātā (mother of Nakula). She tells the Buddha that she was married to her husband in her youth, and ever since then, she did not even think of transgressing her husband, so no need to talk about physical misconduct (*AN* II.61). A similar statement regarding virtue in sexual behaviour and fidelity to husband was made by Nandamātā.[23] Not only physical restraint but also mental restraint concerning evil conduct is required by the Buddhist teaching. Further, referring the virtuous character of the treasure of woman of the universal monarch, it is said:

> That pearl among women too, Ānanda was never, even in thought unfaithful to the Great king of Glory: how much less then could she be so with the body. – *MN* III.175

---

[21] *Sn* 116: *itthidhutto surādhutto akkhadhutto ca yo naro-laddhaṃ laddhaṃ vināseti, taṃ parābhavato mukhaṃ* ।

[22] *Mahāvagga Pali*, BJTS, p. 175 in Gamage 1998: 121.

[23] *AN* IV.66: *yato 'ham bhante sāmikassa daharass 'eva daharā ānitā, nābhijānāmi sāmikaṃ manasā pi aticarittā, kuto pana kāyenā 'ti* ।

A woman who is defiled by the thought of lust for other men is considered as a slayer in disguise of wife:

Who is pitiless, corrupt in mind
Neglecting husband and unamiable
Inflamed by other men, a prostitute
On murder bent
Let her be called: a slayer and a wife.
– *GS* IV.57

It is clear that a wife has to maintain her purity in character and faithfulness to husband both physically and mentally. All the scriptural guidelines given to promote the well-being of marriage are conducive to protect the norm of chastity and thereby to strengthen the institution of marriage to fulfil personal as well as social expectations.

The most pathetic person who suffered due to being suspicious of committing adultery, mentioned in the Buddhist literature, is Aṅgulimāla (man with garland of fingers). Ahiṁsaka was a very clever student under a teacher who had many students. They were jealous of Ahiṁsaka's ability and conspired against him; they carried a tale to his teacher making a false accusation of having him a secret affair with the teacher's wife. The teacher being upset about it, planned to get rid of the enemy strategically. So, he asked Ahiṁsaka to offer a garland of thousand fingers in gratitude. The student trusting the teacher killed many persons to collect fingers to perform the duty. Finally, the Buddha interfered to avoid killing his own mother and brought him back to his real senses (*MN* II.98ff.). This episode reveals that adultery can be used as a serious accusation against a person. The psychological aspect of sexual jealousy plays a very important role in this story.

In addition to the moralistic approach to unconventional sexual behaviour involving adultery in Buddhist literature, we can find that it has been seen as a forgiveable offence requiring the treatment of offenders from a humane viewpoint. Particularly the Jātaka literature is characterized by this approach to the problem of adultery. Rape cases, incestuous relationships and other forms of sexual aberrations are very rarely mentioned in this collection of stories. The majority of stories refer to adultery as the common form of sexual misconduct. And also, there is an attempt to examine various issues arising from illicit sexual conduct.

The discussion carried out in the *Durājāna Jatāka* is concerned with the psychological imbalance that could occur within an adulterous person. A lay follower was very much troubled due to the incomprehensible behaviour of his wife. One day she behaved like a servant to him, but the next day she behaved completely differently, by being very cruel to him. Finally, he informs of her puzzling character to the Buddha. Revealing the secret of this unusual behaviour, the Buddha explains that on days that she has committed adultery she shows kindness to him in order to conceal her feeling of guilt. After she finds that he is not aware of her misconduct, she reverts to the rude mannerism. However, on hearing that the Buddha had come to know her illicit relationship, she abstains from continuing with her evil conduct (*J* I.299f.). The adulteress in the story seems to have been suffering from her guilty conscience for betraying the husband. On account of her remorse, she loses psychological integrity. The two patterns of behaviour expressed by her, subservience and aggressiveness, both exhibited an abnormal mentality. The reason for her irregular behaviour can be understood in the aforesaid manner. An important factor to which attention is drawn here is that her giving up of misconduct was due to shame.

According to the Buddhist understanding of any moral wrong, the possibility of awakening oneself to the requirements of the moral life sooner or later is granted. Even if one commits adultery, he is not considered as an incorrigible sinner. This woman was conscious of shame and fear to do evil even though due to her weakness of will she succumbed to temptation. This consciousness might have caused her to mentally suffer about her wrong. The interference of the Buddha brought her to the predominant trait in her character, which is morality. It is notable that there is no mention of retribution for her offence in the after life.

Buddhism has tried to understand adultery as a common weakness of human character. In the *Bandhanamokkha Jātaka*, a queen sexually misbehaves with sixty-four persons in the absence of the king who was devoted only to her.[24] The judgement given for her guilt is humanistic; after knowing the event, the king commands to execute all the sixty-four adulterers; *bodhisatta* points out that they are not guilty because they followed the queen's need. When the queen was accused of the offence the *bodhisatta* reasoned that it is the nature of gentle-sex to commit adultery and that she should not be punished (*J* I.437ff.). Even though from the feminist point of view this is an insult for women, yet, the element of understanding about human nature with regard to sin reflected in this text is praiseworthy.

In many cases, adulterous persons have been forgiven for the offence and restored to morality. In the *Culla-Paduma-*

---

[24] This number could be an exaggeration and can be connected to the idea that a woman has sixty-four kinds of charms to entice a man.

Jātaka, Prince Culla-Paduma saves his wife's life tactfully and quenches her thirst by giving his blood. Later, the wife who was loved so much falls in love with a mutilated criminal and commits sin with him. Subsequently, she plans to kill her husband. The prince could escape death and became the king of his kingdom. His wife maintained her paramour from public support and finally came to the king who recognized his former wife. Then, he revealed in public that she was his former wife who betrayed him and tried to kill him. Instead of punishing or seeking to take revenge from her, the king expels her from his kingdom (*J* II.115-21). Two important points are derivable from this story. One is the risk of committing violent acts like killing due to adultery and the other is the understanding of the offence from a humanistic angle.

Forgiveness for the guilt of adultery is mentioned in the *Gahapati Jātaka* too. This story takes a realistic approach to the problem of adultery. The wife misbehaved with the village headman; one day her husband caught both as they were committing the offence and beat the paramour and threatened the wife with dire consequences if she ever did behave in that manner again. The conflict simply ended and no serious moral punishment was given (*J* II.134f.).

The *Ucchiṭṭha-bhatta-Jātaka* is also very similar to this story. While the husband is away, the wife commits adultery with another person. The story ends with the discovery of the secret and the husband punishing both the adulterous persons. In this case, the wife found the chance to sin as her husband was away for business (*J* II.167ff.).

According to the Jātaka literature, persons who engaged in business activities have to spend long time outside their houses and families. It is evident from the *Apaṇṇaka* and

Vaṇṇupatha Jātaka (*J* I.95ff., 106-10). With this kind of long absence of husbands, it is natural that it causes loneliness in the life of wives at home and consequently an urge develops in their minds to seek love and affection from others. In such a context it is not very surprising that an offence like adultery might be committed. Even though the Jātakas do not reason out why adultery occurs, the attitude to it has been humanistic.

Buddhism recognizes marriage between young girls and old males as a reason for one's decline. The *Parābhavasutta* states that if a man past his youth brings a very young lady as his wife (whose breasts are like *timbaru* fruits) he cannot sleep at night because of (sexual) jealousy. That is a cause of decline for a man.[25] The problem of this type of marriages can be seen in the *Vessanatara Jātaka* and *Sattubhatta Jātaka.* In the latter story, an old brāhmaṇa takes a young lady as his wife. The young woman falls in love with a young person and harasses her old husband (*J* III.341-51). The *Vessantara Jātaka* is the best illustration of conflicts between old husbands and their young wives (*J* VI.488f.).

In early Buddhism, desire to gratify senses has been explained on a gender-free basis. When the Buddha preaches about sensory process and subsequent conceptualizing activity of the mind, he makes no reference to man or woman, but to the term *sattā*. The Buddhist genesis story uses the term *sattā* to indicate the pre-gender stage of human evolution (*DN* III.85).

A person afflicted with ignorance and desire is liable to fall into sin. In contrast to this common nature of human beings, there is a particular devaluation of the human female in

---

[25] *Sn* 110: *atītayobbano poso āneti timbaruttaniṃ,*
tassā issā na supati, taṃ parābhavato mukhaṃ ।

connection with evil in many cultures. Discriminative attitude towards women was largely practised in Indian society by the time of the Buddha. Even the Buddhist literature could not completely avoid this influence and consequently attitudes expressing the idea that women are inferior have been included in the Pali *suttas*.

Concerning adultery, wrong is attributed in many cases to the women and there is an attempt to generalize that women are naturally inclined to commit sin. Previously, we have referred to the *Bandhanamokkha Jātaka* which emphasizes this attitude to woman.[26] The *Anabhirati Jātaka* states that "naughtiness of women is natural" (*J* I.301-02). In the *Mahāsupina Jātaka*, a prediction is made of human kind that women will betray their husbands and spend the family wealth to enjoy life with paramours (*J* I.334-45). Another reference reads that it is impossible to keep a guard over a woman; no guard can keep a woman in the right path (Chalmers 1981, vol. I: 151). The culmination of idealizing woman as given to adultery is seen in the *Andhabhūta Jātaka*: the king plays dice with his old brāhmaṇa counsellor uttering the verse:

'Tis nature's law that rivers wind;
Trees grow of wood by law of kind;
And, given opportunity,
All women work iniquity.[27]

The old brāhmaṇa takes a young girl who was brought up since her foetus stage keeping in his own house, avoiding her

---

[26] *J* I.440: *itthiyo nāma methunadhammena atittā, jātisabhāvo hi esā, etāsaṃ bhavitabbayuttakaṃ hoti* ।

[27] *J* I.289f.: *sabbā nadī vankagatā sabbe kaṭṭhamayā vanā-*
sabbitthiyo kare pāpaṃ labhamānā nivātake ।

contact with the outer world. The only male whom she knew was the old brāhmaṇa. Finally, the king employs a person to pollute her chastity to confirm his view which brought victory in the play. An attempt is made to convince that no means can protect women kind from committing adultery when there is opportunity.[28]

Edward Westermarck points out that adultery had been almost exclusively a problem for married women: the serious problem arising from woman's adultery is the purity of offspring.[29] The other reason is the idea that a wife's transgression can bring about more severe emotional breakdown in marriage than that of husband. This conclusion is made on the assumption that man's adultery is only a sensual act whereas that of woman is more than that of bodily attachment (Westermarck 1934: 136 quoted in Lawson 1990: 48). Kinsey (1953: 143) points out that there is attitudinal inequality concerned with adultery for man and woman. He says:

> Most societies recognize the necessity for accepting some extramarital coitus as an escape value for the male, to relieve him from the pressures put on him by society's insistence on stable marital relationships. These same societies, however, less often permit it for the female.

The conclusions quoted from modern sexological researchers prove that stigma on women for adultery is a cross-cultural phenomenon and it is still influential among human societies,

---

[28] In the Sinhalese literature, this idea was put into verse by the poet Totagamuwe Rahula: *avasarakal rahas tena-gahanu kavuruda varada nobadenna* । — *Kāvyaśekhara Mahā Kāvyaya* p. 488

[29] The idea of having a pure birth (parental purity) is mentioned in Buddhist literature too.

despite scientific and rationalistic advancements made regarding knowledge of facts about human nature.

However, Buddhism attempts to bring some balance in such attitudes by the inclusion of canonical admonitions to males not to commit adultery by transgressing one's wife. In some places, male is advised not to go against his wife's will while other places in the texts have tried to interpret adulterous behaviour as an inherent characteristic of women. A more reasonable perspective on this matter in Buddhism can be seen in the *Saṃyutta Nikāya*. The Buddha himself states that in the world a few persons practise restraint in respect of sexual misconduct whereas the majority does not do so (*SN* V.469). This statement makes no indication of gender difference. This is also indicated in the third precept in the canon.

Monogamy and Polygamy

In Indian society of the Buddha's time, there were both monogamy and polygamy in vogue. According to Hindu scriptures, a brāhmaṇa was entitled to marry three women, the kṣatriya two, and the vaiśya and the śūdra one.[30] S. Tachibana based on the Sanskrit texts comes to the conclusion that Brāhmanism accepted the practice of polygamy (Tachibana 1986: 155). L.P.N. Perera points out that Tachibana's remark is somewhat misleading because the Vedic ideal of marriage had been monogamy.[31] It should be mentioned that even though

---

[30] Quoted in Tachibana 1986: 155 fn. 1: *Va* I.24; *Manu* III.13; but according to *Manu* III.23, the brāhmaṇa may marry six women, the kṣatriya four, the vaiśya and the śūdra each one; and according to the institute of *Viṣṇu* XXIV.1-4, the brāhmaṇa four, the kṣatriya three, the vaiśya two and the śūdra one.

[31] Perera 1993: 133 fn. 1; he makes this remark based on the discussion by Horner 1990: 35 fn. 1.

Tachibana says that Brāhmanism approves of polygamy, he does not assert that polygamy was the ideal of Indian culture.

In the canonical material as well as commentarial literature, there are references to polygamy. In the Jātaka, there is reference to polyandry as well (*J.* V.425). Depending on one's economic condition, it was permissible for a male to marry several women. The *Laṭukikopamasutta* (*Simile of the Quail*) reports the custom of having a vast number of wives by rich persons (*MN* I.452). In the *Aṅguttara Nikāya*, we find the wanton life of a householder with four wives depicted. His sensualistic life is explained in this passage and it also shows how a person becomes subject to mental and physical suffering due to such a way of life (*AN* I.137). The householder, Ugga is reported to have had four wives prior to his conversion (*AN* IV.210).

In the *Kulāvaka-Jātaka*, it is mentioned that the *bodhisatta* had four wives in the human world and three of them were born in the divine abode together with him after death. The story carries no condemnation of polygamy as morally wrong and it is also granted that they can continue in *saṁsāra* together (*J* I.198ff.). References to the kings' harems are found in several places of the Pali canon and in the commentarial literature (*J* I.262; II.125, 206; III.13, 168). The chief consort of a king was called *aggamahesi*. We find reference to Mallikā who was the chief consort of Pasenadi, the king of Kosala.[32] The *Kuṇāla-Jātaka* mentions polyandry. The Princess Kaṇhā is married to the five princes of the King Pāṇḍu. Being not satisfied with them, she sins with her hump-backed crippled attendant (*J* V.424-25).

[32] *J* I.381; II.206; *DN* II.187: Queen Subhaddā was the chief of eighty-four thousand wives of king Mahāsudassana.

The position of Buddhism regarding the morality of polygamous marriage is not clear. Tachibana contends that most of the references made to marriage emphasize the virtue of monogamy and it can be a good ground to conclude that Buddhism denies the practice of polygamy (Tachibana 1986: 157). C. Gamage also points out that throughout the texts, it is difficult to find a place where the Buddha criticizes or praises this practice (Gamage 1998: 119). In the present story of the *Sādhusīla Jātaka*, a brāhmaṇa had four daughters whose hands were sought by four candidates. Among the suitors one was of noble birth, another handsome, the third, wealthy and the last was virtuous. The brāhmaṇa asks the Buddha who is the most qualified suitor for his daughters. The Buddha's answer was that the virtuous one. Then, the daughters were given to him (*J* I.137f.).

In contrast to the general assumption that Buddhism only approves of monogamy, the *Sādhusīla Jātaka* indicates that the Buddha has given guidance even regarding a good polygamous marriage. Moreover, the *Kuṇāla Jātaka* establishes a positive attitude towards the practice of polygamous marriage. However, it is well-known that the *Jātaka* literature is a later development in the Buddhist history. In examining the commentator's attempt to show that the Buddha did provide guidance for successful polygamous marriage, we can assume that the silence of texts on the matter might have allowed room to do so.

In spite of the assertion made by both Tachibana and Gamage that Buddhism does not approve of polygamy, it is safer to hold the position of Peter Harvey that Buddhism is tolerant of polygamy (Harvey 1990: 206). A modern famous propagandist of Buddhism, K. Dhammananda also states that

Buddhism does not reject polygamy. Since there is no law made by the Buddha as to the number of women that a man can marry, it depends on the law of a country.[33]

The position in connection with monogamy is clear. Many teachings given for the betterment of married people are directed to the monogamous marriage. In the *Sigālovādasutta*, the Buddha advises the householder Sigala to have a respectable and intimate relationship between wife and husband. We can be assured of conjugal harmony existing in such a union. The wife is said to be the best friend that one has.[34] In the *Aṅguttara Nikāya*, the ideal of monogamy, the couple of Nakulamātā and Nakulapitā, is praised by the Buddha (*AN* III.295-98). Satisfaction with a single wife is always mentioned as praiseworthy moral virtue (*sehi dārehi santuṭṭhi*). The Buddha states, "Let him not share a wife with another" (*J* VI.286-87). In reference to the virtuous married life of the ancient brāhmaṇas, the Buddha says that they did not marry a woman from a different caste, that they did not buy a wife, and that they chose living together with mutual love after having come together.[35] It is indisputable that Buddhism upheld the monogamous marriage.

Premarital Sex

According to sexological classifications, premarital sex (fornication) is categorized as a normal deviant sexual behaviour (Hensley and Tewksbury 2003: 5). If a sex act is not legally wrong and practised by a small number of persons,

[33] Dhammananda, http://www.geocities.com/CapeCanaveral/Runway/5787/marriage.htm

[34] *SN* I.37: *bhariyā ca paramā sakhā* ।

[35] *Sn* 290: *na brāhmaṇā aññaṃ agamum na pi bhariyaṃ kiṇimsu te,*
sampiyen 'eva samvāsaṃ sangantvā samarocayuṃ ।

such a sex act is called as normal deviation. It becomes a non-conformal act because the larger society does not accept it. In Buddhist literature, there is no explicit discourse prohibiting sex before marriage. However, according to the list of women to whom one should not go, one cannot have premarital sex. A man and woman should enter a formal bond to live as wife and husband and to have sexual relationship.

The *Aṅguttara Nikāya* (*AN* III.76; *J* III.395) refers to the young girls who are matured enough (*thullakumārikā*) to be given in marriage but not yet married. Monks are advised not to go to the houses where such girls dwell. Here, we can see the recognition of the possibility of the occurrence of premarital sexual relationships in such cases and monks are prevented from exposing themselves to such a danger. In the list of minor virtues (*cūla-sīla*), it is mentioned that ascetic Gautama did not accept women and young girls. The commentary to *Dīgha Nikāya* states that the term *itthi* (women) means who have had sex with a male and *kumārikā* stands for others (who have not had sex with a male).[36] According to this definition, we can assume the Pali term *kumārikā* has been used for virgins.

In the canonical works, we cannot find a definite view on premarital sex and information about it. Only a few Jātakas have touched on the issue. In the *Pannika Jātaka*, a father tests his daughter's purity (virginity) before she was given in marriage to a husband. The father pretends that he amorously loves her; then she said that such a thing would be as monstrous as fire rising out of water (Chalmers 1981, vol. I: 244). In the past story related to this event, what the

[36] *DA* I, p. 72 (Devanāgarī): *itthikumāri paṭiggahaṇāti ettha itthīti purisantaragatā, itarā kumārikā nāma* ।

role of a father in guarding his daughter's purity (virginity) is well expressed:

> *He that should prove my buckler strong,*
> *My father, worketh me this wrong.*
> *Forlorn in thickest wood I cry;*
> *My helper proves my enemy.*

The daughter was questioned for her virginity by her father. The duty of a father towards her daughter and parental expectation of their daughters to be virgins until they enter marriage is explained in this story (Chalmers 1981, vol. I: 244).

Premarital sex is denied because of the problems it might cause in a later marriage relationship. The *Kaṭṭhahāri Jātaka* makes a realistic investigation into the undesirable effects of fornication. This *Jātaka* story deals with the destiny of children born from illegal sexual relationships. In its past story, a king enjoys sex with a woman whom he encountered by accident in the forest. The king giving his signet-ring to the woman told her that if a girl would be born, to spend the money earned from selling the ring and if it were to be a boy, to bring the boy with the ring to him. The woman gave birth to a boy who was the *bodhisatta*. Eventually, when the child went to play with his peers, he had to face the stigma of not having a legal father. As a solution, the mother took the child to the king, the father of her child. The king recognizing the woman, but feeling ashamed in front of his court, denied the woman's claim to him as her child's father. The pitiable woman, seeing no help from any quarter, threw the child up into the air. Then the child sitting cross-legged in the air expressed the truth and consequently the king accepted him as his child (ibid.: 27-29).

This story is well illustrative of the issue of momentary

sexual impulses which prompt people to commit sexual acts with no sense of responsibility. And the vision of the Jātaka compiler into the fate of children of illegitimate birth is valid even for modern conditions.

Canonical data is very scant on premarital sex and references found are connected with religious seekers. The few Jātakas that we mentioned have dealt with premarital sex from two different perspectives: (i) virginity, and (ii) illegal child birth. The last mentioned Jātaka is more concerned with fornication which means voluntary sexual intercourse between two unmarried persons or persons not married to each other.

Masturbation

Masturbation is the device of reaching sexual orgasm through the manipulation or other frictional contact with the genitalia without copulation. This is a mode of expression of auto-eroticism (Menuhin 1996: 9). This exists among both male and female members of society. Sexologically, it is considered as a normal stage of sexual development (ibid.: 10)[37] and free of any harm to the person unless one becomes fixated on it for fear of heterosexual relationships. In the *Vinaya Piṭaka*, both kinds of masturbation, male and female, have been recorded.

According to the classification of Gagnon and Simon, masturbation is classified under normal sexual deviation. A sex act is recognized as normal deviation for the reasons of low visibility and involvement of a significant number of

[37] Masturbation begins very early in some infants, who stimulate themselves by rocking backwards and forwards on the genitals when less than one year old. For the great majority of men active masturbation to orgasm begins at thirteen or fourteen with the onset of puberty.

participants in it. And also statistically, it is a normal sexual behaviour because more than 50 per cent of members in society are reported to have experienced it at least one time in life and many adults have engaged in it (Hensley and Tewksbury 2003: 5).

Since two researchers have examined regarding the prevalence of masturbation in monastic community and in the contemporary Indian society prior to the present research (Gamage 1998: 62ff.; Perera 1993: 167f.), I will try to understand the reasons why this is prohibited for monks and nuns in the Order, paying attention to ethical and doctrinal teachings related to sensual desire. Masturbation is a manifestation of auto-eroticism and, according to psychology, auto-erotic impulse may or may not be directed to one's self (Perera 1993: 167 fn. 2). In the *Saññogasutta* of the *Aṅguttara Nikāya*, it is explained how auto-eroticism exists in one's psyche and it leads to seek sexual pleasure in opposite sex. The text reads:

> A woman attends inwardly to her feminine faculties, gestures, manners, poise, and desires, etc. On being excited and delighted by that she attends outwardly to masculine faculties, desires and charms, etc. Being excited and delighted by that she wants to be bonded to what is outside her, wants whatever pleasure and happiness that arise based on that bond. – *AN* IV.57

It is clear from this that the beginning of erotic feeling is directed towards oneself, which we referred to as auto-eroticism. In accordance with this early Buddhist psychological explanation, masturbation can be considered as an expression of deep-rooted tendency in the mind. According to sexological writings, masturbation is associated with sexual fantasies about opposite sex partners. Even desires, which cannot be materialized in the practical life, are present in this practice (Ge 1982: 593).

In view of sexual fantasies, Buddhism holds the position that if a recluse enjoys memories concerned with members of the opposite sex, derives pleasure from them and longs for them, though he is devoid of actual contact with them, his celibacy is not perfect and celibacy is torn (*AN* IV.54-56). Even though, the Vinaya is silent about the element of sexual fantasy in the act of masturbation, according to Buddhist psychology, the presence of sexual fantasies is unavoidable in an unrestrained mind.

In the section called *saṅghādisesa* (require formal meeting of *saṅgha*) of the *Suttavibhaṅga*, the rule prohibiting intentional emission of semen (*sañcetanikā sukka visaṭṭhi*) was laid down by the Buddha because of a monk who engaged in masturbation by himself. Ven. Seyyasaka was displeased with following the holy life because of intense desires and thoughts of sensuality. As a consequence of displeasure, his physique changed and lost pleasantness in appearance. Seeing this change, another monk advised him to lead a relaxed life and to release sexual tension by masturbation when desire arises. That monk, as the Vinaya says, ate as much as he wanted, bathed, slept and when passion assailed his heart, emitted semen by using his hand.[38] Then in a short time, Ven. Seyyasaka was nice looking with round features, of a bright complexion and a clear skin. So, his fellow monks asked him the reason for his change for the better. He frankly replied to them saying that no medicine was used (*na kho ahaṃ āvuso bhesajjaṃ karomi*) but followed a relaxed life given to pleasure

[38] *Vin* III.110: ... *yadā anabhirati uppajjati rāgo cittaṃ anuddhaamseti tadā hatthena uppakkamitvā asuciṃ mocesi* ।

practising self-masturbation.[39] Hearing this, the virtuous monks became angry and criticized his act:

> *kiṃ pana tvaṃ āvuso Seyyasaka yen 'va hatthena saddhādeyyaṃ bhuñjasi ten 'va hatthena upakkamitvā asucim mocesīti.*
>
> – *Vin* III.111
>
> But do you reverend Seyyasaska, eat the gifts of faith with very same hand as that you use to emit semen?

This statement is useful to understand the reason why masturbation is prohibited for monastic members. A religious person is supported by the laity by providing food and other requisites. Consequently, society expects monks to lead a celibate life.

In the *Aggikkhandhopamasutta* of the *Aṅguttara Nikāya*, the Buddha states to the monks that it is better to thrust a burning iron ball into mouth to destroy organs up to the anus because such an act would cause only death to the person but if some one with a mind obsessed with lust and desire enjoys alms, gifts of faith offered by devotees, would be reborn in hell. The former is better than the latter (*AN* IV.118f.). Even though this statement caused a crisis in the community, still it reflects the early Buddhist attitude to receiving offerings from others and expectation of inner purity to become qualified for them.

The *Piṇḍapātapārisuddhisutta* advises monks to review one's mind after their alms round; whether the mind was assailed by desire, lust, hate, delusion, aversion, or desire for five codes of sense pleasures on the path to alms round, and if they were present, one has to make effort to remove them (*MLDB*, pp. 1143f.). Now we can realize the meaning of the

[39] Until recent times, masturbation was deemed as harmful to one's health and causes insanity. This episode in the *Vinaya* shows that Buddhism has not accepted physiological harm at all.

above statement made by monks regarding the misconduct by Seyyasaka and its relation to spiritual quality expected from a person who is dependent on gifts given in faith.

When this moral breach was reported to the Buddha, the culprit monk was rebuked and was explained why one should refrain from any act leading to sensual gratification:

> *Dhamma* has been taught for stilling passion in various ways, for the subduing of conceit ... for the elimination of attachment, for the cutting through the round of becomings, for the destruction of craving, for passionlessness. ...
>
> – *BD* I.194f.

This statement of the Buddha indicates how the act adversely affects the final goal of Buddhism, which is to eradicate desire and stop the continuity in *saṁsāra*. From the Buddhist doctrinal point, masturbation is not a simple and ethically neutral action, but one which directly affects the ultimate aim of monastic life in Buddhism. Further, referring to the effect of this act upon society, the Buddha says that it is not conducive to increase the faith of the converted or win over the faith of the unconverted (*Vin* III.111).

The complete rule promulgated to restrain intentional emission of semen reads as follows:

> Intentional emission of semen except during a dream is an offence requiring a formal meeting of the Order.[40]

In spite of the fact that masturbation is also a sexual act, it is not counted to be as grave as the first *pārājikā* of heterosexual behaviour. So, masturbation is perceived secondary to the sex connected to bodily orifices. The special characteristic in the Buddhist monastic code is the necessary involvement

[40] *Vin*. 112: *sañcetanikā sukkavisaṭṭhi aññatra supinantā saṃghādiseso ti*।

of the element of intention in determining an act as being offensive; it is present in this case too (the term *sañcetanikā* indicates this). It is a natural thing among adults to experience nocturnal emission of semen and the *Vinaya* reports some monks who have experienced it during dream. They were given verdict of guiltlessness as there was no conscious attempt to emit semen (*Vin* III.112).

Committing the first *pārājikā* offence entails irrecoverable defeat in the holy career but for the offence of masturbation (and auto-erotic activities not concerned with sexual orifices), the *Vinaya* imposes only a short-term prohibition of membership; the culprit can restore to the original position in the *saṅgha* after undergoing a probationary period.

Vinaya seems to have some kind of liberal attitude to moral breach caused by self-erotic activities (if they are not orificial). The main intention of the *Vinaya* is to restrain acts of body and speech. (In a deep sense *Vinaya* is aimed at restraining all the three doors, body, word and mind.) To categorize a sex act as a grave offence, the *Vinaya* applies the criterion of intentional sexual engagement in threefold sexual orifices. In a woman, there are three channels: genital organ, mouth and anus, while in a man there are only two orifices: mouth and anus.

According to the Freudian concept of erogenous zone, these three channels are considered to be highly sensitive and they are connected with psychosexual development.[41] The entrance of genital (male) into these orifices causes the defeat for a monk. In the practice of masturbation, orgasm is reached through stimulation caused by touch (by oneself or by another) without involvement of sexual orifices. According to the understanding in *Vinaya* and fact revealed by scientific

---

[41] http://psychology.about.com/library/weekly/aa111500b.htm

investigations, we can assume that the highest level of sexual gratification is achieved from intentional entrance of genitals into orifices (no matter man or woman). This can be clarified from the imposing rule of defeat for those who practise self-fellation — putting genital into one's own mouth (*Vin* III.35) or self-pederasty — entering genital into one's own anus (*Vin* III.35). This shows that no matter where the sexual orifices are available whether in one's own body or in others.

According to these data, it seems that the *Vinaya* takes into consideration the physiological value of bodily parts when it introduces a rule for sexuality. Higher the degree of sensitivity of a particular sexual channel, higher the severity of offence. On account of lower degree of sensitivity involved in masturbation, the *Vinaya* has reduced the degree of severity of the act.

According to Buddhist psychology, the unwholesome root of *rāga* is involved in intentional emission of semen. J.C. Holt in his analysis of *Vinaya* rules according to the three basic unwholesome roots, shows that the first *saṅghādisesa* rule is considered as dealing with acts rooted in *rāga* (Holt 1981: 94). As mentioned authoritatively, in the *Pañcapparanaṭṭhakathā* (p. 117 in Perera 1993: 168), auto-eroticism is invariably associated with sensuality: *sukkavisaṭṭhi nāma rāgasamuṭṭhānā hoti* Sāratthadīpanī, pt II, p. 642, in Perera 1993: 168). The presence of passion in masturbation has been explained thus:

> The body becomes a temple of passionate pleasure, almost innocent in its return to first sexual experience, auto-eroticism or masturbation. – Menuhin 1996: 18

The operation of *rāga* in human mind is active until all the cankers are permanently eradicated. Attachment to sensuality originates in passion and it is acceptable if it occurs within an ethical frame. *Rāga* involved in an accepted way of deriving pleasure (sensual or sexual) is not a moral offence likely to produce retribution in unhappy states. It is evident that by the approval of sexual contact between marital couples this was granted. This can be said as release of passion in a normatively permitted way (*rāga* within *dhamma*).

In the case of the monks and nuns, they themselves have made a self vow of complete abstinence from sexual gratification. Buddhist monasticism is aimed at destroying sensual desire. Therefore, any act conducive to sense gratification is rejected as unwholesome (*adhamma*). Therefore, if one transgresses the vow of celibacy (or norm) by engaging in any kind of sex act, that act is perceived as caused by improper passion (*adhammarāga*). For a monk, his body cannot be used for sexual needs. If it is so used, that becomes a sexual abuse of one's own body. So, in the context of Buddhist monasticism, masturbation is a sexual deviation.

No canonical information is found regarding the practice of masturbation by lay persons. Before the twentieth century, medical science and religious dogmas considered masturbation as abnormal sexual behaviour. Modern sexologists point out that it is a myth to consider masturbation as harmful. Medical scientific classification of sexual disorders (paraphilias) does no longer include masturbation into the list. Under the new knowledge revealed by different branches of science, it is interesting to examine the Buddhist standpoint regarding whether the practice of masturbation is acceptable or not for the lay community.

The definition of the third precept is given in such a way as to reflect its social importance as it is necessarily connected with a second person. With regard to masturbation (self), there is no interference with the body of another. In the attempt to derive the implications of the Buddhist ethical principles on a practice like masturbation, the *Ambalaṭṭhikā-rāhulovādasutta* seems significant. This *sutta* presents a moral criterion based on harm and benefit brought about by doing an action. The first yardstick to measure an action is to consider the harm that would result to oneself. The second is to consider the harm caused to others (society); and the third is to consider likely harm to both oneself and to the others. If an action brings about affliction to oneself, to others, and to both parties, such an act definitely should not be done because it is unwholesome (this criterion is equally applied to bodily, verbal and mental deeds). And if an action is beneficial to oneself, beneficial to others, and to the both parties, such an act is acceptable.[42] To clarify whether this particular sex act is compatible with moral yardstick given here, we are to seek the scientific view on it:

> All the information revealed by modern science indicates that masturbation is a perfectly normal act, both biologically and psychologically, and that it causes no ill effects whatsoever. As a matter of fact, the argument continues, it is probably one of the earliest and best ways that human beings can become familiar with their own bodies and their own sexuality. – Thiroux 1995: 356

In a close look into this statement which is a summary of modern scientific knowledge on masturbation, it becomes clear that it makes neither harm to the person psychologically or physically, nor to the other persons (society). Further, it

---

[42] *MN* I.416: *n'eva attabyābādhāya samvatteyya na parabyābādhāya samvatteyya na ubhayabyābādhāya samvatteyya, kusalaṃ idaṃ kāyakammaṃ* ...।

is helpful for the person to build a healthy sexual life. So, it is clear that masturbation is compatible with the moral criterion given in the *Ambalaṭṭhikārāhulovādasutta*. To further our knowledge on this, it is useful to refer to J.L. Menuhin, a medical practitioner. Tracing to the history of changing of ideas on masturbation, he describes:

> Almost forty years passed before Stekel (1951) declared the "disturbance" in masturbation to be unnecessary guilt feelings when inhibition failed to stop it. This was thought to connect fantasies of oedipal conflicts with father or mother and with the superego incorporation of parental prohibitions towards masturbation. Attitudes were finally moving towards a positive acceptance of masturbation as a norm in child and adolescent development. Kinsey (1948) had extended to argue that adult masturbation is a harmless form of sexual behaviour from heterosexual intercourse, but rather the second most often performed sexual activity, practised by adults in parallel with heterosexual activity, and both preceding this sexual activity in adolescence and often succeeding it in older age. – Menuhin 1996: 11

The views based on medical scientific researches, reveal that masturbation is a harm-free sexual act. A recent writer on sexual ethics brings a criterion similar to the Buddhist judgement of moral action advocated in the *Ambalaṭṭhikārāhulovādasutta*. Ben Neal Ard puts it as:

> It is still helpful to inquire as to what are the consequences for a person of a given pattern of sexual behaviour, and whether the behaviour contributes to or detracts from the person's happiness in the long run.
>
> – Quoted in Ard 1989: 163

If we are based on new findings and ethical criteria (very

similar to Buddhism), the practice of masturbation is acceptable as a harmless sex act.

When considered from the Buddhist moral point of view, masturbation is not more different from a legal heterosexual genital act because of its non-involvement in creating harm to oneself, to others and to both sides. Therefore, it is free from morally ill effects. According to Buddhist psychology, *rāga* is necessarily present in the reciprocal sexual contact between wife and husband; so is it in the emission of semen through masturbation. As a legal heterosexual act brings no harm, masturbation is also completely innocent.

Lay people are recognized as given to sensual gratification and it should be enjoyed within an ethical frame which aims at avoiding harm to oneself, to others and to both parties. And also, an act should not be generative of suffering in this life and in the next life. Any such harm cannot be seen in the act of masturbation. In the case of the issue of *saṁsāra*, any sexual act is problematic whether it is heterosexual, homosexual or of any other mode because of involvement with *rāga*. Moreover, this practice is used by oneself for one's own pleasure without producing three forms of harm given in the above-mentioned Buddhist moral criterion. Then, we can arrive at the conclusion that masturbation for a lay person is not morally wrong.

To sum up the chapter, we dealt with the subject of sexual deviation from two approaches. In the first section, the two norms of celibacy and chastity were discussed in relation to the Buddhist monks and the laity. Under the norm of celibacy, any kind of sex act becomes deviant for monks. It is involved from the doctrinal, ethical and sociological goals and expectations put on the religious seeker of Buddhism.

The norm of chastity is given for the laity and the third precept of abstaining sexual misconduct is to be followed by them. The lay person enjoys sex within the marriage and chastity is practised within it. There are teachings advocating the betterment of the family and instructions to avoid adultery. Adultery is the major form of violating the norm of chastity and it is connected with the Buddhist *kamma* theory. Buddhism has adopted a multi-faceted approach to its theory on adultery and the Jātaka is more humanistic in its approach to the problem. While monogamous marriage is accepted, Buddhist teachings reflect a tolerant attitude towards polygamy. In the last part of the chapter, two forms of normal sexual deviation, premarital sex and masturbation were discussed. Parental expectation of virginity of girls and the issue of illegal children born from fornication have been discussed. In view of masturbation, it is prohibited for monks on the grounds of celibacy norm, doctrinal aim and social expectation of spiritual virtue of monks and nuns. Finally, an attempt was made to recognize the Buddhist position on masturbation as a practice of laity and the conclusion was drawn that it is acceptable for lay people as the Buddhist moral criterion is based on facts compatible with scientific knowledge.

5

Pathological Deviant Sexual Behaviour

Introduction

THE second class of sexual deviation is pathological deviations. These are considered as clinical conditions and mental disorders. The *Diagnostic and Statistical Manual of American Psychiatric Association* (*DSM*-IV, 1994) classifies paedophilia, exhibitionism, voyeurism and some other forms of sexual disorders as paraphilias which require clinical treatments. Even though rape has not been included by the *DSM*-IV as a paraphilia, researchers of sexual deviance hold that it is of enormous clinical and forensic value. Incest is recognized as a subcategory of paedophilia by psychiatrists. Incest is considered as a criminal offence as well as a psychological disorder.

In the legal sphere, all these five forms of sexual deviations are included under sexual crimes. W. Simon and J. Gagnon regarding this category of sexual deviations state that they are considered by many as harmful, are usually against the law and are practised by relatively few individuals (Hensley and Tewksbury 2003: 5f.). Pathological deviance is similar to normal deviance in that it does not have significant or sizeable supportive group structures to maintain the participants of the activities. This category of deviations is characterized by sexual arousal in response to objects or situations that are not part of normative sexual arousal activity patterns. So, they become problematic to the individual as well as to society.

Milder forms of this type of sexual behaviour are practised by many people and fall within the normal range of human sexuality. Such a form of behaviour is not considered to be a mental disorder by clinicians. Another element found in all pathological deviations is fantasy, unrealistic desires imagined and beyond the sphere of reality. If a person is constantly depressed by fantasies related to abnormal sexual stimuli (children or non-consenting adult women, etc.) for more than six months, it is diagnosed as a pathological condition (Doctor and Neff 1994: 174). If the fantasies (raping, etc.) are put into practice, the person is involved in a violation of law and becomes a threat to society. Moreover, he is committing a moral offence.

On this ground, it seems that pathological sexual deviation is a multifaceted phenomenon related to psychopathology, law and religion. In this chapter, I have selected only five forms of pathological sexual deviations, namely, rape, incest, child molestation (paedophilia), exhibitionism and voyeurism from the spectrum of psychosexual disorders as I am following the classification produced by Simon and Gagnon. Within the following discussion of this chapter, data available in the selected sources are examined in the light of modern sexological views with the purpose of recognizing the Buddhist position regarding the category coming under pathological deviant sexual behaviour.

Rape

Rape is a form of sexual violence of greater frequency in many countries in the modern world. It has been witnessed in ancient times too under various conditions and people have tried to avoid the bitter consequences of it by establishing religious laws and state laws against perpetrators. Records of rape cases have been included in the Pali canonical and post-canonical material in discussions relevant to the monastic life. The community of nuns could not escape the threat of being sexually assaulted by male members of the Order itself and by lay persons. Miserable experiences and constant threat to celibate life of nuns led the *Vinaya* authority to discuss the issue of rape and to promulgate rules to protect the females from sexual victimization. In this section, the data found from the selected sources related to rape are examined using modern sexological views with the purpose of recognizing the Buddhist explanation on the matter.

In Pali, the verb *dūseti* is used to refer to the act of rape against a woman. The synonym given to *dūseti* is *padhamseti*.[1] *Dūseti* is formed from the root *duṣ* meaning "spoil" (Whitney 1885: 76). To this term, Rhys Davids and W. Stede give the meanings of "to spoil, ruin, to injure, hurt, to defile, pollute, and defame" (*PED*, p. 328). We can see that these meanings are expressive of impurity, stigma and physical damage of raping. The other verb *padhamseti* has the meanings of "to destroy, assault, violate and offend" (ibid., p. 411) which are more concerned with the violent nature of the act. It can be stated that the terms utilized in Pali to deal with the issue of rape are indicative of the problematic nature of the act.

Modern definitions of rape are based on the English common law "carnal knowledge of a female forcibly and against her will" (Koss et al. 1987: 162), wherein carnal knowledge refers quite specifically to penile–vaginal penetration (Hudson and Ward 1997: 333). Legally there are two types of rape: statutory rape and forcible rape. Statuary

[1] *Chaṭṭasaṃgāyanā* CD-ROM, Vipassana Research Institute: *dusetīti padhamsesi.*

rape laws specify inappropriate opposite-sex partners (underaged partners). Statutory laws criminalize sexual intercourse with a female who is younger than a statutorily defined age of sixteen or eighteen years.[2] Even though the victim gives her consent for the act, it does not negate her partner's criminal liability. However, the underaged female who consents to sexual intercourse is not criminally liable for her behaviour (Ward et al. 1994: 312). Forcible rape is an act of sexual intercourse without female consent. Victims are women of all ages, offenders are men, and female consent negates male criminal liability. Definition of forcible rape has been expanded than it was in the common English law. In addition to penile–vaginal intercourse, cunninglingus, fellation, anal intercourse and other bodily intrusions inflicted upon a woman by force constitute a rape (Hudson and Ward 1997: 333). The elements discussed in relation to rape based on modern views can be seen more or less in the rape cases reported in the Pali sources as it will be evident from the following discussion.

In the *Bhikkhuvibhaṅga*, there is a reference to an incident of rape of which Uppalavaṇṇā, who was an enlightened disciple of the Buddha, happened to be the victim:

> ... a certain brāhmaṇa youth was in love with nun Uppalavaṇṇā. Then this brāhmaṇa youth, when the nun Uppalavaṇṇā had gone into the village for alms, entered the hut and sat down, concealed. The nun, Uppalavaṇṇā, after the meal and when she had finished eating, washing her feet and entering the hut, sat down on the couch. Then the Brāhmaṇa youth, taking up the nun Uppalavaṇṇā raped her. The nun Uppalavaṇṇā told this matter to the nuns and

[2] Grero 1996: 76. According to Sri Lankan Penal Code, age is twelve.

> they through the monks reported the event to the Master. He declared: "There is no offence, as she was not willing".
> – *BD* I.53f.

According to the story mentioned in the *Dhammapadaṭṭhakathā*, an young man was the cousin of a nun and had been in love with her during her lay life. He hid in the residence in Andhavana and, in spite of her protest, deprived her of chastity. It is said that he was swallowed up by the fires of *avīci* (*DhA* II.49f. in *DPPN*, vol. II, p. 419).

If we try to sexolgically understand the case regarding Uppalavaṇṇā, the assault on her did not come from an unknown person but from an acquaintance (Russell 1984: 61-62). It is accepted that the majority of rape cases take place within a known relationship. In the *Vinaya*, both types of rape, from the known and from strangers have been reported. From the legal perspective, the present case falls into the category of forcible rape. In this case, Uppalavaṇṇā was declared to be free of guilt as there was no "overt genuine consent".[3]

Psychologically, fantasy is an integral part of not only "normal" sexual relations but also of deviant and criminal sexual acts. Fantasy is defined as a series of thoughts that preoccupy the individual into the rehearsal of the script. As the fantasy evolves, it may include feelings, emotion and dialogue (Hensley and Tewksbury 2003: 98).

The concept of "fantasy" can be understood in terms of the Buddhist psychological concepts of *kāmasaññā* and *kāmavitakka* which refer to the fundamental perceptions and thoughts related to sexual gratification.[4] Prior to a sexual

---

[3] *Vin* III.35: *anāpatti bhikkhave asādiyantiyā* ।

[4] *MN* III.125: The Elder Bakkula in answer to question whether he had sexual intercourse during recluse life, states that he had no even a →

intercourse (normal or pathological) psychological process regarding the pleasure of the act and means to achieve might be contemplated upon in one's imagination. This process can be understood as thoughts of sense gratification (*kāmavitakka*).[5] As long as this process runs smoothly without obstruction, there is no element of anger (*vyāpāda*). If the individual perceives an obstruction to his end (sexual pleasure), he becomes violent (*vihiṁsā*) first mentally and second physically. The growth of cruel thoughts ends up in various forms of action (physical attaches, rape or even killing).

Moreover, it may be assumed that fantasy is a basic longing for pleasure followed by a mental map. In the case of Uppalavaṇṇā, the commentary mentions that her rapist had been of a sexually excited (aroused) mind for a long time (*kālato paṭṭhāya rattacitto*).[6] Uppalavaṇṇā's leaving of lay life obstructed the fantasy which could otherwise have smoothly resulted in final gratification of the imagined desires. The result was that the young man had turned out to be pathological (probably due to frustration) to the extent of criminality.

← perception of sexual desire (*kāmasaññā*). Again he mentions that there was no thought of sensual desire *kāmavitakka* (contextually sexual) in him. As this *sutta* implies, perception of sexual desire appears prior to thought of sensual/sexual desire. According to the definition of "fantasy", even in normal sexual relations, it is present.

[5] The negative sphere of human thinking (*saṅkappa*) consists of three lines of thoughts: (i) sensuous thoughts (*kāmavitakka*), (ii) hating thoughts (*vyāpāda-vitakka*), and (iii) violent thoughts (*vihiṁsā-vitakka*).

[6] *Chaṭṭhasamgāyanā* CD-ROM: Vipasssana Research Institute: the term *paṭibaddhacitta* has been defined thus.

A remarkable reference to the Buddhist conception of *kamma* is found in the pathetic episode of Uppalavaṇṇā. Buddhaghoṣa explains that the seriousness of sexual misconduct is decided by the inner moral quality of the sexual object.[7] Uppalavaṇṇā was an *arahanta* (a worthy person). As the rapist got down from her bed, fire came from the *avīci* hell and swallowed him.[8] In Buddhist literature, Devadatta is reported to have a similar retribution for his crimes against the Buddha and creating schism in the community (*DPPN*, vol. I, p. 1110). It seems that sexual crime against an *arahanta* nun has been held by the tradition as having equal gravity as the five gravest moral breaches.[9]

After the incident regarding Uppalavaṇṇā came to be known among the *saṅgha*, there arose a doubt regarding whether *arahants* too enjoy sensual pleasures because they also have the same physical make-up like any other people. In response to the question, the Buddha emphasized that *arahantas* do not enjoy sensual pleasures for they do not cling to objects of sense and to sensual pleasures, just as water does not cling to the lotus leaf or the mustard seed to the tip of an awl (Daw Mya Tin 1990: 493f.).

---

[7] *DhA* II.49f.; *MA* I, p. 207 (Devanāgarī): *so panesa micchācāro sīlādiguṇarahite agamaniyaṭṭhāne appasāvajjo, sīlādiguṇasampanne mahāsāvajjo* ।

[8] *Chaṭṭhasaṃgāyanā* CD-ROM: Vipasssana Research Institute: *ayaṃ mahāpaṭhavīsinerupabbataṃ dhāretuṃ samattāpi taṃ byāmamattakaḷevaraṃ dhāretuṃ asakkontī viya vivaramadāsi* ।

[9] *Vin* I.136: there is a list of persons with whom, the *pātimokkha* should not be held; *na mātughātakassa, na pitughātakassa, na arahantaghātakassa, na bhikkhunidūsakassa, na saṃghabhedakassa, na ubhatobyañjanakassa nisinnaparisāya pātimokkhaṃ uddisitabbaṃ ...* । if one pretends to be a matricide, parricide, a slayer of one perfected, a seducer of a nun, a schismatic, a shedder of (a truth finder's) blood, a hermaphrodite, the entire purity should be declared to another. — *BD* IV.159-60 (*AN* V.70-71)

Following the Uppalavaṇṇā's episode, a preventive measure was taken by the Buddha so that there would be no awkward happenings to his female disciples. King Pasendi of Kosala was summoned by the teacher and he was alerted to the situation by saying to him:

> Your Majesty, in this religion young men of family, as well as young women of family, renounce many kinsfolk, and much wealth, and retire from the world, and take residence in the forest. In case women reside in the forest, it is possible that evil-minded men inflamed by lust may conduct themselves towards them with disrespect and arrogance, do them violence and bring their religious life to naught. Therefore a place of residence for the Community of Almswomen should be erected within the city.
>
> – *Vin Texts* IV.264, quoted in Horner 1990: 156 fn. 1

After the construction of this residence, it is said that almswomen dwelled only within the city. Introducing regulations against their going about singly and prohibiting nuns to dwell in forests were among the other preventive measures taken to avoid sexual assaults on almswomen. Horner considers that precautions such as these were necessary for the safety of the weaker sex (1990: 157).

The case of Sundarīnandā is not a clear rape. At the beginning, the text says, the Migāranattu and the nun had a mutual attraction towards one another. So, the man was looking for a chance to rape (*dusetuṃ okāso*) her.[10] Finally, he plans to do it within a secret place in his own house. Sundarīnandā realizing the danger of their misdemeanour

[10] In this context, *dūsetuṃ* does not seem to mean inflicting a sexual assault but perceiving the sex act as impure which is held by general community regarding sex (for example the terms like *gāmadhamma* and *vasaladhamma* represent the repulsive attitude to sexual intercourse).

becoming public, stays in the temple. The man comes to the temple looking for her. There is no element of force inflicted upon the nun by the man. When he inquired her reason to become sick, her answer was inviting for him:

> *evan h 'taṃ āvuso hoti yā anicchantaṃ icchatīti* ।
>
> I like something that should not be liked.

This statement expresses her inner struggle between the adherence to morality and the carnal desire. They commit sexual intercourse with mutual consent in aroused mind (*avassuto avassutāya sundarinandāya bhikkhuṇiyā kāyasamsaggaṃ samāpajji*). The intention for having sexual pleasure is indicated by the term *avassuta* (sexually aroused). The term *avassuta* is defined in the *Suttavibhaṅga: avassutā nāma sārattā apekkhavā paṭibaddhacittā.*[11]

Perera (1993: 108) refers to this incident as a rape. The basis for such a characterization is not clear. According to our definition of rape, this case does not fall into the first type of statuary rape for the victim was a mature woman (one obtains *bhikkhuṇī* ordination after twenty years). Second, the text shows that the *bhikkhuṇī* was awaiting the sexual association with the man and whatever they did was with mutual consent.[12] Therefore, there is no element of force used against her. Further, the text shows that she was reprimanded for her act because she intentionally participated in the act (*Vin* IV.213). Even though she was accused of committing a breach of the celibacy vow, she was not commanded to leave

---

[11] *Vin* 214; *BD* III.161: Filled *with desire* means: infatuated, full of desire, physically in love with.

[12] Ward et al. 1994: 312: female consent negates male criminal liability.

the order.[13] Later on, she had to leave the community because of her pregnancy (*Vin* IV.216).

The monks are reported to have perpetrated forcible rape against nuns. In the *Mahāvaggapali*, it has been recorded that a novice called Kaṇḍaka, Ven. Upananda Sākyan's student, had raped a nun called Kaṇḍakā. In causally explaining why a monk is inclined to such a moral violation as forcible rape, sociologists point out that where the lack of resources to obtain opposite-sex relationships is greatest, forcible rape is most likely to occur (Clark and Lewis 1997: 130). In the *Vinaya*, it is mentioned that some monks have expressed their deprivation of access to sex.[14] When the case of Kaṇḍaka was reported, the Buddha laid down the rule to get rid of (*nāsetuṃ*) a novice who commits tenfold offence:

> I allow you, monks, to expel a novice who is possessed of ten qualities: if he is one who makes onslaught on creatures, takes what is not given, who is unchaste, tells lies, takes strong drinks, speaks dispraise of the Awakened one, speaks dispraise of the *dhamma*, speaks dispraise of the Order, holds false views, and if he is a seducer of nuns.[15]

The *Vinaya* commentary explains the reason for establishing two rules for the same offence within the same code, which

---

[13] Wijayaratna 1990: 141f.: It is not necessary to command a person to leave the Order because on committing an offence of defeat, one automatically loses the membership. Moreover, it is like a suicide; therefore, no need arises to punish the culprit.

[14] *Vin* I.96: *dullabho kho pabbajitānaṃ methuno dhammo*। (also *Vin* III.39, 67).

[15] *Vin* I.85: *anujānāmi bhikkhave dasah 'angehi samannāgataṃ sāmaṇeraṃ nāsetuṃ: pāṇātipātī hoti, adinnādāyī hoti, abrahmacārī hoti, musāvādī hoti, majjapāyi hoti, buddhassa avaṇṇaṃ bhāsati, dhammassa avaṇṇaṃ bhāsati, sanghassa avaṇṇaṃ bhāsati, micchadiṭṭhiko hoti, bhikkhunidusako hoti*।

are the third rule and the last concerned with sexual misconduct. Ven. Buddhaghoṣa says that the third case and the tenth are distinguished here, because a person that has simply committed an impurity may receive the ordination, if he is willing to refrain himself in future, but a seducer of nuns cannot be ordained in any case.[16]

A passage in the *Mahāvaggapali* mentions three persons who should not be granted with higher ordination: a seducer of a *bhikkhuṇī*, one who causes a schism among the *saṅgha* and a bloodshedder of a Truth finder (*VinA* 1024). If any of these persons is not already ordained, he should not be ordained; if he is already ordained, he should be expelled.[17] The term *bhikkhuṇīdūsaka* is an important term associated with sexual assault on almswomen of the Order. The *Samantapāsādikā* commentary gives the following explanation on the term:

> The person who rapes a nun of genuine character, through one of her three sexual orifices, he is called a *bhikkhuṇīdūsaka*. For him both minor ordination and major ordination are prohibited (1). Even if someone makes a nun lost in virtue through physical contact, for him minor ordination and major ordination are not prohibited (2). Having forced to wear white clothes, without getting consent, if one rapes a nun, he is also a nun-rapist (3). Having forced to wear white clothes, but with consent, if

[16] *Mahāvagga-Aṭṭhakathā*, p. 281 (Devanāgarī): *bhikkhunidūsako cettha kāmaṃ abrahmacāriggahanena gahitova abrahmacāriṃ pana āyatiṃ saṁvare ṭhātukāmaṃ saraṇāni datvā upasampādetuṃ vaṭṭati*। *bhikkhunidūsako āyatiṃ saṁvare ṭhātukāmopi pabbajjampi na labhati, pageva upasampadanti*।; *Vinaya Texts*, I.215 fn. 1.

[17] *BD* IV.113; *Vin* I.89: *bhikkhunidūsako bhikkhave anupasampanno na upasampādetabbo, upasampanno nāsetabbo, samghabhedako … lohituppādako bhikkhave anupasampanno na upasampādetabbo, upasampanno nāsetabbo*।

> one has sexual-intercourse with a nun, he is not a nun-rapist (4). The reason for this is that on accepting the lay life, she loses her nun-hood. One does not become a nun-rapist by violating one who is once lost in virtue or females undertraining or female novices (5). He is not deprived of minor ordination and major ordination.
>
> – *Mahāvagga Aṭṭhakathā*, p. 289

In this passage, five occasions of having sex with a nun or a religious woman are indicated. One becomes a nun-rapist through the involvement with only two out of the five. The first instance is raping (by force) a nun of genuine character (one who has not lost her *upasampadā* and wearing robes) using one of her erogenous zones (1); the second instance is having sex without the consent of the nun, after making her wear white clothes (3). Both the cases are concerned with the unblemished virtue in the victim and the consent.

In Buddhist theory, a sexual offence becomes more serious for the offender when the inner purity of the victim is higher. The two instances that constitute the wrong of "nun-violating" are involved in harming an enlightened person. The importance given to full-status monk/nun (*upasampadā*) is similar to that given to the Buddha because they also share his vision of *dhamma* by adhering to the discipline.[18] As John C. Holts puts:

> In short, the *bhikkhu* community shares the charisma of the master by virtue of the fact that they emulate the model he provides through adhering to discipline. – 1981: 112

On this ground, raping a nun by force, entails refusal

[18] The moral conduct given in the *suttas* of *Sīlakkhandhavagga* was the lifestyle adopted by the Śākyamuni Buddha. It was the same model established for monks and nuns in various forms of rules.

of entrance to the Order and such a culprit is seen as a completely defeated person in the moral life like in the cases of matricide, parricide and other grave offences. In the scriptures, the character of nun-rapist was seen with a strong sense of denial and repugnance; it is evident from the promulgation of a rule to suspend the performance of *pātimokkha* ritual (*pātimokkhaṭhapana*), when a nun-rapist was present in the company and a debate relevant to such an incident was unfinished (*AN* V.70-71; *GS* V.50-51). As the second item implies (2), a sexual/physical contact with a nun having consent, does not make the male a nun-rapist. This can be clarified from the episode of Migāranattu, who had sex with Sundarīnandā with her consent. Here, he is not referred to as *bhikkhuṇīdūsaka*.[19]

For the most part, the criterion applied to determine culpability of nun-rape is based on the degree of inner virtue possessed by the female victim: the second and the fifth item are supportive for this idea. The fifth item refers to three kinds of religious women: 1. defeated nun (*sīlavipannaṃ*), 2. a female under training, and 3. a female novice. All these three do not have the full status of a nun, who is sharing the charisma of the master. In the fourth item (4), two criteria have been counted to release a person from the guilt of nun-rape: 1. accepting lay dress which entails automatic loss of nun-hood, and 2. giving consent to the act. It seems that the *Vinaya* commentator had made the assumption that this offence is not a rape but adultery with a lay woman. So, the male is free of the fault of nun-rape (Ward et al. 1994: 313).

[19] Ward et al. 1994: 312: The principle followed here to make the rapist free of charge seems to be "female consent negates male criminal liability" in law.

However, from the feminist point of view, any act of sexual intercourse where the female's "genuine affection and desire" is absent and there is male coercion, it should be counted as a forcible rape. In a deep analysis into the fourth possibility of a nun-rape, it seems that we can agree with feminist definition of rape because the approach to the act is characterized with violence (*balakkārena*), so, the female consent cannot be natural. In this sense, the fourth item also should constitute the offence of nun-rape. Nevertheless, the commentator seems to have looked at only half of the event, which is acceptance of white clothes and giving consent but not the initial crucial factor of employing coercion against a nun. However, even the *Suttavibhaṅga* has not gone to that extent of feminists, that is, if the consent of victim (in any way) is present, he or she is also taken to be responsible.[20]

An incident of rape was reported by the nun Mettiyā who of course was bringing a false allegation against the monk, Dabba Mallaputta. Although the accusation was false, the manner in which it was reported reflects the vicious nature of sexual assault against a woman. As Mettiyā described the event:

> Where there is calm now there is gale. It seems the very water is blazing. I have been assaulted by… . [21]

The calm and gale evidently refer to the calmness and virtue of the nun as against the brutality and violence of the rapist.

---

[20] *Vin* III.40: *tena kho pana samayena vesāliyaṃ licchavikumārakā bhikkhuṃ gahetvā bhikkhuniyā vippaṭipādesuṃ* ı *ubho sādiyimsu: ubho nāsetabbā* ı

[21] *Vin* III.162: *idaṃ bhante nacchannaṃ na paṭirūpaṃ, yāyaṃ bhante disā abhayā anītikā anupaddvā sayaṃ disā sabhayā saītikā saupaddavā, yato nivātaṃ tato pavātaṃ, udakaṃ maññe ādittaṃ, ayyena 'mhi dabbena mallaputtena dūsitāti* ı

The burning passion of rapist is reflected in the phrase "the very water is blazing". There can be seen a continuous attempt to disgrace the Arhanta Dabba Mallaputta by Mettiyabhummajaka monks. They persuaded the Licchavi Vaḍḍha to charge the *arahanta* of rape associating his own wife (*Vin* II.124f.).

The *Bhikhuṇīvibhaṅga* reveals that there was a great danger for nuns from lay persons. Once, two nuns were violated by two ferrymen separately. One was raped after crossing the river and the other was violated before crossing. Finally, they consulted each other and exchanged information of their common fate (*Vin* IV.224). Their conversation depicts how far they were mentally suffering and the empathy for each other. This shows that rapists attack victims when they are defenceless and were rather shy to make the matter known. A nun who missed her companion nuns during the travel was raped by men. This is a gang rape against a single woman (*Vin* IV.229). From the *Vinaya*, it is evident that women had been in a constant threat of being raped if they were as single persons. Robbers (*corā*) and evil-minded persons (*dhuttā*) had tried to sexually assault nuns.[22] According to the *Vinaya* commentary, there had been even common householders who had attempted to take liberties with *bhikkhuṇīs*, female novices and female probationers (*VinA* 790f.; Perera 1993: 108).

Experience of forcible rape is of relatively higher ratio in societies which lack empathy for women and holds the attitude that they are subordinate to men (Donat and D'Emilio

[22] *Vin* I.81, II.278: here it is stated that certain *bhikkhunis* living in the forest were seduced by evil-minded persons.
Vin II.280: *bhikkhunis* bathing at a place other than a ford were seduced by evil-minded persons.

1992: 9-22; Ward et al. 1997: 361). The Indian society during the Buddha's time was patriarchal and the position given to female members was very low. Further, it was an age which practised objectification of women for sex. It is evident from the references in the Pali canon to the harems of kings (*AN* I.137; *J.* III.39-43; Tachibana 1986: 156).

Sexual objectification of women had been practised by powerful persons in many aspects; a passage in the *Vinaya* reads that a woman was used as a tool to sexually intimidate a monk, who was declared free of guilt by the Buddha (*Vin* III.39). The propensity of the Hindu tradition, which was the dominant religious dogma in ancient India, regarding women as mere sex objects and devoid of dignity is well reflected in the *Manusmṛti* (*Laws of Manu*). In the text, women were prohibited from reading the sacred Vedic texts and could not perform sacrifice or worship without men (Dewaraja 1981: 6-7 quoted in Harvey 2000: 355). While it was held that the honouring of women pleased the gods and that family did not prosper without their happiness (*Manu* III.55-57, quoted in Harvey 2000: 355), on the other hand, a female should never be independent (ibid. X.3, ibid.), even in her own house (ibid. V.147, quoted in ibid.). She must be protected by and be subject to her father, in youth her husband and finally her elder son (ibid. V.148, quoted in ibid.). The postulation of this inferior position for womankind was partly because they were seen as highly sexed and ever ready to seduce men (ibid. IX.13-18, quoted in ibid.).

On certain occasions, even early Buddhist texts have not been able to escape the tendency of treating woman as a seductress and a sexual object. As for the seducing power in women, it is said that a female when even going along will stop to ensnare the heart of the man; ultimately she tries to tempt the man even while she is dying (*GS* III.56). To peak the view of woman as highly sexual, a canonical reference states that women die without satisfaction for sex and desiring to beget children (Sanday 1981: 5-27; quoted in Ward et al. 1994: 322ff.). Within a society, where this type of prejudices towards women and sexual enslavement exists, the likelihood of forcible rapes is very high.

Thus, the reason why there are many reports of rape cases in the Pali *Vinaya Piṭaka* can be understood against the contemporary Indian background. Such societies are recognized as "rape-prone" (ibid.) because their male-dominant ideology is conducive to create a mentality in men that inflicting harm upon women is justifiable. The obvious lower positions held by women in the domestic environment as well as in society and the male dominant thinking during this period provide a ground to assume that there had been a great threat against women of being sexually abused and harassed. Their vulnerability was not different by being a lay woman or a religious one.

In the *Vinaya*, there are reports on attempted rapes.[23] A certain nun together with a man, the one with the other, made a boil burst that had formed on the lower part of the body. Then the man attempted to violate the nun.[24] On another occasion, a certain man having seen a beautiful nun, wanted to

---

[23] Sexologically, one classification of rape is attempted rape and completed rape.

[24] *Vin* IV.316: *tena kho pana samayena aññatarā bhikkhuni pasākhe jātaṃ gaṇḍaṃ purisena saddhiṃ eken 'eka bhedāpesi। atha kho so puriso taṃ bhikkhuniṃ dūsetuṃ upakkaṃi।*

seduce her.[25] He invited all the nuns to his home and at night appointed a sleeping place for them, arranging a separate place for this particular nun away from the others. The nun having understood the threat coming from the man went to another place to spend the night.[26] This shows how rapists plan strategically to capture their victims.

According to the modern definition of rape, inserting (forcibly) any object into the female sexual organ (vagina) is a rape. A monk was aroused by seeing a young girl sitting on a chair and put his finger into her sexual organ. Consequently she was dead (*Vin* III.34). To the *Vinaya*, this was not as serious an offence as penile–vaginal or other forms of genital sexual intercourse (*anāpatti bhikkhu pārājikassa, āpatti saṅghādisesassa*). The text refers to the girl by the term *dārikaṃ* which means small girl not yet reached maturity. In modern law this can be categorized as a statutory rape (Fn. 2).

In the *Suttavibhaṅga*, it is mentioned of a mass rape. Once, slaves of Sākyans came to be out of hand (*avaruddhā*). Sākyan women wanted to make a meal in jungle lodgings. The slaves of the Sākyans heard that Sākyans women were desirous of making a meal in jungle lodgings. They infested the way (*pariyuṭṭhiṁsu*). Sākyan women, taking sumptuous solid food, soft food, went off to jungle lodging. The slaves of

[25] Felson and Krohn 1990: 222-42 in Ward et al. 1994: 326: There is no unanimous agreement of reasons why people commit rape; these two writers suggested that many rapes are sexually motivated. They argue that rape victims are targeted because they are young and presumably attractive. It is agreeable with this idea in connection with the case discussed here.

[26] *Vin* IV.229: *atha kho sā bhikkhuni sallakkhetvā pariyuṭṭhito ayaṃ puriso, sace rattiṃ āgacchissati vissaro me bhavissatīti bhikkhuniyo anāpucchā aññataraṃ kulaṃ gantvā seyyyaṃ kappesi*।

the Sākyans, having issued forth, robbed the Sākyan women and violated them.[27]

This was not due to any personal insult from women. It was a problem of two classes, between slaves and masters (Sākyans were the lords and slaves were under their control). As revenge upon the enemy, slaves turned their anger towards womenfolk of their enemy. This situation seems to reflect a social situation where the society was undergoing a crisis due to the clash between the two classes. In such situations of instability, women are naturally put in to danger of sexual violence even in modern societies.[28]

One category of motives for rape is referred to as "The Punishment Model" in which rapist views his act as a legitimate form of revenge. In these rapes, men are seeking to hold females accountable and punish them for some action that the rapist subjectively perceives as an insult. The action may have been committed directly by the victim, or she may be a victim of "collective liability" in which the victim is a representative of a larger class of individuals (Black 1983: 34-45; Scully and Morolla 1984: 530-44 in Hensley and Tewksbury 2003: 92f.). Clifford Allen points out that the sexual harassment taking place in war time is connected with fantasy and is a form of sadistic deviation (1961: 805).

---

[27] *BD* III.115; *Vin* IV.181: *tena kho pana samayena sākiyadāsakā avaruddhā honti*। *sākiyāniyo icchanti āraññakesu senāsanesu bhattaṃ kātuṃ*। *assosuṃ kho sākiyadāsakā sākiyaniyo kira āraññakesu senāsanesu bhattaṃ kattukāmāti*। *te magge pariyuṭṭhimsu*। *sākiyāniyo paṇītaṃ khādanīyaṃ bhojanīyaṃ ādāya āraññakaṃ senāsanaṃ agamamsu*। *sākiyadāsakā nikkhamitva sākiyāniyo acchindimsu ca dūsesuṃ ca*।

[28] MacKinnon 1994: 190-91: It is a well-known fact that raping women as a crime against a particular ethnic group was practised in Serbia to destroy Muslim ethnicity in the recent history.

The *Mahāparinibbānasutta* of the *Dīgha Nikāya* throws light on the abuse of political power in India of its time, to victimize married and young girls. The Buddha states in this *sutta* that the kingdom of Licchavis is unconquerable until they adhere to seven principles that prevent decline (*satta aparihāniyā dhammā*) (*DN* II.73ff.). Abstention from forcible abduction of others' wives and daughters and compelling them to live with rulers is given as one of those seven principles conducive to prosperity and avoid the decline of a state.[29]

It can be assumed that the contemporary rulers' behaviour might have influenced the views of the Buddha to propose abstention from abducting women as a state policy. In the *Dhammapadaṭṭhakathā* (p. 251), it is mentioned that King Pasenadi attempted to possess a woman of another person. The *Maṇicora Jātaka* narrates a king employing a wicked plan to kill a man so that he could take the man's beautiful wife (*J* II.121-25). These stories portray the amorous character of rulers and wicked tricks that they played to satisfy their desires regardless of morality.

During the Buddha's time, there were two forms of government in India, republican and monarchical. Even though the Buddha did not interfere with politics, in his social project, he made an attempt to reform the ideology of rulers through ethical teachings. The ethical guidance given to monarchs of the time is reflected in the *Cakkavattīsīhanādasutta* wherein the wheel-rolling king (*cakkavattī rājā*) governs the country according to the five precepts (*DN* III.62). If a ruler or any other person observes them, he cannot violate sexual

---

[29] *DN* II.74: *yāvakīvañca ānanda vajjī yā tā kulatthiyo kulakumāriyo tā na okkassa pasayha vāsessanti, vuddhi yeva ānanda vajjīnaṃ pāṭikankhā no parihāni*।

morality. For the republican rulers, the teaching given by the Buddha was the sevenfold non-declinable principle which directly advises rulers to restrain from undesirable sexual behaviour, or not to use the political power to satisfy carnal desires.

The commentary to the *Mahāparinibbāṇasutta* describes that if rulers carry away women and girls by force, citizens become displeased and leave for remote places and turn out to be rebels and destroy the country. Buddhism in this context makes a socio-psychological analysis of forcible rape against female members in a community. When beloved mothers, wives and daughters are victimized by rapists, the male relatives of the victims are naturally affected by anger and feeling of revenge upon enemy (their psychological melancholy is well depicted in the commentary). Consequently, they start to hate society finally leading to chaotic situation in the whole country.[30]

The Buddhist attitude towards rape can be understood in the words of a modern expert on law, Hari Singhe Gour (1987, vol. II: 1673):

> Rape is the forcible ravishment of a woman. It has been always regarded as an offence of great heinousness and as such, meriting even the death. ... The offence owes its enormity to the defilement and dishonour of their women, and their forcible ravishments arouses all those feelings of retaliation and revenge which have accounted for so much bloodshed in history.

---

[30] *DA Mahāvaggaṭṭhakathā*, p. 98 (Devanāgarī): *evan hi karontānam vijite manussā– "amhākaṃ gehe puttamātaropi, khelasinghāṇikādini mukhena apanetvā saṁvaḍḍhitadhītaropi ime rājāno balakkārena gahetvā attano ghare vāsentī" ti kupitā paccantaṃ pavisitavā corā va corasahāyā hutvā janapadaṃ paharanti* ।

According to the foregoing discussion, the majority of rape cases in the selected sources are concerned with nuns with some exceptions. The inner virtue of a *bhikkhuṇī* makes her offender so grave that he cannot get entrance to the community and if the victim is a liberated one like Uppalavaṇṇā, the kammic retribution is very serious. A variety of rape as categorized by modern law, feminists and sociologists can be seen in the *Vinaya* source. It is remarkable that the stigma of being raped is not directed at the female victim as evident in the case of Uppalavaṇṇā.

As we noted, in addition to introducing certain rules to be followed by nuns to avoid sexual harassment, practical solutions like establishing a monastery within the city indicate the concern shown by the Buddha regarding the protection of his female disciples. By imposing strong rejection against one who seduces nuns (like Kaṇḍaka), the early Buddhists had tried to avoid sexual crimes inside the monastic community. Finally, in relation to major society, Buddhism recognizes abusing political power to victimize females in a state as having the consequence of decline of state authority and also as a cause for a chaotic situation in the country.

Incest

Incest is a worldwide sexual taboo which prohibits sexual relationship between close relatives. This is the only universally accepted sexual deviation. All societies see incestuous (incest in Greek "impure") sexual contact as undesirable. Clinically it is accepted as a sexual disorder and according to criminology, it is a crime. The root of incestuous behaviour exists in a deep-layer of psyche of a human being. Psychoanalysis theory tries to explain this behaviour in terms of Oedipus complex of Sigmund Freud which means unusual sexual desire for mother seen in a young son. Modern literature on incest has been focused on father–daughter (or stepfather) and definition of the concept is not clear. It is not classified as paraphilia and included as subcategory of paedophilia (child sexual abuse). Most researchers and practitioners consider incest different from child sexual abuse, with incest viewed as *intrafamilial* and child sexual abuse *extrafamilial* sexual relations. In the Pali sources, there are references to incestuous relationships and they have been seen as immoral acts.

The *Aṅguttara Nikāya* describes an incestuous sexual contact between mother and son who were celibates within the Order for long time. They constantly met each other and became so intimate that they were tempted to have incestuous sexual intercourse.[31] This can be seen in the light of Oedipus complex. According to the concept, the son loves his mother in the sexual sense and hates the father.[32] However, in the present episode, there is no element of hate against the father. The fact that two persons who were undergoing the training in the spiritual path fell into a condition, of which, even the

---

[31] AN III.67: The *Nibbedika Pariyāyasutta* explains how sensuality comes into play: "*Phasso bhikkhave kāmānaṃ nidānasambhavo* — contact is the cause by which sensuality comes into play" (*AN* III.410 sq.). Kalupahana 1994: 33: According to Buddhist psychology, contact is understood as "familiarity" based on which one's mind begins the process of being obsessed of a sense-object. In the present episode, familiarity between the mother and son has led them to commit sin.

[32] Lewinsohn 1958: 331 in Perera 1993: 104. The Oedipus complex is defined as the "high-spirited love of a youth for his mother. Often used in the sexual sense of ideal or actual incest between mother and son, coupled with an extreme dislike for the father. Named after the legend of Oedipus, wherein the youth killed his father and married his mother".

ordinary person is seriously careful, calls for a deep analysis of the human psyche.

The character of Gaṅgātīriya is another similar case to legendary Oedipus Rex.[33] Gaṅgātīriya was a householder called Datta of Sāvatthī. On discovering that he had, though unwittingly, committed incest with both his mother and sister, he was overcome with anguish and left the world. After Gaṅgātīriya's conception, his mother was driven out of house by her mother-in-law suspecting her of infidelity. Heading along the highways all alone in search of her husband, she felt the onset of labour, and in a way side hut delivered a son, Gaṅgātīriya. While she was away bathing, a merchant came there, stole the child from her, and brought up the child as his own.

Later, Gaṅgātīriya's mother was taken in by a robber chief. By him, she bore a daughter. Then one day, by mistake, she injured the child, and fearing the husband's wrath, she fled from him, leaving her daughter behind. On coming to Rājagaha, she became a courtesan and later was married by Gaṅgātīriya who was unaware of his relationship to her. Sometime afterwards he was married to the robber's daughter as well. One day, to her horror, the elder wife discovered the scar on her young co-wife's head, which identified the woman as her own daughter. Filled with shock, both mother and daughter became nuns, and Gaṅgātīriya gave up the worldly life as mentioned above (*ThagA* I.248f. in *DPPN*, vol. I, p. 735). In this case, incest has been perceived as an unbearable disgrace and understood as a result of desire for sensual gratification which can lead one to a lot of tragic mistakes.

In the *Vinaya Piṭaka*, one instance mentions that a monk

[33] http://www.users.globalnet.co.uk/~loxias/myth.htm

had incestuous sexual relationship with his own mother, daughter and sister in the belief that such relationship would not incur guilt.[34] The *Pannika Jātaka* reports a pseudo incestuous attempt by a father towards his daughter. On seeing her father's behaviour, she told that such an attempt would be as monstrous as fire arising out of water. Further she says: "My helper proves my enemy" (Chalmers 1981, vol. I: 244). Inhumanity of incestuous behaviour of fathers to their own daughters is well depicted in the statement of the daughter here.[35] In the story, it is said that the father had no such intention to harm her but to know her purity in character as he was arranging a marriage for her.

The *Mahā Paduma Jātaka* reveals a disaster brought about by a stepmother to an innocent prince.[36] According to the story, after the death of Prince Paduma's mother, the father-king got married to another queen. In the absence of the king, the queen invites the prince saying: "Just until the king comes,

[34] *Vin* III.35: *tena kho pana samyena aññataro bhikkhu evaṃ me anāpatti bhavissatīti mātuyā-pe-dhītuyā-pe-bhaginiyā methunaṃ dhammaṃ paṭisevi*।

[35] *Introductory Lectures of Psychoanalysis*, 1933 quoted in Herman with Hirschman 1981: 7. Sigmund Freud states that many women patients had complained that they were seduced by their fathers. He says that such complaints were not true and there exists in women's psyche a fantasy of being seduced by their fathers, which is the expression of the typical Oedipus complex in women; Herman with Hirschman 1981: 7-9, based on clinical experiences, argue against the Freudian view and inconstancy of his own statements regarding incest and female hysteria.

[36] Horton et al. 1990: 20. This event falls under the category of incest between step-parents and stepchildren. The most discussed topic on this category in modern days is concerned with the abuse of stepdaughter by stepfather. The present story deals with its opposite side; the stepmother becomes the threat to the stepson's life.

let us both enjoy the bliss of love" (Rouse 1981, vol. IV: 118). The prince denies her unusual request: "Mother, my mother you are, and have a husband living. ... How I can do such a deed of pollution with you?" (ibid.) After three times being refused by the prince, the queen threatens to slander against him misleading the king but the prince kept to his morality. Being misled by the slanderous words of the queen, the king orders to execute death punishment against the prince.[37]

In contrast to frequent incestuous seduction by the male, the initiative by female is revealed here and its disastrous results are pointed out. If we try to understand why the queen was motivated to make an incestuous request, there can be seen two reasons: the physical attraction of the prince[38] and the safe opportunity available due to the absence of the husband (king). According to Henry Amoroso, this sort of opportunity is called "chance circumstances". He says that such circumstances are considered to be "an excellent stimulus in sexual matters, probably because inhibitory mechanisms fail to function when sexual relations take place suddenly and unexpectedly. It is as though the partners did not have time to remember prohibitions that normally weigh down on them" (Amoroso 1965: 102). Even though, incest is related to clinical conditions, all the forms of incestuous relations are not considered as psychopathic (Nathan and Harris 1975: 368). Then, we can apply the observation made by Amoroso to understand the psychology involved in certain incestuous relationships like that of what we referred to here.

---

[37] Meyer 1930: 253. It had been a very difficult task for the incest offender to regain his purity in character. For that one had to undergo death by fire, castration, expulsion from the caste and the like.

[38] The Jātaka states that the name Paduma (lotus flower) was given to him because of his extraordinary comeliness. —*J* IV.189

There is a canonical reference to brother-sister incestuous relationship in the *Ambaṭṭhasutta*. As the legend states, the origination of the Sākyans had taken place from a brother-sister relationship.[39] L.P.N. Perera contends that it is impossible to accept this story as truth because the Sākyans were very proud of their clan and purity. So, the story may be a mere legend.[40] As the cross-cultural researches indicate, even though many cultures consider incestuous relationships as deviant, there is evidence in certain groups in society which encourage incestuous marriages.

Peter E. Nathan and Sandra L. Harris point out that incestuous relationship was found in the royal families of ancient Greece and England, because it guaranteed an uncomplicated royal lineage (Nathan and Harris 1975: 368). Even though the legend of Sākyans may not be a complete truth, we cannot deny at least its possibility when it is examined in a cross-cultural historical context. Incest is considered a psychopathological state of one's sexual behaviour and medical experts point that all the cases are not to be counted so. For example, exploratory sexual play of a brother and sister may progress to intercourse. Where such occurrences are isolated events, they may not involve psychopathology. But where they are continuing relationships – substitutes for more appropriate or more mature relationships, they may well be signs of serious mental disorder (ibid.). In ancient times, certain incestuous

[39] *DN* I.92; it is a noteworthy similarity between the ancestries of Śākyans and that of Sinhalese people who trace their origin to the couple of Sinhabāhu and Sinhaseevalī who were brother and sister.

[40] Perera 1993: 105 and Horner 1990: 178f.: also refer to the family pride of Śākyan clan and how they avoided giving a pure Śākyan lady to King Pasenadi.

relationships were a result of the social norm of maintaining one's progeny and strong regard felt by people towards it.

Buddhism recognizes the appearance of incest as a result of larger-scale moral degeneration in a society. The *Cakkavattīsīhanādasutta* explains the degeneration of human civilization on a political basis. Due to wrong political principles, a country falls into poverty and consequently there appears a range of crimes in society (*DN* III.70). The beginning of one immoral act gives rise to a number of issues in affecting the entire social structure. Prior to the appearance of incest, false views spread over the society (*micchā-diṭṭhi vepullam agamāsi*) (ibid.). In this context, *micchā-diṭṭhi* is defined in terms of denial of moral theory.[41] The destructive effect of wrong view is examined by the Buddha:

> No other thing than evil views do I know, Oh monks! whereby to such an extent the unwholesome things not yet arisen arise, and the unwholesome things already arisen are brought to growth and fullness.
>
> – *AN* I.22, in Nayantiloka, 1991, *Buddhist Dictionary*, p. 52

According to the *cakkavattī* discourse, in a society wherein false views are abundant, three things increase: incest (*adhammarāgo*), excessive greed (*visama lobho*)[42] and deviant practices (*micchā dhammo*) (*LDOB*, p. 401). The term *adhammarāga*[43] refers to the incestuous practice. The

---

[41] *DA Pāṭikavaggaṭṭhakathā*, p. 33 (Devanāgarī): *micchādiṭṭhīti natthi dinnantiādikā antaggāhikā paccanīkadiṭṭhi*।

[42] Perera 1993: 126 fn. 2. He points out that *visamalobha* (and *visama*) in certain contexts implies moral discrepancies with a sexual overtone.

[43] Ibid. He interprets the term as direct allusion to adultery; but it should be as'incest; both Maurice Walshe (*LDOB* 401) and T.W. Rhys Davids (*Dialogues* III.69) translate *adhammarāga* as "incest" not as adultery.

commentary explains the term:

> *adammarāgoti mātā mātucchā pitucchā mātulānīti ādike ayuttaṭṭhāne rāgo*
>
> – *DA*: *Pāṭikavaggaṭṭhakathā*, p. 33 (Devanāgarī)

If we try to see this commentarial reference to incest in the light of sexology, this widens the possibilities of incestuous relationships which were not found in the canon. Incestuous contacts with (including mother) mother's sister (*mātucchā*), father's sister (*pitucchā*) and with maternal uncle's wife (*mātuḷānī*) indicate close relatives who have blood relation.

In addition to one's own parent, brothers and sisters, in Buddhist understanding, incestuous relationships extend to other close relatives who are respected with high esteem within the family. In absence of child's own mother, her sister takes care of the child. The most esteemed *mātucchā* was Mahā Pajāpati Gotamī, the Buddha's god mother and his mother's sister. All the women mentioned in the list are high-ranked persons in the Buddhist community.

Modern literature on incest is largely devoted to discuss the issue of child molestation within the family by father and other closest relatives. Within the Buddhist literature, there is scanty of data regarding child molestation within the family. The cases we discussed are concerned with adult incestuous relationships. The element of mental disorder in the behaviour of those persons is obviously absent in our readings. By Buddhism, incest is viewed as a problematic sexual act and it is seen as a result of decline of morality and concerned with one's ideological basis (*diṭṭhi*).

Exhibitionism

Exhibitionism is exposing one's nudity or sexual organ to

others in order to get sexual arousal or gratification. Legally, it is referred to as "indecent exposure" because of the shock or offensive nature of the act in relation to others (Doctor and Neff 1994: 175). Exhibitionists (flashers) are largely males and victims are primarily females; a few cases of female exhibitionism also have been reported (Murphy 1997: 23). Flashers expect reaction on the part of onlooker (Allen 1961: 807).

In the *Bhikkhuvibhaṅga* is included a case of exhibitionism under *Nissaggiya* IV. One day, Ven. Udayi went to see his former wife who also was a celibate in the Order. Having arrived at her place, he showed his genitalia to the nun; in response, she also did the same and they engaged in mutual exhibitionism.[44]

According to the clinical definition of exhibitionism, an exhibitionist suffers from recurrent, intense, arousing fantasies of exposing his genital to an unsuspected stranger (Murphy 1997: 22). The cited case is free from the element of "stranger". The victim was the previous wife of the perpetrator. A study conducted among college girls indicate that a third (36 per cent) of incidences was committed by acquaintances, relatives or "good friends" of the victim (Nevid et al. 1995: 560). The quoted episode from the *Vinaya*, though in the ultimate sense, is exhibitionism, it may be said to consist of scopophilic element, i.e. the "pleasure derived from looking" (Perera 1993: 190 fn. 7) and mere substitute for coitus.

A case of group exhibitionism is reported in the *Cullavaggapāli*. It is mentioned that the Chabbaggiyā monks

---

[44] *Vin* III.205: *atha kho āyasmā udāyi . . . yena sā bhikkhunī tenupasamkami upasamkamitvā tassā bhikkhuniyā purato angajātaṃ vivaritvā āsane nisīdi, sā pi kho bhikkhunī udāyissa purato angajātaṃ vivaritvā āsane nisīdi* ।

on one side and the Chabbaggiyā nuns[45] on the other, engaged in mutual group exhibitionism.[46] It is said that the intention of this practice was to explore the possibility of attracting the opposite sex: *app'eva nāma aṃhesu sārajjeyyunti.*[47] Exhibitionism becomes abnormal only when it takes extreme, fixed, or obsessive-compulsive form. When the nature of the punishment imposed by the *Vinaya* authority for these offences is considered, it appears that they have been treated with a less degree of severity. Sexologically, a normal human sexual interaction consists of four stages: (1) location of a partner, (2) pre-tactile interactions, (3) tactile interactions, and (4) genital union (Freund 1990: 195-207). An exhibitionistic act reaches only the second phase wherein no physical contact whatsoever occurs, which is an invariable element in sexual contact.[48] In the *Vinaya*, even if an act reaches the third stage of tactile contact, it is considered as a violation of *saṅghādisesa* or *pārājikā*.[49] We can conclude that exhibitionism is an offence

---

[45] Nevid et al. 1995: 562: A number of exhibitionists have reported that they hoped that the women would enjoy the experience and be impressed with the sizes of their penises.

[46] *Vin* II.262-63: *tena kho pana samayena chabbaggiyā bhikkhū kāyaṃ vivaritvā bhikkhunīnaṃ dassenti uraṃ vivaritvā ... angajātaṃ vivaritvā bhikkhunīnaṃ dassenti ... tena kho pana samyena chabbaggiyā bhikkhuniyo kāyaṃ vivaritvā bhikkhūnaṃ dassenti thanaṃ vivaritvā ... uraṃ vivaritvā ... angajātaṃ vivaritvā bhikkhūnaṃ dassenti* ।

[47] Ibid.; *BD* V.363: "Perhaps they may be attracted to us".

[48] *MA Mūlapaṇṇāsa-aṭṭhakathā*, I. p. 207 (Devanāgarī): *maggenamaggappaṭi-pattiadhivāsanaṃ* ।

[49] *Vin* III.120: *bhikkhuvibhanga sanghādisesa* rule II is an example of tactile contact which is only second to the defeat wrong (for monks); *Vin* IV.220: the eighth *pārājikā* in the *Bhikkhunivibhanga* considers tactile contact of opposite sex partner by a nun with a passionate mind as severe as sexual union.

in the *Vinaya* but not taken seriously as it lacks an actual physical contact.

Voyeurism

Voyeurism is deriving sexual satisfaction from watching people undressing or nude, or observing them during sexual acts without their knowledge or consent. Voyeurs (from the French verb meaning "to see") or Peeping Toms are usually unmarried males in their 20s and 30s. They generally prefer to peep at women who are strangers and are most often sexually excited when the risk of being discovered is high. Many voyeurs confine their sexual activity to masturbation while peeping or while fantasizing about previous peeping escapades.[50] In the Pārājikā section, it is reported that Licchavi youths taking hold of a monk, made him commit sexual intercourse with a nun (female probationer, female novice, prostitute, a eunuch, a woman householder) (*Vin* III.39). The *Samantapāsādikā Vinaya* commentary states that these immoralities were practised by Licchavis for the sake of pleasure.[51] This episode concerns voyeuristic tendencies of looking at others' sexual act and deriving sexual pleasure without engaging in the act oneself. The Buddhist attitude to this type of misdemeanours by rulers is expressed by saying that after this event the decline of Licchavi kingdom started.[52]

The *Khaggavisānasutta* of the *Sutta Nipāta* explains how

---

[50] http://sexuality.jbpub.com/ref_links_visit.cfm? WeblinksID=3583& URL=http://wylde.com/paraphilia.html

[51] *Chaṭṭasangāyanā* CD-ROM: Vipassana Research Institute: *bhikkhunī-sampayujanādisu te licchavī kumārakā khiddāpasutā attano anācārena evaṃ akamsu* ।

[52] Ibid.: *tato paṭṭhāya ca licchavīnaṃ vināso eva udapādi* ।

affection comes into being from *saṁsagga* (association).[53] The *Cullaniddesa* in its exposition of the meaning of the term *saṁsagga* has given two forms of union (sexual): *dassanasaṁsagga* and *savanasaṁsagga*.[54] Two modes of deriving pleasure are defined in terms of sex: one sees (*passati* = voyeur in French means to see) a beautiful woman or a young girl; then he desires and considers various bodily parts in the woman or girl as beautiful or attractive (*anubyañjanaso nimittaṃ gaṇhāti*). On considering characteristics of bodily parts he becomes overjoyed, and this is called desire out of seeing (*dassanakāma*).[55] One derives pleasure from listening to being said that there is a beautiful woman or a young girl in a particular village or a place. By listening to the description of her characteristics, he becomes delighted. This is called desire out of listening (*savanakāma*) (*Cullniddesa*, p. 272).

It is clear that both of these modes of deriving pleasure are concerned with sexual desire. This idea of various forms of achieving sensual/sexual gratification has been developed

---

[53] *The Group Discourses*, II, p. 4: K.R. Norman translates the term *samsaggajātassa* (*samsaggajātassa bhavanti snehā* ... in the *Khaggavisāna-sutta*) as "who has associations".

[54] *Cullaniddesa*, p. 272: *dve samsaggā: dassana-samsaggo ca savanna-samsaggo ca* ।

[55] Hirschfield 1935: 127. Sexologically, there are fivefold sexual stimulus which are liable to grow up to sexual deviations: (a) Visual sexual stimuli (*dassanasamsagga*), (b) auditory sexual stimuli (*savanasamsagga*), (c) olfactory sex stimuli, (d) gustatory sex stimuli, and (e) tactile sex stimuli (*kāyasamsagga*). The extreme manifestation of attachment to these five sexual stimuli forms the five forms of sexual deviants: voyeurs (Peeping toms), ecouteurs (listeners), renifluers (smellers), lechuers (lickers) and frotters (rubbers). This classification is same with the Buddhist classification of sexual stimulus found in the opposite sex partners. – Cf. *AN* I.1

in the *Paramatthajotikā* commentary. It has produced a list of five kinds of ways from which one becomes sexually delighted:

i. *dassanasaṁsagga* — sexual desire born out of seeing (*aññamañaṃ disvā cakkhuviññāṇavīthivasena uppannarāgo dassanasaṁsaggo nāma*)

ii. *savanasaṁsagga* — sexual desire born out of listening (*parehi pana kathiyamānaṃ rūpādisampattiṃ attanā vā hasitalapitagītasaddaṃ sutvā sotaviññāṇavīthivasena uppanno rāgo savanasaṁsaggo nāma*)

iii. *kāyasaṁsagga* — sexual desire born out of body (*aññamaññaṃ aṅgaparāmasanena uppannarāgo kāyasaṁsaggo nāma*)

iv. *samullapanasaṁsagga* — sexual desire born out of conversation (*aññamaññaṃ ālapanasamullapane uppanno rāgo pana samullapanasaṁsaggo nāma*)

v. *saṁbhogasaṁsagga* — sexual desire born out of co-consumption (*bhikkhubhikkhuṇīhi saddhiṃ paribhoga-karaṇe uppannarāgo saṁbhogasaṁsaggo nāma*).[56]

The *Paramatthajotikā* commentary illustrates the disastrous nature of voyeuristic desire in sexual affairs. The text presents a story in order to explain the issue: a lady of the village, Kāḷadīghavāpi in Sri Lanka, fell in love with a young monk who was going for alms. Due to some reason, she could not win over him and was dead of anguish. Shortly after her death, the monk happened to see a dress worn by her and was assailed by melancholy born out of not achieving a chance to come to union with such a lady. He died of heartbreak.[57]

---

[56] *Paramatthajotikā*, I, p. 56f. (Devanāgarī).

[57] Ibid.: *tattha sīhaladīpe kāḷadīghavāpigāme piṇḍāya carantaṃ kaḷyāṇavihā-ravāsīdīghabhāṇkadaharabhikkhuṃ disvā paṭibaddhacittā kenaci upāyena* →

From the perspective of sexology, this episode cannot be counted as an indication of a full-fledged instance of voyeurism. "Voyeurism" is viewing some form of nudity or sexual activity, accompanied by sexual arousal. In this episode, the most influential factor is fantasy (imagining an experience of sexual pleasure with a certain person which never occurred in the real life). It is clear that intensified sexual arousal is present in both the characters that we referred to; they were so overwhelmed by desire that they were dead. The *Diagnostic and Statistical Manual of Mental Disorders* (*DSM*-IV) produces the criteria to decide a patient as voyeur. To meet *DSM*-IV criteria (p. 532) for voyeurism, the client's voyeuristic tendencies must also be personally distressing or must interfere with social or occupational functioning. The criteria are:

A. Over a period of six months, intense sexually arousing fantasies, sexual urges or behaviours involving the act of observing an unsuspecting person who is naked, in the process of disrobing, or engaging in sexual activity.

B. The fantasies, sexual urges or behaviours cause clinically significant distress or impairment in social, occupational or other areas of functioning.

It is clear that the incident does not meet the criterion A of the *DSM*-IV. But it is concerned with the criterion B, and we can say that functioning of fantasy and distress born out of sexual attachment are apparent both in the woman and in the monk. Distress caused by attachment arisen from seeing the person and things related to the person had

---

← *taṃ alabhitvā, kālakatā kuṭumbhiyadhītā, tassā nivāsanacolakhaṇḍaṃ disvā "evarūpavatthadhāriniyā saddhiṃ samvāsam nālattha"nti hadayaṃ phāletvā kālakato*।

caused impairment in all the aspects of these two persons and consequently they died.

How an ascetic was distressed due to sexual desire by seeing the beauty of a queen's lower part of body is mentioned in the *Mudulakkhaṇa Jātaka*. An ascetic possessing divine powers was attended upon by a king for sixteen years. One day the king had to go outside the palace to put down a rebel that had arisen in the frontier. Before setting out, the queen (named Mudulakkhaṇā — gentle heart) was charged with providing the ascetic with requisites when he comes to the palace.

The following day, the queen having prepared alms for the ascetic was waiting. Seeing his delay in arriving, she took a bath and dressed in beautiful clothes and lay down on a small couch awaiting his arrival. The hermit getting up from his *jhāna* and noting that he was late for lunch, transported himself by air to the palace. On hearing the noise of his clothes, the queen hurried to receive him. In her hurry to rise, her tunic slipped down, so that her beauty was revealed to the ascetic as he entered; and at the sight, breaking precepts, he looked at the queen for pleasure's sake. Lust was kindled within him and he lost all psychic powers. He received food but did not eat and left the palace with the bowl, trembling with desire. Coming to his dwelling in the royal garden, set the bowl down beneath his couch and thereon lay for seven days a prey to hunger and thirst, enslaved by the queen's loveliness, his heart aflame with lust.[58]

[58] R. Chalmers (tr.), 1981, *The Jātaka*, vol. I, p. 163; *J* I.304: ... *mudulakkhaṇā vākacīvarasaddaṃ sutvā va "ayyo āgato" ti vegena uṭṭhahi। tassā vegena uṭṭhahantiyā maṭṭasāṭako bhassi। tāpaso sīhapañjarena pavisanto derviyā visabhāgārammaṇaṃ indriyāni bhinditvā subhavasena olokesi। ath'assa abbhantare kileso cali ... so āhāraṃ gahetvā abhuñjitvā va kilesakampito pāsādā oruyha uyyānaṃ gantvā paṇṇasālāṃ pavisitvā phalakattharasayansa* →

This story depicts clearly the psychological distress caused by the passion that sets in due to seeing the physical beauty of a person of the opposite sex. Although, there is no pathological voyeuristic behaviour attributed to the hermit, it is indicative of voyeuristic tendencies which cause impairment in personal as well as other areas of functioning.

Paedophilia

Paedophilia is (in Greek "love for child") is preference to children of either sex for erotic gratification. This is also called "child sexual abuse" and "child molestation". In the *Vinaya*, one instance appears related to a case of sexual abuse of a female child by a monk. A certain monk going on his round for alms, being inflamed by sexual arousal at the sight of a small girl reclining on a chair, thrust his finger into her genitalia.[59] In consequence of his act, she died.[60]

In deciding punishment for the act, the monk was not guilty of committing a homicide because of the absence of intention and for touching the female organ he was punished with *saṅghādisesa* (offence entailing a formal meeting of the Order) which is only second to the offence of defeat (*pārājikā*) in severity (*Vin* III.34). Sexual abuse of children is a crime (Araji 1992, *Sp.* 1775) as well as a psychopathological condition in the offender. Paedophiles (child molesters) are said to experience:

← *heṭṭhā āhāraṃ ṭhapetvā visabhāgārammane bhaddho kilesagginā dayhamāno nirāhāratāya sukkhamāno sattadivsāni phalakattharake nipajji* ।

[59] Doctor and Neff 1994: 174. Child molesters most often are males and they perform actions such as manipulation of the child's genitalia, stroking of the body, etc.

[60] *Vin* III.34: *tena kho pana samayena aññataro piṇḍacāriko bhikkhu pīṭake nippanaṃ dārikaṃ passitvā sāratto anguṭṭhaṃ angajātaṃ pavesesi, sā kālaṃ akāsi* ।

> recurrent, intense sexually arousing fantasies, sexual urges, or behaviours involving sexual activity with a prepubescent child or children (generally age 13 years or younger).[61]

There is no reference whatsoever as to whether the culprit monk was suffering from any kind of long-term psychological depression (which is indicated by the standard phrase *anabhiratiyā pīḷito*) so that his condition meets this criterion in medical science.

According to Buddhist psychology, the consciousness (the whole perceptional process) of ordinary person is burning with sexual desire, hatred, ignorance and many other negative tendencies.[62] Therefore, we cannot deny the existence of various kinds of fantasies in their seed form in human psyche until a relevant stimulus brings them into reality by losing self-control (*sāratto*) as it was in the case of the monk. As this episode implies, in the Buddhist monastic law, there is no room whatsoever for child molestation because it is involved in breaking the vow of celibacy.

To sum up the chapter, all the five forms of pathological deviant sexual behaviour have been seen as going against Buddhist moral theory. Especially, forcible rape against nuns has been considered as a very serious offence and persons committing such an offence must undergo bitter retribution (like the perpetrator of Uppalavaṇṇā) after death, and in this life they are deprived of access to the Order. A notable

---

[61] American Psychiatric Association (*DSM*-IV 1994), p. 528. Regarding the age, another criterion is presented by *DSM*-IV: paedophiles, attracted to female children, prefer 8 to 10 years old, whereas those attracted to males usually prefer slightly older children (p. 527).

[62] *SN* IV.19: *sabbam ādittaṃ . . . kena ādittaṃ? rāgagginā dosagginā mohagginā ādittaṃ* ।

characteristic of the Buddhist approach to the issue is that the stigma of being raped is not attached to the victimized woman. Buddhism holds that rape and sexual harassment is a menace to society and conducive to socio-political degeneration. Incest is denied with repugnance and seen as a result of socio-cultural decline and supported by morally wrong views. Psychologically, it is understood as a misery coming from sense desire.

Exhibitionism is wrong in the *Vinaya* but not so serious because it lacks the element of physical contact which is required to complete a sex act. There is a dearth of data regarding voyeurism. Voyeurism is recognized by the Buddhist texts as a major way of gratifying sexual desire (*dassanakāma*). The case of Licchavis is important to understand the Buddhist attitude to such immoral practices; the commentary recognizes sexual intimidation involving voyeurism as the cause of the decline of Vajjian kingdom. Child sexual abuse is also mentioned in the *Vinaya Piṭaka* and culpability is seen as serious. Based on the data relevant to the selected pathological sexual practices, it can be said that Buddhism sees them as problematic both to oneself and to the whole community.

6

Sociological Deviant Sexual Behaviour

Introduction

THE discussion attempted in this chapter is concerned with three forms of deviant sexual behaviour which have been categorized under sociological deviation. Even though, they have been discussed theoretically by sociologists, I do not intend to deal with those diverse theories presented regarding these three phenomena. My attempt is to see the Buddhist scriptural explanation of them and to examine the possibility of deriving certain implications from the Buddhist point of view regarding the selected sexual practices.

The third category of sexual deviance is the sociological one. Both sociological and pathological deviances violate cultural and religious standards, but sociological deviance involves behaviour that creates a structure to produce or recruit participants, socialize them, gather people together to perform the act and provide social support for the actor. For example, some homosexual men engage in and depend on contact with other homosexual men to develop a homosexual identity. Pornography, prostitution and swinging are the other examples of sociological sexual deviances (Hensley and Tewksbury 2003: 6).

Prostitution

Prostitution is known to be the oldest profession in the history of human civilization. It is recognized as a sex-offence because most of the countries have prohibited it by law. *The Encyclopaedia of Sexual Behaviour* defines prostitution as engaging in coitus or other sex relations for monetary gains (Ellis and Abarbanel 1961: 950). And also, under the law, brothel-keeping-managing a house of prostitution is a criminal offence (ibid.). "Sex for pay" is a well-known phenomenon to the Pali canonical literature and it reveals that many factors contributed to maintain it as an institution in Indian society of the Buddhist age. Secular matters as well as references to the spiritual career of prostitutes are discussed in this section with a view to clarifying the Buddhist perception of prostitution.

According to Hindu scriptures, the existence of prostitution is pre-Buddhistic and had continued into the Buddha's time. I.B. Horner makes valuable observations on the matter how female community earned their living during the Buddhist era. As she reveals, in addition to duties performed in the domestic life as wives, mothers and sisters, there was a considerable number of female professional workers who largely consisted of domestic-slaves, nauch-girls and women musicians. In addition to these groups, a large part of the female community was engaged in sex work. In spite of the importance given to marriage during the Vedic period, prostitution also had been in existence in India. For some girls who had no protection from a responsible relative or from some other guardian, prostitution had been the way of living. However, the larger society was not pleased with this practice. Aśvapati states that his kingdom is free from many evil forms of conduct such as theft, drug abuse, adultery and prostitution (Keith, quoted in Horner 1990: 88).

The adverse attitude held towards prostitution is reflected in the *Laws of Manu*. In it, courtesans are portrayed as ceremonially unclean and brāhmaṇas are instructed not to eat food offered by harlots (*Manu* IV.209 quoted in Horner 1990: 88), for such action is said to exclude person from the (higher) worlds (*Manu* IV.219 in ibid.). Further, a king should know clever harlots to be a thorn on the side of his people (*Manu* IX.259-60 in ibid.). He should instigate them to commit offences, then bring them under his power (*Manu* IX.261 in ibid.) and punish them (*Manu* IX.262 in ibid.).

In spite of public aversion towards it, the profession of prostitution continued into the Buddha's day and in the Buddhist texts there are two subgroups engaged in it, *gaṇikā* and *vesī*. *Gaṇikās* (courtesans) were super-grade prostitutes whose clientele was drawn from the court or wealthy class. A courtesan's life condition was very high and was similar to the modern equivalent of call girls (Murcott 1991: 120). Ambapālī, Aḍḍhakāsī, Sirimā and Sālavatī were from this subgroup of prostitutes in the Buddha's time. The term *gaṇikā* is defined as "one who belongs to the community or clan", harlot, courtesan and prostitute (*PED*, p. 241). According to the Buddhist literature, *gaṇikā* was a special institution established by the state and the first state to do so, seems to be that of the Licchavis of Vesālī (Perera 1993: 214). Ambapālī (Ambapālikā) was the courtesan of the Licchavi clan in the city of Vesālī.

The second subgroup of prostitutes was *vesī* or *vesiyā* — a woman of low caste, a harlot and prostitute (*PED*, pp. 650f.). The present-day equivalent of her is a streetwalker. Her life condition was not as good as that of a *gaṇikā*. Her charges might have been quite low because she was to cater to the requirements of ordinary society. There is no particular reference to the charges of this subcategory of prostitutes.

The only available data to guess the rate of their payment is found in the *Cullavaggapāli*. On a certain occasion, the elder Piṇḍolabhāradvāja exhibited his psychic powers in order to get a wooden bowl. In criticism of the act, the Buddha compares him to a woman who would display her charms for a miserable *māsaka* (a low-priced coin).[1]

The image of the prostitute of this class reflected in the canonical material is not as high as that of the super-level prostitute. The *Mahāvaggapāli* reports that the Bhaddavaggiya princes employed a prostitute for one prince who had no wife. The prostitute, seeing an opportunity, stole the valuables of the princes and escaped (*Vin* II.112). We can assume that their level of education as well as general nurture had not been very high. However, they appear to have lived in accordance with the customs of civil society. They had offered food and support to religious people.

In the *Vinaya Piṭaka*, it is mentioned that for a monk who is under the observance of rainy-retreat (*vassā*), temptation to sensuality could come from a variety of persons belong to many walks of life. Among them, a prostitute has also been mentioned as a threat to *brahmacariya*.[2] There is admonition not to visit a dwelling of a prostitute because there would appear public criticism against such a monk.[3] Moreover, it is advised not to go in single person to accept food from the house of a prostitute and a monk may go there with other

---

[1] *Vin* II.112: *seyyathāpi bhāradvāja mātugāmo chavassa māsakapūrassa kāraṇā kopinakaṃ dasseti, evеṃ eva kho tayā bhāradvāja chavassa dārupattassa kāraṇā gihīnaṃ uttarimanussadhammaṃ iddhipāṭihāriyaṃ dassitaṃ* ।

[2] Ibid. 150: *idha pana bhikkhave vassūpagataṃ bhikkhum vesī nimanteti* ।

[3] *VinA* 992: *so nacirass'eva asukavesiyā saddhiṃ gato ti vattabbaṃ pāpunāti* ।

monks (*VinA* 992). In giving these warnings, it seems that two factors had been considered; adverse public opinion and the possibility of seduction that could result from sensualist women.

A more important point that comes to light in this reference is that the lower grade prostitute had attended upon monks as any other normal devotee did, such as householders, merchants and kings. However, monks were expected to be very mindful whenever they interacted with prostitutes.

It is noteworthy that all the "pleasure women" who entered the Order were from the higher-level group (*gaṇikā*) but none from the lower-grade public women (*vesī*). Due to the irregular way of life as well as poor life condition, the prostitutes of menial service have become an object of stigma even among their own kind in comparison with the super-grade prostitutes.[4] However, in the Pali scriptures, there is no reference to the class of courtesans (*gaṇikā*) looking down upon the subcategory of harlots (*vesī*). It is clear that the disapproving attitude towards poor prostitutes was more than towards those of the higher level since ancient times.

It is necessary to examine why in Indian society there were a large number of courtesans. According to the I.B. Horner's observation, for such girls who were without protectors, a life of prostitution was an obvious course to pursue (1990: 88). The majority of prostitutes should have come from women who faced the challenge of economic survival. The opportunities to earn a livelihood through righteous ways had been limited

---

4 Nathan and Harris 1975: 379: Harold Greenwald (1970) stated that call girls (higher level prostitutes) were scornful of the streetwalkers than the most puritanical reformer.

for women because the labour force (both physical and intellectual) was the monopoly of males in ancient times. It may be assumed that in ancient India, a large proportion of prostitutes entered the profession for economic reasons. Recent researches conducted on the life of prostitutes have recognized a range of causes for the entry of women into this profession among which economic instability is perceived as one. Hardman (1997: 19-31) reports:

> Because of restricted access to financial and material resources, some women may resort to prostitution as a resistance to poverty.
>
> – quoted in Hensley and Tewksbury 2003: 169

To explain the reasons of women's entry into prostitution, two concepts were used by a group of researchers (Dalla 2003: 168). They were: susceptibility and exposure. The susceptibility model contends that psychological characteristics (e.g. alienation, feelings of worthlessness) in conjunction with traumatic events (e.g. incest), make some women vulnerable to the lure of prostitution. The exposure model predicts that interpersonal contact with, and inducement from, others involved in the sex industry leads to personal involvement (ibid.: 169). As to the first model, there is no special reference within the selected sources. Yet, regarding the second model, i.e. exposure, there is mention in the *Mahāvaggapāli*. At one time, nuns and prostitutes were bathing naked in the same ford of the River Aciravatī. The prostitutes mocked the nuns saying:

> Why are you young women living the holy life? Why not enjoy pleasure now and renounce the world when you are old? Then you can experience both. – *Vin* I.293

Even though, this was a clear encouragement by the sensual

women to anti-sensual counterparts to enjoy sexuality, there was no prohibition to bathe together with them afterwards. A preventive measure was taken to stop such unsuitable mocking by promulgating a rule to wear a bathing costume for nuns (*Vin* I.293). This instance is supportive of the assumption that prostitution may sometimes have tempted other females to fall into sensualistic life, which was freely enjoyed by them.

Tendency of runaway behaviour in certain persons has been recognized as one of the reasons to fall into prostitution. An investigation conducted in Canada on boys, who were in the service of streetwalkers, indicated that many of them were more likely to be or to have been runaways (Dalla 2003: 168f.). Helplessness and independence both come together to one who escapes from one's house and protectors. Loneliness is an inevitable psychological characteristic dominant in those escapers. All these factors may be more active in a city environment. The escape behaviour can be illustrated in relation to prostitution through the story of Gaṅgātīriya's mother. One day, while she was quarrelling with her husband, was happened to place her child on the bed in a hurry whereby the infant was injured. In fear of the husband's rage, she escaped from home to the city of Rājagaha and led a life of a courtesan over there.[5]

In considering the sociological facts regarding the prevalence of prostitution in Indian society as reflected in the Buddhist scriptures, it is clear that in spite of the common stigma attached to it, there had been a supportive structure to sustain it. According to the Indian caste system (*varṇa dharma*), one's profession is determined by birth and

---

[5] *Therigāthā-Aṭṭhakathā*, p. 220 (Devanāgarī): *tato sāpi sāmikaṃ bhayitvā rājagahameva paccāgantvā serivicārena vicarati* ।

previous *kamma*. Through this theory, it appears that the continuation of the institution of prostitution had been eternalized by Indian society. The story of Aḍḍhakāsī given in the *Therīgāthā* commentary refers to the term *gaṇikākule*.[6] According to this, there should have been a separate caste of prostitutes like other castes whose profession was determined by birth. Prostitution was assumed by Sirimā (*SnA* I.144) and Vimalā on a hereditary basis (*Therīgāthā*, XXXIX in Honer, 1990: 88 fn. 1). Sirimā was the daughter of Sālavatī, who was the first courtesan of Rājagaha. Later she was succeeded by her daughter, Sirimā (*Vin* I.268f.). Ambapālī, the courtesan of Vesālī, after attaining enlightenment, said that she happened to be reborn ten thousand times as a courtesan due to an evil deed done in a previous birth.[7] If we remove the religious element from the utterance of Ambapālī, it becomes clear that the existence of prostitution had been in vogue justified by the theories of caste and *kamma*.

Society in India by the time of the Buddha was subject to exclusive male domination. Uma Chakravarti observes the society reflected in early Buddhist scriptures as follows:

> Women were ideally expected to be like slaves and be obedient to their husbands. They were under the control of various bodies like the king, the *saṅgha*, the *seṇī* (guild) or *pūga* (company). – Chakravarti 1987: 33

All the power projects were under the control of men and consequently the life of woman was decided by them. Certain

---

[6] *Therīgāthā-Aṭṭhakathā, Chaṭṭhasamgāyanā* CD-ROM: *tena kammāvasesena, ajāyiṃ gaṇikākule, bahusova parādhīna, pacchimāya ca jātiyaṃ। disvāna dassanīyaṃ maṃ, giribbajapuruttame, gaṇikatte nivesesuṃ, akkosanabalena me।*

[7] *Therīgāthā-Aṭṭakathā, Chaṭṭhasamgāyanā* CD-ROM.

women were compelled to take to prostitution by these male authorities. For instance, Ambapālī was established in her position of courtesan by the Licchavi clan (*Vin* I.268f.). Sālavatī became the super-grade prostitute in Rājagaha because of the decision taken by the state (ibid.). And also, Aḍḍhakāsī was positioned in courtesanship by her government.[8]

There is no mention whether any of these women entered sex industry by self-inducement. Their way of lives was decided by external forces. Researches conducted about prostitution point out that no one was willing to become a prostitute by her or his own will in the absence of a serious crisis in one's life. Even though Aḍḍhakāsī was a highly valued figure, after her enlightenment, she refers to the extremely pitiable nature of her previous life as a prostitute (*ajāyiṃ gaṇikākūle, bahusova parādhīna*).[9] The desire to be free from this worthless profession and lead a respectable life with one's own husband has been expressed by Sulasā, the super-grade prostitute of Benares:

> One day she saw a stout person who was subjected to corporeal punishment. Seeing him, she thought: If I can free that stout-fighting man, *I will give up this bad life of mine and live respectably with him.* — Francis and Neil 1984, vol. III: 261

It is evident that the entrance to prostitution was not due solely to one's free will but due to social influence upon womankind.

A characteristic seen in the sociological deviant sexual behaviour is the existence of certain groups that recruit new members, train them and have sexual contacts with them in

---

[8] *Therīgāthā-Aṭṭhkathā*, p. 33 (Devanāgarī).

[9] Ibid.

a particular sexual pattern. In the Jātaka stories, regarding prostitution, the training of new members in the profession is mentioned. A prostitute called Sulasā who lived in Benares, had 500 courtesans as trainees (ibid.). The courtesan, Kālī met in the *Takkāriya Jātaka* also had women under training as prostitutes. The nature of the brothel kept by her is described in the story as follows:

> Now in that house of ill fame the fashion was this: out of every thousand pieces of money received 500 were for the woman, 500 were the price of clothes, perfumes and garlands; the men who visited that house receive garments to clothe themselves in, and stayed the night there, and on the next day they put off the garments they had received, and put on those they had brought, and went their way.
>
> – *J* IV.248; Rouse 1981, vol. IV: 157

Specially, courtesans who were in the post of *nagarasobhinī* (beautifier of the city) had to master aesthetic arts such as music, singing and dancing. Ambapālī and Sālavatī are portrayed as having thorough mastery in those areas of entertainment. The *Mahāvagga* gives a vivid account of the talent possessed by Ambapālī in these arts:

> ... the courtesan Ambapālī, beautiful, good to look upon, charming, she was possessed of the utmost beauty of complexion, was dancing and singing and lute-playing, much visited by desirous people and she went for a night for a fifty, and through her Vesālī shone forth all the more.
>
> – *BD* IV.379

In addition to physical attraction, the mastery over aesthetic arts was necessary for super-grade courtesans because their clients came from high-class societies, who had great interest in sensualistic activities.

The children born to prostitutes were kept with their mother only if the child was female. Sālavatī first had a boy and asked the servant girl to throw him away. He was saved by Abhayarājakumāra and later the child was known as Jīvaka Komārabhacca who became the physician of King Bimbisāra (*Vin* I.268ff.). The female child was nurtured as they could carry on their mother's profession (e.g. Sirimā and Vimalā). The social structure in place to maintain prostitution in Indian society thus can be understood on two bases. One was hereditary and the other was systematic training under an expert in the profession. This further affirms that prostitution had been flourishing in that society and factors that caused women to turn into this problematic behaviour had been largely present.

The economic importance of the courtesan was recognized during the Buddha's time by rulers, and they were eager to establish the position of courtesan as a device to attract many people to their countries. Once, the urban officers (*negama*) (Perera 1993: 221 fn. 3) of Rājagaha went to Vesālī for a certain matter and saw that the city of Vesālī was flourished so well. The delegation noticed the cause behind that prosperity as the courtesan Ambapālī, who was a stunning beauty and highly skilled in music, singing and dancing. She charged for one night fifty pieces of money (*paññāsāya ca rattiṃ gacchati tāya ca vesālī bhiyyosomattāya upasobhati*). On return to Rājagaha, the officers suggested to King Bimbisāra to establish a courtesan in his city too. The king accepts the idea and assigns them with the duty of finding a suitable maiden. Sālavatī was endowed with all those qualities required to become the belle of the city (*nagarasobhinī*) in physical splendour and talents in aesthetic arts. According to the *Mahāvagga* account, Sālavatī was the first courtesan in Rājagaha appointed by the state (*Vin* I.268f.).

The main cities such as Ujjenī and Kośāmbī also had courtesans. Padumavatī who was the courtesan of Ujjenī gave birth to a child conceived from King Bimbisāra. Their son, Abhaya, later entered the Order and became an *arahanta*, through whose influence the mother also attained enlightenment. She was known as Abhayamātā (*ThigA* 31-32, quoted in *DPPN*, vol. I, p. 134). Sulasā was also a courtesan (*nagarasobhinī*) of Rājagaha (*J* III.435-39). The courtesan, Kālī was living in Benares (*J* IV.248). A virtuous courtesan is reported to have been living in the city of Indapatta (Rouse 1981, vol. II: 260).

The courtesans of this era had earned much wealth. As it was said above, Ambapālī charged for one night fifty pieces of money (*Vin* I.268) and Sālavatī had got 100 (*Vin* I.269). Sirimā (*DhA* III.104f.; *VvA* 74ff.), Sulasā (*J* III.435-39), Kālī[10] and Aḍḍhakāsī had to be paid 1,000 per night or day. About Aḍḍhakāsī, it is said that originally she had charged 1,000 for one day and later because it was very expensive, many customers used to pay 500 and stay for half-day with her. So, she became known as "Aḍḍhakāsī" literally means "half *kāsī*". Buddhaghoṣa defines the term *kāsī* as 1,000 and, anything worth 1,000 is called *kāsiya* (*DPPN*, vol. I, p. 50).

An important explanation of Aḍḍhakāsī is given by Dhammapāla. The revenue which accrued to the king for one day from Kāsī (kingdom) was 1,000. Aḍḍhakāsī's customers had to give a like sum to spend a night with her. For this reason, she was called Kāsī. But later many men, being unable to pay 1,000, would pay half the amount and spend the day with her. As a result she became known as Aḍḍhakāsī

[10] *J* IV.248: *pubbe kira kāli nāma gaṇikā ahosi ... kālī ekadivasam sahassaṃ gaṇhāti* ।

(*DPPN*, vol. I, p. 35). In spite of being subject to censure by the religious groups, the secular groups such as state rulers and wealthy persons were in support of higher level prostitution. King Bimbisāra had two sons from courtesans, Abhaya from Padumavatī[11] and Vimala-Kondañña from Ambapālī.[12]

It is not mentioned whether the courtesans of the Buddha's time had to pay taxes to the government. With the passage of time, the state had directly interfered with the earnings of prostitutes. The *Arthaśāstra* states that in addition to certain occasional fines which may be imposed on the courtesan,[13] she had to make payment of twice the amount of a day's earning, to the state.[14] As we referred to earlier, because of Ambapālī, Vesālī became more and more prosperous. So, the urban council of Rājagaha (*negama*) was tempted to propose a counterpart in their city too. This was due to being convinced of the economic potential of the institute. Thus, we can see a gradual evolution of the institute of prostitution in India to an extent of becoming an essential element in the economy of the country.

The reason for one's rebirth as a prostitute could be seen in two ways: as a consequence of bad *kamma* and as a consequence of good *kamma*. There is no comprehensive discourse to explain the reason for one's fate as a prostitute. Ambapālī was one of the most celebrated courtesans in the Buddha's time of India.

---

11 *Paramatthadīpanī: Dhammapāla's Commentary on the Therīgāthā*, p. 40.

12 Ibid., p. 207.

13 *Arthaśāstra* II.27: 9, 11, 12; 19, 20 and 21 in Perera 1993: 221 fn. 2.

14 *Arthaśāstra* II.27: 27; 27: 24: *rūpajīvā bhogdvayaguṇaṃ dadyuḥ*: She also had to make statements of her income to the government: in Perera 1993: 221 fn. 2.

In the *Apadānapāli* and in the *Therigāthā* commentary, it is mentioned that she happened to be born as a prostitute because of insulting an *arahanta therī* by calling her *gaṇikā*. In the Sikhī Buddha's time, she had been a nun.[15] One day, she took part in a procession of *bhikkhuṇīs* and was doing homage at a shrine when an *arahanta* nun in front of her hastily spat in the court of the shrine. Seeing the spittle and not knowing who had committed the fault, she said in blame, "what prostitute has been spitting here?" (*kā nāma gaṇikā imasmiṃ ṭhāne khelapiṇḍaṃ pātesī 'ti*).[16] Owing to this insulting remark made regarding the *arahanta* nun, she happened to undergo severe retribution in horrible purgatory. After retribution therein, she was 10,000 times born as a prostitute in the human world still having the residue of her bad *kamma*.[17]

Aḍḍhakāsī, who was put the highest value by people, later receives the ordination under the *bhikkhuṇī* community and attains enlightenment. The commentary to the *Therīgāthā* explains why she became a courtesan. In the Kassapa Buddha's time she had been a nun well established in the precepts. But she reviled an *arahanta* nun by calling her a prostitute, and by way of retribution for it, she was born in purgatory. In the last life, she was the daughter of a rich and distinguished citizen of Benares but, because of her former evil speech, was appointed a prostitute in Rājagaha.[18] These two accounts relate the life of a courtesan to retribution resulting from bad *kamma* done in the past.

---

15 *DPPN* I.155f. mentions as "novice" but the commentary mentions as: *upasampannā hutvā bhikkhunīsikkhāpadaṃ samādāya viharanti* (*Therīgāthā Aṭṭhakathā*, p. 237 (Devanāgarī).

16 *Therīgāthā Aṭṭhakathā*, p. 237 (Devanāgarī).

17 Ibid.

18 Ibid., p. 33.

In contrast to the above position, rebirth as a courtesan has been mentioned as a result of merits accumulated by a person. The courtesan Vimalā's rebirth as *gaṇikā* is said to be a consequence of a meritorious deed done by her at the time of one of the previous *Buddhas*.[19] A similar cause is given in the commentary with regard to the birth of Padumavatī (Abhayamātā), the courtesan of Ujjenī. Dhammapāla in the *Therigāthā* commentary explains that in the past, Abhaya's mother acquired merit by giving alms to former *buddhas*. Due to this merit, she was born as a courtesan named Padumavatī (Lotus-like).[20] Later, she became a consort of King Bimbisāra.

These commentarial descriptions might have been based on an observation of the luxurious life that they led and the value attributed to super-grade courtesans at that time in India. Such a person from the secular point of view was enjoying sensual pleasures to the highest degree, and therefore one cannot assume that sort of life to be miserable. The life of Vimalā was prospered with all the worldly assets such as beauty and fame to the extent that she looked down on other women (*Th* II.72). Padumavatī became a consort of King Bimbisāra.[21] Horner (1990: 94) states that in the period represented in the Buddhist scriptures, one's *kamma* was perceived as the cause of rebirth as a prostitute. According to Pali Buddhism, *kamma* and its consequences are twofold, pleasant and unpleasant. In the Pali canonical and commentarial works, the birth as a prostitute has been traced to both these kinds of *kammas* and their consequences.

---

19 *Chaṭṭhasamgāyanā* CD-ROM, Vipassana Research Institute: *purima buddhesu katādikārā ... vivaṭṭhupanissayaṃ kusalaṃ upacinitvā imasmiṃ buddhuppāde vesāliyaṃ aññatarāya rūpajīvitthiyā dhītā hutvā nibbatti* ।

20 *Therīgāthā Aṭṭhakathā*, pp. 31-32 (Devanāgarī).

21 Ibid.

In early Buddhist texts, one cannot see a strong antipathy towards courtesans. The Jewish law commands death as a punishment for prostitution. Leviticus 21:9 states:

> If a priest's daughter defiles herself by becoming a prostitute, she disgraces her father; she must be burned in the fire.[22]

However, Jesus has denied Jewish laws against prostitutes and has forgiven them[23] while he did perceive prostitution as an evil. In Buddhist scriptures, there is no mention of prostitution as requiring such a serious punishment. The *Parābhavasutta* of the *Sutta Nipāta* states that seeking the company of prostitutes and adultery are causes of one's decline (*Sn*, p. 108).

For monks, it is prohibited to be closely associated with prostitutes. Yet, such warnings have been made in regard to lower level prostitutes (*vesī*) (Perera 1993: 217). And also, certain prostitutes had tried to seduce monks. On a certain occasion, a monk was meditating in a pleasure park. A courtesan, who had an arrangement with a certain person to meet in the park, awaited his arrival there, but the man did not turn up. As she was strolling about, she happened to see the monk and attempted to seduce him (Narada Thera 1993: 94). Vimalā attempted to tempt the elder Moggallāna (*ThagA* II, p. 178) and another courtesan who ran her own restaurant attempted to seduce the elder Anuruddha (*Vin* IV.17f.). As previously mentioned, prostitutes mocked at nuns on a

---

[22] http:// bible.gospelcom.net/passage/?search=Lev%20- 21:9& version=31

[23] Mattew 21:32-33: Tax collectors and prostitutes will get to the kingdom of heaven before you. URL: bethinking.org/bible/bible-scandals/4-prostitutes

certain occasion tempting them to pursue a sensuous life (*BD* III.283). In spite of the inclusion of such kinds of problematic episodes and moral prohibitions related to prostitutes, Buddhism has accepted them as normal as any other person in society. For example, Sirimā and Ambapālī were pious lay devotees and their offerings were accepted by the Buddha and his disciples.

It is said that when Ambapālī heard of the Buddha's visit to Koṭigāma, near Vesālī, she and her retinue drove out of city in magnificent chariots to meet him, and after listening to a *dhamma* talk by him, invited him and his disciples to a meal the next day. The Buddha accepted this invitation and had, as a result, to refuse that of the Licchavis of Vesālī.[24] It was after this meal that she donated her park, the Ambapālīvana, to the Buddha and the Order. The Buddha accepted the gift and stayed there some time before going to Beluva (*Vin* I.231-33; *DN* II.95-98). The Buddha never criticized Ambapālī for her career and she also is not reported to have ever repented about it.

Sirimā was a stream-enterer (*sotāpanna*) (*Dha* III.104f.; *VvA* 74ff. in *DPPN*, vol. II, p. 1144) and had conducted offering food for eight monks every day at her house. Her career has not been considered a blemish in Buddhism as revealed in the evaluation of her spiritual cultivation. As such, she was honoured by recognizing as one of the eminent *upāsikās* (*AN* IV.347; *AA* II.791). In Buddhism, one becomes *upāsikā* by taking refuge in the tripple gems and observing five precepts among which the third item is abstinence from sexual misconduct. If Buddhism treats Sirimā's career as a violation of the chastity

---

[24] *DA* II.545: The *Dīgha Nikāya* commentary says that just before Ambapāli's visit to him, the Buddha admonished monks to be steadfast and mindful, lest they lose their heads about her.

norm, she should not have been honoured as a worthy lay disciple.

This raises the problem, whether Buddhism does not consider prostitution as a moral breach or considers it as one among the variety of professions. As I assume, a large part of female population in the time of the Buddha were sex workers, so their pathetic condition was seen by Buddhism with sympathy and the wrong has not been attributed to the victim but to relevant causes ranging from doctrinal, which includes the rational of *kamma*-retribution to socio-economic factors which clearly have been perceived as conducive to numerous evils in society.

The whole Indian society, according to the Buddha's realization was dominated by two ideals: asceticism and sensualism. Any person who gives up these extremes becomes free from ignorance and craving which causes one to be trapped in the sāṁsāric cycle. Prostitutes were indulging in the extreme of sensuality and their risk was considered to be relatively higher to continue in the round of deaths and rebirths than of those who were in the other extreme of asceticism. Buddhism acted for the redemption of both these categories overlooking a person's caste, gender or profession. Four courtesans who attainted enlightenment realizing the Buddha's teaching have been mentioned; Ambapālī, Padumavatī (Abhayamātā), Aḍḍhakāsī and Vimalā have been included in the *Therigāthā* as the enlightened nuns who were formerly courtesans. It is evident that Buddhism does not exhibit an attitude that negates a person's capacity of achieving final liberation because of the nature of his or her career. What is implied from this position is that a stigma need not be attached to a person simply because of one's profession as a male or female prostitute.

Homosexuality

Homosexuality is a sexual conduct between two persons of the same sex. According to erotic orientation, a homosexual is any individual, whose choice of sexual object is someone of the same sex (Ward et al. 1994: 210). Homosexuality among females is called "lesbianism" while the males who engage in the same-sex conduct are known as "gay". The term gay is sometimes used to refer to both male and female homosexuals. In the modern Western culture, any man who engages, or has engaged in homosexuality is identified as "a homosexual". It becomes sexually deviant because of non-conformity to heterosexual behaviour and non-conformity to the requirement of reproduction. While one's sexual orientation may be homosexual, in behaviour one may be heterosexual. Therefore, the sexologist A.C. Kinsey points out that it is difficult to divide persons as homosexual or heterosexual (ibid.).

In the Pali scriptures belonging to the early period as well as the commentarial age, homosexuality has been mentioned as a practice among both males and females.[25] In this section, let us consider the views expressed in Pali texts in order to recognize the scriptural position regarding this deviant phenomenon.

In a discussion of homosexuality in the Pali scriptures, it is required to pay attention to two concepts, hermaphrodite and eunuch. A hermaphrodite is defined as:

> a male or female whose external genitalia are modified in such a manner that they resemble those of the opposite

---

[25] However, Buddhism shows a restriction to unusual sexual deviants like nun-rapists, the restriction is not limited only to homosexuals.

sex. Usually the sex glands are abnormal. ...

– Ford and Beach 1951: 281

The Pali term *ubhatovyañjanaka* (one having the sexual characteristics of both sexes) refers to the modern term hermaphrodite. In Buddhism, for a person having masculinity or femininity, the perfect membership in the Order is permitted. But, for one who is having both characteristics, the case is different. The first *pārājikā* rule mentions that a hermaphrodite is sexually available in three channels, that is, genital, oral and anal.[26] The *Vinaya* accounts for the reason why a hermaphrodite is not allowed to enter to the Order.

The *Mahāvaggapāli* states that because of the possibility of a hermaphrodite enticing a fellow monk or nun to have sex, a hermaphrodite should not be ordained (*Vin* I.89; II.271). According to Buddhaghoṣa, hermaphrodites can be divided into two as males and females because they are endowed with only one capacity (*indriya*, either *itthindriya* or *purisindriya*). When a female hermaphrodite is sexually aroused, she desires a sexual relation with a woman, manifests male sexual organs and retracts and hides her own female sexual organs, whereas the converse situation obtains for the male hermaphrodite. It is said that female hermaphrodites can both impregnate and give birth, and male hermaphrodites cannot give birth yet can be sexually attractive to both males and females.[27] L. Zwilling, in connection with the Buddhaghoṣa's comment, says that he has conflated hermaphroditism and bisexuality (1992: 206).

---

[26] *Vin* III.28: *ubhatobyañjanakassa tayo magge methunaṃ dhammaṃ paṭisevantassa āpatti pārājikassa vaccamagge, passāvamagge mukhe* ।

[27] *Asl* 322-23; *Vinaya Aṭṭhakathā-Mahāvagga* (Devanāgarī), p. 290: *itthiubhatobyañjanako sayañca gabbhaṃ gaṇhāti, parañca gaṇhāpeti* । *purisaubhatobyañjanako pana sayaṃ na gaṇhāti, paraṃ gaṇhāpeti* ।

As the *Milindapañha* 310 says, a hermaphrodite is an "obstructed" person for he is incapable of attaining the understanding of *dhamma* in spite of the right practice. The Buddhist monastic institute bars the entrance of hermaphrodite into the Order on the assumption that he is a seductive power, who may spoil the celibacy of monks and nuns leading to the expulsion from the Order. The psychological reason given regarding the hermaphrodite can be understood as an indirect support for the prohibition of his entrance to the Order.

A detailed examination has been made in the commentarial work on the concept of *paṇḍaka*. L. Zwilling points out that *paṇḍaka*, which is translated as eunuch, does not mean "someone deliberately castrated" as eunuchs were virtually unknown to pre-Muslim India. Zwilling states *paṇḍaka* should be known as "man without balls" (1992: 204). Further, he states that the term *paṇḍaka* was used in the metaphorical sense, "as we do in English when it is said of a weak or pusillanimous person that he (even she) 'has no balls' ". In a writing published in the Internet, L.A. De Silva points out that *paṇḍaka* does not refer to homosexuals in general but rather to the effeminate, self-advertising and promiscuous "homosexual".[28]

In the first *pārājikā* rule, a list of sexual outlets has been produced (*Vin* III.28f.). Four major persons are given as follows:

1. Female – human, non-human and animal,
2. Hermaphrodite – human, non-human and animal
3. Eunuch – human, non-human and animal

[28] De Silva, www.budddhanet.net/homosexu.htm

4. Male — human, non-human and animal.

With the exception of the first category, all the other sexual objects are recognized as homosexual partners for the male. As we discussed in the fourth chapter, the problem regarding sexual behaviour in the monastic institute arises concerning penetrative sex. For a man in the female body, three sexual channels are available (genitals, anus and mouth). Male homosexuality is also seen in the texts as relating to the same issue, that is, sexual contact with a male homosexual is involved in sexual orifices and whose penetration entails expulsion from the community. The texts recognize two possibilities of penetrative sex between a perfect male and a eunuch, oral and anal.

In addition to referring to the man who lacks masculinity, the term *paṇḍaka* has been used to refer to a woman lacking normal characteristics of femininity (*itthipaṇḍaka*) (*Vin* II.271). According to the information included in the texts, hermaphrodite possesses the characteristics of both sexes whereas *paṇḍaka* lacks characteristics of either sex. A common commentarial explanation for the term *paṇḍaka* is *napuṁsaka*, the non-male, which indicates a person lacking both maleness and femaleness, i.e. a neuter (Harvey 2000: 414). It is stated that if a nun has sexual contact either with a non-human male or with a *paṇḍaka*, it is only a lesser offence. This proves that *paṇḍaka* is a non-male human (*Vin* IV.215, 233, 269). As the *Vinaya* texts mention both *paṇḍaka* and *itthipaṇḍaka*, it seems that even though *paṇḍaka* is lacking the sexual organ, in outer appearance, he/she has the characteristics either of a male or of a female. The term *paṇḍaka* might have been employed as the common word to refer to both the categories, males and females in appearance only, but lacking the characteristic sexual organs.

Zwilling points out that the pre-Buddhist *Atharvaveda* distinguishes *paṇḍakas* from ordinary males and females, and implies that they were transvestites (1992: 205). Perera (1993: 116) argues that *paṇḍaka* was a castrated man (or woman – *itthipaṇḍaka*) used especially for homosexual activities such as federacy and oral sex, etc. As Buddhaghoṣa sees, it is not definite whether *paṇḍaka* was a castrated person used for homosexual activities.

Ven. Buddhaghoṣa's comment on *paṇḍaka* in the *Vinaya* commentary is presented in relation to an episode that mentions an incident that occurred within the monastic community during the Buddha's time. The *Mahāvagga* reports that a *paṇḍaka* after ordination in the community approached monks and invited them to defile him. Being denied and chased away by them, he asks young novices to defile him. They also chased him away; finally, he went to the elephant keepers and grooms to get himself defiled. After defiling him, they became angry at his act and accused the Buddha's followers:

> These recluses, sons of the Sākyans, are eunuchs and those of them who are not eunuchs, they too commit offences with eunuchs. Thus they are one and all unchaste.
>
> – *BD* IV.108; *Vin* I.85

Because of this criticism against his *saṅgha* community, the Buddha decided to prohibit the ordination of *paṇḍakas* and commanded to expel if anyone is already ordained (ibid.). A similar prohibition is made to female *paṇḍaka* and *animittā* (who lack female organ) (*Vin* II.271). However, Buddhaghoṣa in commenting on this passage, takes *animittā* to mean "without sexual organs" (*nimittarahita*) and then glosses *itthipaṇḍaka* as *animittā* (*Smpk* II, p. 546 quoted in Zwilling 1992: 208). Zwilling points out that in rendering the term *pandaka* as eunuch in the ancient times as well as in modern times there has been some confusion. Such confusion seems to have had an effect on Buddhaghoṣa too, as it is clear from the above definition of *itthipaṇḍaka*.

Buddhaghoṣa in the *Samantapāsādikā* (III.1068-69 quoted in Zwilling 1992: 208) produces a list of five kinds of *paṇḍakas*:

1. *Napuṁsakapaṇḍaka* — a congenitally impotent person (*yo pana patisandhiyamyeva abhāvako uppanno, ayam napuṁsakapaṇḍako*).
2. *Usūyapaṇḍaka* — a person, who out of frustration, satisfies his desires by watching others engage in sexual relations (*yassa paresaṃ ajjhācāraṃ passanto usūyāya uppannāya pariḷāho vupasammati, ayaṃ usūyapaṇḍako*).
3. *Pakkhapaṇḍaka* — in retribution of immoral acts, one becomes temporarily impotent for fourteen "black days" of the month but regains his potency during the fourteen "white days", that is from the new to the full moon (*ekacco paṇa akusalavipākānubhāvena, kālapakkhe paṇḍako hoti, junhapakkhe panassa pariḷāho vupasammati, ayam pakkhapaṇḍako*).
4. *Asittapaṇḍaka* — a person who satisfies his sexual desires by fellating another to ejaculation (*yassa paresam aṅgajātam mukhena gahetvā asucinā assitassa parilāho upasammati, ayam asittapaṇḍako*).
5. *Opakkamikapaṇḍaka* — one who attains ejaculation by means of a certain effort or artifice (*yassa upakkamena bījāni apanītāni, ayaṃ opakkamikapaṇḍako*).

Zwilling, based on this explanation of Buddhaghoṣa,

concludes that for the Buddhist commentarial tradition the term *paṇḍaka* did not signify eunuch (castrated person) because except the first category which is lacking the capacity to experience any sexual activity, the rest have the potential for either erection, ejaculation or the experience of sexual pleasure (1992: 205).

Under the term *paṇḍaka* several types of sexual dysfunctions and variations have been included for the reason that they all share the common quality of being *napuṁsaka* (lacking maleness). All the five types are unable to meet the normative sex role expectations for a male adult. In the Vinaya literature, references to *paṇḍaka*s are made almost invariably within the context of sexual, specifically homosexual behaviour, and in many societies a tendency to label a boy or man who participates in homosexual activity as not being a "real man" can be found (Karlen 1971: 478). In India, since the *Atharvaveda* period, *paṇḍaka*s had been considered as a distinct group, different from ordinary males and females, and apparently transvestite. The Pali Vinaya scriptures also recognize '*paṇḍaka*'s' as a distinct group. The term '*manussa-paṇḍaka*' refers to '*paṇḍaka*s' and *manussapurisa* (human-male) refers to ordinary male (*Vin* III.35ff.).

Regarding the psychological make-up of *paṇḍaka*s, Buddhaghoṣa states that they are full of intensified passions (*ussannakilesa*); that their lusts are insatiable (*avūpasantapariḷāha*) and that they are dominated by libido (*pariḷāhavegābhibhūta*) and the desire for lovers like prostitutes (*vesiya*) and coarse young girls (*thūlakumārikā*) (*Smpk* III.1042 quoted in Zwilling 1992: 212). Zwilling points out that the psychological view presented of *paṇḍaka* is more concerned with behaviour and the psychological characteristics of the stereotypical "bad" woman (Zwilling 1992: 205). Vasubandhu says that *paṇḍakas* are incapable of religious career (*saṁvara*) because they are obsessed with the defiling passions of both sexes (*ubhayāsrayakilesādhimātrat ā*), and they lack the sense of modesty and shame necessary to cancel out them (*Abhidharmakoṣa* IV.43 quoted in Zwilling 1992: 212). Neglected by the parent, a *paṇḍaka* does not develop the strong emotional ties to them which would make him capable of committing the heaviest sins of matricide or patricide (ibid. IV.97a-c).

The *Vinaya* punishes all intentional sexual conduct by monks or nuns, providing a hierarchy of penalties depending upon the nature of the offence. Penetration with emission calls forth expulsion from the Order, regardless of the gender or species of the partner or the orifice penetrated (*Vin* III.15f.). Under the first *pārājikā* rule, possibilities of homosexual contacts among the male community have been mentioned:

> A monk commits sin with a sleeping monk. Awakened he agrees; both should be expelled. Awakened he does not agree; the defiler should be expelled. A monk commits sin with a sleeping novice. Awakened he agrees; both should be expelled. Awakened he does not agree; the defiler should be expelled. A novice commits sin with a monk. Awakened he agrees; both should be expelled. A novice commits sin with a sleeping novice. Awakened ... should be expelled.
>
> – *Vin* III.33; *BD* I.50f.

In the *Mahāvagga*, there is a reference to sodomy by two novices who were under the care of Ven. Upananda (*BD* IV.99). However, in this case there is no special punishment given to the culprits but measures were taken to avoid such practices within the community (ibid. fn. 1). Non-orifice sexual contacts such as mutual masturbation between two monks, even though a serious offence, do not lead to defeat in the spiritual career. And also non-orgasmic contacts such as touching one's genitals have been seen as less severe offences (*Vin* III.166).

In regard to the prevalence of homosexual practices within the female community (lesbianism), it is mentioned in the *Bhikkhuṇīvibhaṅga* that two nuns who were sexually aroused, indulged in the sexual practice called *talaghātaka.*[29] Sexologically, this practice is known to involve the apposition of the sexual organs of two females in the posture referred to as "Venus Observa feminae" (Perera 1993: 202 fn. 6).

In addition to the above interpretation of *talaghātaka*, another suggestion has also been made. The term *tala* has the meaning of "palm" of one's hand, and as defined by both Pali and Sanskrit dictionaries (*PED*, p. 298; William 1990: 440) and by Horner (*BD* III.248), *talaghātaka* could imply a form of manual caress. To support this suggestion, the term *tala* has occurred in the sense of the "palm" of the hand (*Vin* IV.147). Buddhaghoṣa in the *Kaṅkhāvitaraṇī* has interpreted the term *talaghātaka* as touching female sexual organ using hand or any other object.[30] On this textual basis, we can conclude that this particular practice might have been a "manual caress" rather than a sexologically recognized practice. Moreover, *talaghātaka* has been allowed by the *Vinaya* in case of sickness (*anāpatti ābādhapaccayā ...* — *Vin* IV.261). The practice would not be allowed if it were found only in sexual activities.

There is no a definite indication to homosexual behaviour in the early Pali Nikāyas. However, the *Puggalappasādasutta* in the *Aṅguttara Nikāya* can be considered as a warning to guard

---

[29] *Vin* IV.260: *tena kho pana samayena dve bhikkhuniyo anabhiratiyā pīḷitā ovarakaṃ pavisitvā talaghātakaṃ karonti* ।

[30] *Kankhāvitaraṇī*, p. 172 in Perera 1993: 204.

against homoerotic feelings among the monks. The Buddha warns that a monk devoted (*abhippasanna*) to another, who thinks: "This person is dear and pleasing (*piyo manāpo*) to me" will be adversely affected if his friend is suspended or expelled by the Order, leaves, becomes mentally unbalanced or dies (*AN* III.507-08). Buddhaghoṣa, in the commentary to the *Cakkavattīsīhanādasutta* (*DN* III.70), describing the progressive degeneration in the lifespan of human beings following upon their increasing corporeality and sinfulness, takes the expression "wrong conduct" (*micchādhamma*) as "the sexual desire of men for men and women for women".[31] It is clear that the Pali tradition regarding homosexual behaviour holds a negative attitude concerning both the lay and the clergy.

The *Papañcasūdanī* in its definition of the third precept of abstaining from sexual misconduct (*kāmesumicchācāra*) first refers to persons who should not be sexually associated with (*agamanīyaṭṭhāna*). At the head of the list of such persons, male partners are mentioned as those who should not be sexually associated with.[32] The unknown author of the commentary to the *Abhidharmasamuccaya*[33] also sees gay sexuality as a breach of the third precept. Even though, the female's sexual activity with another female is not mentioned, we can assume that the rule is equally applicable to both sexes. According to Buddhaghoṣa, such kinds of sexual union is extremely blameworthy (*ekanta nindito*) and is a lower practice (*lāmakācāro*) (fn. p. 129).

[31] *Sumaṅgalavilāsinī*, III, p. 172 quoted in Zwilling 1992: 213.

[32] *Mūlapaṇṇāsa — Aṭṭhakathā*, I, p. 207 (Devanāgarī): *tattha agamanīyaṭṭhānam nāma purisānam tāva* ... ।

[33] *Abhidharmasamuccayabhāṣyam*, ed. Natmal Tatia, p. 63 quoted in Zwilling 1992: 213.

There are preventive measures taken to remove homosexual behaviour from the monastic community. As we have earlier mentioned, for a monk, any sexual act involving orifice-penetration with genitals ensues expulsion from the order. Any other sensual or sexual contact, with a woman, *paṇḍaka*, or man, does not amount to the expulsion from the Order. A homosexual act such as getting a novice to masturbate a monk is a serious offence (*Vin* III.117). If a monk touches a novice's privacy, it is a minor offence (ibid.). It is forbidden for two nuns to sleep in the same bed (*Vin* IV.288f.) and to share the same bedcover (*Vin* IV.289) which can be seen as preventive measures of potential homosexual behaviour. It is a lesser offence, or wrongdoing, for monks to eat from the same dish or to share the same couch (*Vin* II.124). The prohibition of the entrance of *paṇḍakas* into the community was because sexual blemish could arise due to their unusual sexuality.

Pali Buddhist texts have not ignored the causes of one's rebirth either as a hermaphrodite or as *paṇḍaka* or of being castrated. According to the *Aṭṭhasālinī* (pp. 264-65 quoted in Harvey 2000: 414) and *Visuddhimagga*, the birth as a hermaphrodite or as a eunuch (*paṇḍaka*) is a result of inadequacy shown in the performance of meritorious activities (*Vism*, p. 457; Ñāṇamoli 1991: 514). The story of the nun Isidāsī in the *Therīgāthā* draws a reason from the realm of sexual morality for one's rebirth as a *napuṁsaka* (neither a male nor a female) and for being castrated (*Thig* verses 435-47). As a consequence of seducing another's wife in a previous life, she happened to suffer castration (*nillacchesi*)[34] in several

[34] *Paramatthadīpanī* (Devanāgarī), p. 296: *nillacchesīti purisabhāvassa lakkhaṇabhūtāni nillacchesi nīhari* ।

lives in the animal plain and was born as a *napuṁsaka* (*neva mahilā na puriso* — neither a female nor a male).[35] A similar story is found in the *Mahānāradakassapa Jātaka*. In consequence of committing adultery, a person first happens to suffer in hell, then becomes subject to castration in several existences in the animal realm, and is born in the human world as a *napuṁsaka* (*n'ev'itthi na pumsakasiṃ manusatte sudullabhe, tassa kammasa nissando paradāra-gamanassa me* — *J* VI.238).[36] It is clear that the losing of sexual organ is a condition that appears at one's birth due to previous unskilful acts, particularly due to sexual misbehaviour. Castration is also seen as a result of sexual misbehaviour.

Putting homosexual behaviour in the monastic code as well as lay sexual ethics shows that there is no room for the practice. For monks, if the homosexual act involved orifice — penetration, it deserved expulsion from the Order. Any kind of homosexual act done by a monk or a nun is a violation of celibate vow, so, there are rules in the monastic code in order to prevent even potentialities of homosexual behaviour. The persons like hermaphrodites and *paṇḍaka*s were perceived as homosexual potentials and consequently were prevented from gaining entry to the monastic community as a measure of curbing the intrusion of such practices.

As for the laity, the commentarial literature sees gay sex as a breach of the third precept while the phenomenon of homosexuality is perceived as a condition arising in the course of moral degeneration. It can be concluded that Buddhism recognizes homosexuality in the same degree of

---

[35] *Paramatthadīpanī* (Devanāgarī), p. 296: *neva mahilā na purisoti itthīpi purisopi na homi, jātinapumsakoti attho* ।

[36] *J* VI.239: *nevitthi na pumāti napumsakattaṃ sandhāyāha* ।

gravity as heterosexuality. In the words of Zwilling, in Indian Buddhist writings, homosexuality was derogated to much the same degree as heterosexual acts (1992: 209).

Pornography

Pornography is defined as written or visual material that stimulates sexual feelings whose primary aim is to sexually arouse the observer or the reader. It is also referred to as porn, smut and obscene material. The term "pornography" is derived from *porneia*, the Greek word for prostitute, and means "the writings of and about prostitutes".[37]

In most countries, obscene literature, art, film or live display are legally prohibited. The word obscene usually means morally offensive according to the general and prevailing standards of morality in any particular culture, society or group. The Supreme Court of United States has attempted to provide a standard definition of pornography; pornography is that which appeals to the prurient interest (lust and desire for the impure in thought and deed) and which has no redeeming social, literary, or artistic value (Thiroux 1995: 357).

In the *Vinaya Piṭaka*, under the *bhikkhu pācittiya* rule XXVI, there is a reference to an obscene picture drawn by a monk (*Vin* IV.60f.). The story says that Ven. Udayin was skilled in the making of robes. A certain nun having approached him, requested to make a robe for her. Then he, having sewed a robe for her, having made it well dyed and well worked, raised up (or painted) in its middle "an imaginative design" (*paṭibhānacitta*) (*Vin* IV.61). Buddhaghoṣa has explained the

---

[37] http://sexuality.jbpub.com/ref_links_visit.cfm?WeblinksID=3583 and URL= http://www.wylde.com/paraphilia.html

term *paṭibhānacitta* as *vippakatamethunaṃ ittipurisarūpaṃ* (*VinA* 804). Rhys Davids and W. Stede translate the phrase as "interrupted intercourse" (*PED*, p. 628). Based on this rendering, Horner translates the expression as "the form of a woman and a man in interrupted intercourse" (*BD* II.285 fn. 5). Perera does not agree with the translation "interrupted" in this context and contends that it should be as "uncompleted" (1993: 177). Through a reading of several contexts wherein the term *vippakata* occurs within the canon, he concludes that a meaningful translation of *vippakatamethuna* would be (a scene of a woman and a man in) unfinished intercourse – which really means a scene of man and a woman indulging in the sex act (Perera 1993: 177).

Another interpretation may be suggested on the basis of the etymology of the word. The past participle passive *pakata* (Sanskrit *prakṛta* – *pra+kṛ*) could mean "natural", or "by nature" and accordingly *vippakata* (*vi + prakṛta*) may also mean "unnatural", "out of normalcy" and therefore of diverse forms. In Sanskrit, the form *viprakṛti* gives the meanings of "change" or "variation" (Williams 1990: 975). On the ground of this linguistic analysis, Perera states that *vippakatamethuna* could indicate "unusual forms of sexual congress" involving different postures (1993: 178).

It is evident that the drawing made by Udayin, had been an obscene picture because people seeing the nun wearing the robe with the picture criticized the nuns' behaviour as fearless of blame, sly and shameless to the extent to paint "imaginative pictures" (male–female sexual practices) on the robe (*Vin* IV.61). The phraseology employed in this context to describe the unpleasantness of the act conveys the disproval expressed at drawing such pictures even by a person exceedingly given to sexuality (*ye pi te chinnaka dhuttaka ahirika tesaṃ pi evarūpaṃ na sobheyya* — *Vin* IV.61). One of the words used here *dhuttaka* is a person frequently connected with defiling nuns. The Buddhist attitude to that sort of pictures or work of art can be understood from this episode.

A clear prohibition to produce *paṭibhāncitta* is mentioned in the *Cullavaggapāli*. When the group of six monks made *paṭibhāncitta* consisting of "a woman and a man" (or women and men) — *itthirūpakaṃ purisarūpakaṃ* — in their dwelling place, lay people accused the monks saying that they were like laity who indulged in sensual pleasures (*Vin* II.151f.). In response to the public criticism of the act, the Buddha prohibited monks to produce such paintings in the dwelling places (*Vin* IV.151f.). Instead of such drawings, the Buddha allowed other decorative designs such as *malakamma*, *latakamma*, *makaradantaka* and *pañcapatthika* (*Vin* II.152). What is noticeable regarding such paintings is that the *Vinaya* authority holds a strict attitude towards *paṭibhānacitta*, irrespective of the exact meaning of the term. This negative attitude is expressed by giving permission only to forms of arts which promote serene joy (*pasadaniyani*) and conducive to the production of disenchantment with worldly life (*nibbidapatisaṃyuttāni*).

In the *Bhikkhuṇīvibhaṅga*, there is mention of five types of places which were decorated with *paṭibhānacitta*: *rājāgāra*, *cittāgāra*, *ārāma*, *uyyāna* and *pokkharanī*. *Cittāgāra* (sportive arena) as well as the other four places were for the general public's pleasure (*Vin* IV.298). King Pasenadi of Kosala caused to draw a *paṭibhānacitta* in the *cittāgāra* of his garden and many people went to see it, including the *chabbaggiya* nuns.

Later, due to public opinion, it was prohibited for nuns to visit *cittāgāra* because the place had been decorated with *paṭibhānacitta*. Buddhaghoṣa refers to a *rājāgāra* having *paṭibhānacitta* built for the pleasure of kings (*DA*, p. 42 quoted in Perera 1993: 179). Nuns are prohibited to visit all the five places because of their being decorated with such drawings.

In this episode, the interest shown by people to visit such paintings (called *paṭibhānacitta*) is remarkable and the government's attention to fulfil such needs of people is evident. In the *Vinaya*, there is no prohibition whatsoever applying to the laity regarding visits to such places and it is recognized as a part of sensual life. The proscription has been imposed only on the monastic community. However, there had been a certain degree of disapproval at making such things even by the people given to excessive sensuality as we referred to the instance of Udayin.

To conclude the discussion on the Buddhist conception regarding sociological deviant sexual behaviour, it is clear that prostitution, homosexuality and pornography are seen as offences within the monastic code of law in Theravada Buddhism. As for the laity, any sexual act violating the third precept is a moral offence entailing harmful effects in future lives. Buddhism conceives prostitution as a lower grade profession but the prostitute is not held with stigma for a variety of reasons. Homosexuality is prohibited with all potentialities within the monastic community as any heterosexual orifice penetration sex act. However, there was a slight mildness shown for homosexual behaviour if the act is non-penetrative. Due to the threat of infiltration of homosexual practices into the monastic community, hereditary homosexuals such as hermaphrodites and *paṇḍakas* are not allowed to get the monastic membership. Such persons are recognized as mentally inadequate to pursue a spiritual career. The commentarial tradition perceives homosexual behaviour as a phenomenon appearing in a morally degenerated society and both gay and lesbian practices are considered as violations of the third precept in the lay moral code. The data regarding pornography in the scriptures is scanty and such practices are not allowed for the monastic community. For laity, visiting erotic arts is not rejected by any canonical or post-canonical texts. Finally, prostitution and homosexuality as a hereditary condition or a condition forced upon a person is recognized as a consequence of an evil deed done in a previous life, in other words, a consequence of one's bad *kamma*.

Conclusion

In the present study on the concept of deviant sexual behaviour, I have attempted to discuss deviant sexual practices divided into three categories as normal deviant sexual behaviour, pathological deviant sexual behaviour and sociological deviant sexual behaviour. In Buddhism, sexuality is a phenomenon discussed under the concept of sensuality, and therefore, it is necessary to have a Buddhist philosophical understanding of the concept of sensual desire in order to recognize the attitude to deviant sexual behaviour. Having understood the role of sensual desire in connection with a human being's existential condition, Buddhism has introduced a practical path of discipline in order to regulate desires and to completely eradicate the roots of unwholesome desires. So, in this study, both the philosophical conception of sensuality and the ethical scheme introduced to avoid deviant sexual practices within the lay society and the society of monks and nuns were examined with a view to discovering the Buddhist attitude to deviant sexual behaviour. In the final analysis, irrespective of the nature of a sex act, whether it is, acceptable or deviant, Buddhism conceives sexual behaviour as a problematic aspect of human personality because attachment to any sort of sensualistic gratification is directly conducive to suffering in the cycle of existence (*saṁsāra*).

In this discussion, I examined first the Buddhist psychological and philosophical understanding of sensuality and sexuality. Buddhism recognizes sensuality as a latent tendency in the human psyche. The concepts of *āsava* and *anusaya* explain the basic and the deepest structure of human personality within which desire for sensuality is perceived as an integral part (Hamilton 1996: 9). In the discourse of the Turning the Wheel of *Dhamma*, the Buddha states that craving (*taṇhā*) leads to rebirth and causes the sentient being to get attached to desired phenomena (*SN* V.421). Craving manifests in three modes: craving for sensual pleasures (*kāma-taṇhā*), craving for existence (*bhava-taṇhā*) and craving for annihilation (*vibhava-taṇhā*) (ibid.). In accordance with this discourse, the sole cause of suffering is desire and its cessation is the ultimate bliss (*mutti*) (ibid.). Then, it comes to be known that sensual/sexual desire is a crucial factor in the emotional realm of the human psyche and is contributory to suffering. Volitional actions of a human being are aimed at achieving sensual pleasure,[1] leading to sexual gratification. The highest sensual pleasure, according to the Buddhist teaching, is found in sexual gratification (*AN* I.1). Because of the thirst for sensual gratification, a human being is affected by psychological obsession, which is a condition that makes a person blind to ethical values ranging from relative socio-cultural values up to universal values such as not taking another person's life, property, sexual partner and so on. The origin of sexual deviation can be traced to this sort of psychological condition.

According to the early Buddhist theory of cause and effect (*paṭiccasamuppāda*), the realm of human activity (*saṁkhāra* = *kamma*) is conditioned by ignorance (*avijjā*).[2] One's perception

---

[1] *Aṅguttaranikāya*, BJTS, vol. 19, pt. 2, p. 21 in Gamage 1998: 147.

[2] *SN* II.2: *avijjā paccayā bhikkhave saṅkhārā* ।

of the five aggregates (psycho-physical complex) as *atta* ("I" consciousness) leads the human being to perform negative and positive (*kusalākusala kamma*) volitional activities, which condition rebirth consciousness. Even though, in reality, there is no entity at all that can be grasped as permanently existing, due to the collaborative function of the five aggregates, an ordinary person forms the view that there is "I". This ego-centred perception is recognized in Buddhism as the root of continued existence (Kalupahana 1994: 75). The same theory can be applied to the concept of sense pleasures, that is, the erroneous perception that they are really stable things that give permanent satisfaction, the person gets attached to sensual gratification. The *Sutta Nipāta* mentions:

> Forms, sounds, tastes, smells, contacts and all mental phenomena are desired, pleasant and lovely as long as it is said, "They exist".[3]

In the ultimate sense, it is clear that attachment to sense pleasures is a consequence of a fault in one's cognitive faculty. It is clear from the teaching in the *Sutta Nipāta* that sensual desire is involved in the view of existence (*atthitā diṭṭhi*) which is denied by Buddhism as one extreme conducive to the formation of wrong ideologies and consequently the arising of *dukkha*.[4]

It should be said that Buddhism does not deny sense

---

[3] Norman 1993, II: 88;
Sn 759: *rūpā, saddā, rasā, gandhā, phassā dhammā ca kevalā*
iṭṭhā kantā manāpā ca, yāva' 'atthī' ti vuccati ।
The Paramatthajotikā II, p. 509: on the underlined words says: *yāvat'atthī ti vuccatī ti yāvatā ete cha'ārammaṇā "atthi" ti vuccanti* ।

[4] *SN* II.17: *sabbaṃ atthīti kho kaccāyana ayaṃ eko anto* । *sabbaṃ natthīti ayaṃ dutiyo anto* ॥

pleasure as one among several kinds of pleasures achievable by a human being.[5] In early Pali sources, there are instructions for lay disciples to make their sensualistic life more successful. It is accepted that sensual objects are beautiful, pleasant and makes one happy; they are characterized with diversity and consequently the individual is obsessed with desire for them.[6] Every conditioned phenomenon is characterized by impermanence, suffering and selflessness.[7] This nature inherent in sensual objects causes mental and physical pain to the individual (*Sn.* 760; Norman 1993: 88). Being unable to see the reality of sense pleasure and objects, the individual forms the view that sensuality has real existence (i.e. as eternal existence). It is clear that seeking sensual pleasure involves a wrong conception. As a consequence of this misperception, the sentient being becomes subject to the cycle of rebirth and death, which is recognized by Buddhism as suffering.

The Theravada Buddhist concept of the human body was discussed with the purpose of recognizing the relationship between the human body and deviant sexual behaviour. Religious understanding of sexuality and spirituality is closely linked with the attitude towards the human body (Gross 1993: 195). According to the Freudian concept of erogenous zones in the body, one can engage in a deviant sexual act by means other than those of the proper sexual organ (genitals) (Neu 1995: 87). And it is pointed out that various parts of the body

---

[5] *MN* I.398: *yaṃ kho ānanda ime pancakāmaguṇe paṭicca uppajjati sukhaṃ somanassaṃ idaṃ vuccati kāmasukhaṃ* ı *yo kho ānanda evaṃ vadeyya: etaparamaṃ sukhaṃ somanassaṃ paṭisamvedentīti, idamasassa nānujānāmi, taṃ kissa hetu: att' ānanda etamhā sukhā aññaṃ sukhaṃ ...*

[6] *Sn* 50: *kāmāhi citrā madhurā manoramā*
virūparūpena mathenti cittaṃ

[7] *AN* I.286; *MN* I.336: *sabbe saṅkhārā aniccā* ı

are sexually attractive to the person and through them there arises a variety of sexual deviant acts. Anal sex and oral sex can be given as examples. Buddhism recognizes one's own body as a source that can cause deviation from the celibate life (*Vin* III.35). A member of the opposite sex is recognized as a barrier to spiritual development. Specially, the female body is perceived as a danger to a religious career (*itthi malaṃ brahmacariyassa* — *SN* I.38; *MN* I.459f.).

In commentarial Buddhism, Ven. Buddhaghoṣa has developed a clear negativism about the human body. However, even early Buddhism is not completely free from negativism regarding the human body when it emphasizes the analytical approach to it. From the canonical stage to the commentarial development of Buddhism, the human body has been subjected to discussion because of its function as a seductive power for the religious practitioner. The Pārājikā section of the *Vinaya* shows the extent to which the body becomes a source of non-conforming sexual acts. This threat from the human body confronted by the monks led the early scriptural authors as well as commentarial writers to form a negative attitude towards the human body.

In the first part of the fourth chapter, the two norms of the Buddhist ethical code used to determine a sexual act as normal or deviant were explained. The norm of celibacy, complete abstinence from sexual contact is established for the monastic community and the norm of chastity, which involves confining sexual contact only to one's spouse, is prescribed for the lay people. The observance of either celibacy or chastity is left open to individual choice, but after a person opts for the former, any breach of the precept is considered as a moral offence. There are twenty-one rules in the *Vinaya* prohibiting sexual activities for a monastic member and violation of any of these is considered as a deviation from the norm. These rules are concerned with hetero and homosexual penetration and such engagement brings about the loss of membership of the order and falls under the category of spiritual defeat. For a monk, sex not involving orifice-penetration calls forth various kinds of monastic punishments but not the expulsion from the order. The *Vinaya* perceives the severity of such breach of the norm as one leading to suffering in purgatory after death. So, the norm for monks and nuns regarding penetrative sex is connected with the problem of suffering associated with the consequences of bad *kamma*.

The third item of the five precepts is concerned with the sexual life of the laity. Even though there is no particular scriptural reference alluding to the prohibition of polygamous marriage, the third precept is always interpreted as one practised within monogamous marriage. Regarding the sex life of a married couple, Buddhism does not interfere as some other religions do. There is no textual reference emphasizing reproduction as the aim of sexual union by a married couple. The reason for this can be understood in terms of the Buddhist concept of sensuality, that is, the recognition of sexual pleasure as the highest form of sensual gratification. Ethical issues in a married person's sex life in Buddhism are connected with adultery or extramarital relationships. Therefore, sex within marriage is brought into an ethical frame and the individual is encouraged to confine his life of sexual pleasure within it. Buddhism considers adultery as a serious moral breach having the potential of destroying one's sexual life and marriage in many lives, as well illustrated in the story of the enlightened elder nun Isidāsī (*Th* II.435-37).

Through the reading of the Pali canonical and post-canonical texts, it was seen that on certain occasions adultery has been recognized as a slight offence which can be excused by means of simple measures like warning the spouse, intervention of a virtuous third party, and sometimes by beating the culprits without going to legal action. In deciding a sex act as deviant committed either by a clergy or a lay person, as in any other act, volition (*saṃcetanā*) plays the crucial role.

The latter part of the fourth chapter examined the data in the Pali scriptures on premarital sex, which is considered as a normal deviant sex act, and it was seen that monks were not expected to be closely associated with unmarried girls (*thullakumārī*) due to the danger of premarital sex from the side of the female and the resulting harm to the celibate life of the monk.[8] In the Jātaka, premarital sex for the female has not been approved and virginity is appreciated because the loss of purity before marriage could bring about social disgrace to parents (Chalmers 1981, vol. I: 244). Premarital sex or fornication is denied for another practical problem could arise from such sexual contacts, i.e. the birth of illegitimate children.

Masturbation is not allowed for the monks and nuns and is an offence, which is second only to the first *pārājikā* offence. In the first occurrence within the Buddhist order of monks when committing self-masturbation by a monk was reported, the Buddha explains thus why such an act should not be performed:

> *Dhamma* has been taught for stilling passion in various

[8] *Vin* V.129; the term is defined as *pancakāmaguṇika-rāgena-thūlatāya thullakumārīti vuccati* in *PED*, p. 310.

> ways, for the subduing of conceit ... for the elimination of attachment, for the cutting through the round of becomings, for the destruction of craving, for the passionlessness. ... – *BD* I.194f.

This statement indicates how the act is damaging to the final goal of Buddhism, which is the eradication of desire and the cessation of the suffering cycle of *saṁsāra*. From the Buddhist doctrinal point of view, masturbation is not a simple and ethically neutral action; it directly and adversely affects the ultimate aim of recluse life. Further, referring to the effect of this act upon society, the Buddha says that it is not conducive to the enhancement of the faith of those who already have faith and for winning over the faith of those who still do not have faith (*Vin* III.111). As masturbation is not involved in orifice penetration, it is not considered as severe as hetero or homosexual penetration.

However, under the celibate vow, masturbation is not allowed for monks as it is involved in sexual fantasies. An attempt was made to draw the ethical implications of the practice of masturbation in the light of Buddhist ethical criteria and sexological findings. There is no specific moral norm discussed in Buddhism applicable to masturbation in connection with the sexual practices of lay persons.

Any form of auto-eroticism is not allowed for the members of the Buddhist recluse Order. It is evident from the imposition of the rule of defeat for those who practise self-fellation- putting the genital into one's own mouth (*Vin* III.35) or self-pederasty — entering genital into one's own anus (ibid.). In view of monks and nuns, they themselves have made a vow of complete abstinence from sexual gratification. On the other hand, Buddhist monasticism is aimed at eliminating sensual desire, so that any act conducive to sense gratification is denied as unwholesome (*adhamma*). Therefore, if one transgresses the vow of celibacy by engaging in any kind of sex act, that act is perceived as caused by unrighteous passion (*adhamma rāga*). For a monk, his body cannot be used for sexual needs, and if it is used, it amounts to sexual abuse of one's own body. So, in the context of Buddhist monasticism, masturbation is a sexual deviation.

Pathological deviations, rape, voyeurism, exhibitionism, paedophilia and incest are considered as moral breaches in relation to the third precept and the first *pārājikā* rule and other *Vinaya* rules. Many forms of sexual assaults against women and different kinds of rape, which are known to the modern sexologists and psychologists, have been mentioned in the *Vinaya* and in the other texts. It is notable that more the raped is morally higher, the consequences are more serious for the rapist. A considerable discussion regarding nun rapists can be found and such persons were not allowed to enter the *saṅgha* community. However, it is limited to the act of raping a nun who has attained perfection in conduct. Having a forcible sexual contact with a novice or with a *bhikkhuṇī* with her consent does not make the male a *bhikkhuṇīdūsaka*. It is included under adultery. In addition to pointing out its disastrous kammic consequences in the next life, Buddhist monastic community takes preventive measures to avoid sexual offences within the community. Under the discussion of *paṇḍaka*, Buddhaghoṣa refers to a classical voyeur who masturbates while looking others engaging in sexual intercourse (*Smpk* III.1068-69 quoted in Zwilling 1992: 208). In the *Vinaya*, the references to exhibitionism are very few and it amounts only to a slight offence.[9] In this case, according

[9] *Vin* II.262-63; and also a reference to exhibitionism in *Vin* III.205.

to the *Vinaya*, physical contact is a necessary condition for considering a sexual offence as a serious one.[10]

There are references to incest in the *Sutta* and the *Vinaya Piṭaka*. A variety of incestuous contacts have been mentioned and some could not be true but mere imaginary additions by the writers of the Vinaya texts as precautions for future possibilities within the *saṅgha* society. According to the commentarial tradition, incest is a result of social degeneration due to various reasons.

Data regarding paedophilia is very rare and one instance has been mentioned under the first *pārājikā* rule.[11] The *Vinaya* authority had not seen it as a serious offence because there was only physical touch. In contrast to the *Vinaya* position, such an act falls under a criminal offence under the modern legal procedure (Araji 1992: 177). In this case, it is a question why the touch of a sexual organ has not been fallen under *pārājikā* offence? It can be assumed that the partner's full capacity to engage in sex might have been the criterion for considering a sexual offence to be serious. All the five forms of pathological sexual deviations are considered as moral offences and rape is considered a very serious offence which results in dreadful consequences in this very life (*DhA* II.49f. quoted in *DPPN*, vol. I, p. 419).

Finally, I have examined three forms of deviant sexual

---

10 *Vin* III.120: *Bhikkhuvibhanga sanghadisesa* rule II is an example of tactile contact which is only second to the defeat wrong (for monks); *Vin* IV.220: the eight *pārājikā*, in the *Bhikkhunivibhanga* consider tactile contact of opposite sex partner by a nun with a passionate mind as severe as sexual union.

11 *Vin* III.34: *tena kho pana samayena aññataro piṇḍacāriko bhikkhu pīṭake nippannaṃ dārikaṃ passitvā sāratto anguṭṭhaṃ angajātaṃ pavesesi, sā kālaṃ akāsi* ।

practices belonging to sociological sexual deviations. The sociological sexual practice of prostitution is viewed as a problematic form of behaviour and several causal explanations have been given for a person's choice of a life as a prostitute. Through the Pali sources, we can recognize an established social structure that was supportive to the existence of prostitution as a social institution. Ideologically, concepts of *kamma* (Horner 1990: 94) and caste were behind the justification of one's service as a sex worker and Buddhist scriptures have accepted that a person's unskilful actions in a past life can determine her life as a prostitute. As for social structure, in certain cases, the state was directly supportive of establishing courtesanship (*nagarasobhinī*) with the purpose of earning indirect economic profits for the state. Poverty and destitution also were reasons for some women to select the profession. Buddhism accepts the right of religious practice irrespective of one's career and in that sense, prostitutes belonging to both the lower level and higher levels of the social hierarchy could support Buddhism, and some prostitutes did in fact become spiritual winners after reforming their lifestyle.

Homosexual behaviour is familiar to the early disciplinary code and several cases were referred to in the previous chapters. The concepts of *paṇḍaka* and *ubhatovyañjanaka* (eunuch and hermaphrodite) are primarily concerned with homosexual behaviour. Eunuch or *paṇḍaka* is a complicated term and concept because in one instance it stands for a castrated person. According to Buddhaghoṣa, one can become a *paṇḍaka* by birth. And also the term *napuṁsaka* is frequently used to refer to a person who is lacking proper masculinity and femininity. It is not necessary to be castrated to call a person a eunuch.

The *Samantapāsādikā* presents a list of fivefold *paṇḍakas* and they all bear the characteristic of lacking the proper maleness or femaleness and resorted to improper ways of getting sexual gratification instead of heterosexual genital intercourse. One's birth as a hermaphrodite or as a *paṇḍaka* is a result of one's own evil deeds done in a former life. Castration is mentioned in several places in the commentarial sources, but a reference to human castration could not be found. Both the abnormal persons referred to above are prohibited from entering the Order and if they appear in a *saṅgha*'s gathering ready to perform *pātimokkha* ritual, it has to be withheld.[12]

Buddhaghoṣa has examined the psychological make-up of the *paṇḍaka* and has made the observation that such a person is unable to pursue a religious career (*Smpk* III.1042 quoted in Zwilling 1992: 212). However, prohibiting their admission into the society of Buddhist recluses can be understood as a preventive measure to avoid unpleasant sexual practices among monks and nuns causing a blemish to celibacy. Homosexuality among females also has been noted. Homosexuality involved in penetrative sex brings about defeat of spiritual career as any heterosexual penetration. Mild forms like mutual masturbation or touching sexual organs fall under minor offences, which are remediable.

There is a scarcity of information on pornography. However, in the *Vinaya*, there is a reference to a drawing representing *vippakatamethuna* interrupted or uncompleted sexual intercourse between a man and a woman. And also, it is reported that monks on their dwelling places had drawn pictures on walls depicting male–female sexual intercourse.

[12] Vinaya Texts I, p. 276.

The nuns were proscribed from visiting places where *paṭibhāncitta* assumed to be paintings on the walls depicting sensualistic-sexual pictures were found. In the *Vinaya* and commentary, it is stated that there were many such places. Drawing such sensualistic pictures is not permitted for monks but for the lay people, there is no such moral restriction.

The whole discussion carried out in the previous chapters, on the theme of Buddhist attitude to deviant sexual behaviour, can be summed up in terms of the following conclusions arrived at through the available textual data on the issue:

1. According to Buddhist philosophy, deviant sexual behaviour is a phenomenon that is connected with the issue of human suffering. Buddhism recognizes sensual desire as a major aspect of craving, a foremost factor, giving rise to suffering, and also the manifestation of ignorance. Sexual desire is a major aspect of sensual gratification (*kāma-taṇhā*). Sensual objects are boundless in the world and consequently man is obsessed with desire to achieve them. Man obsessed with sensual desire becomes incapable of differentiating between good and bad. In such a mental condition, he pays no regard to social, cultural or moral restrictions. Deviant sexual behaviour is decided by social, cultural and religious norms. Desire for gratification is an inner urge, which can challenge any sort of external constraints.
2. The norm in Buddhism for sexual conformity is twofold: complete sexual abstinence and restriction of sexual contact to one's spouse. Monks and nuns are never allowed to enjoy sex as it directly affects the goal of life in the monastic order, i.e. the eradication of all kinds of

desires. If a monk or nun commits an act giving sexual pleasure, at least in mind, it is a violation of the norm of celibacy. The monastic discipline reflects a stricter attitude to sexual life of the female community. If a nun with sexually aroused mind touches a male body or offers her body, it entails expulsion from the Order (*Vin* IV.220). For a monk these sorts of actions do not amount to an offence resulting in defeat. This shows that within the same society, the application of norms has not been on an equal basis. Whatever is the nature of the sexual act, it is prohibited and penetrative sex acts are considered as leading a person into suffering in hell. If a lay person commits adultery, the result is considered to be very serious, and the consequences of such an act could be a life in a future existence productive of painful results.[13] A classical example to show how Buddhism sees a deviant sex act of adultery is the story of Isidāsī. Sex for the laity is accepted within marriage without restrictions but violation of the norm is a serious offence. The norms for both societies, recluse and lay, are aimed at the betterment of the human being and breaches of the norms are considered as resulting in suffering and deviation from the spiritual path of Buddhism leading to *nibbana*.

3. The Buddhist examination into non-conforming sexual practices was carried out in relation to the code of conduct of monastic community and the third item of the five precepts prescribed for the laity. Admission into the Order and observance of precepts are not

---

13 *Dh* 2 : *manopubbangamā dhammā, manomoseṭṭhā manomayā, manasā ce paduṭṭhena bhāsati vā karoti vā tato naṃ dukkha manveti cakkaṃ va vahato padaṃ* ।

commanded but once a person volunteers to take up the discipline, no one is supposed to make any breach of the norms of celibacy and chastity.

4. The range for deciding a sexual act as unacceptable, according to Buddhist teachings, covers a number of relationships as found in sexological studies, and even go beyond the sexological definitions of deviation. According to sexology, one can have a heterosexual contact with mutual consent between an adult male and female. As this definition implies, even though a couple is not married to each other, they can enjoy sex with mutual consent. Sexological studies are based on observations and bear a certain degree of value-free attitude judgements on them. In contrast, Buddhism, perceives all the unacceptable forms of sexual behaviour in the context of morality and views them in terms of their consequences to a person in this life and the life after.
5. The appearance of non-conforming sexual practices like homosexual behaviour and incest are conceived as a result of moral deviation due to various reasons and the prevalence of wrong ideas in society. Even though certain forms of sexual behaviour like homosexual behaviour and masturbation may be considered as acceptable according to basic principles of determining an act to be *kusala* (acceptable) or *akusala* (unacceptable), there is no strong scriptural basis to justify such practices.

Bibliography

Primary Sources

Aṅguttara Nikāya, The, part I, ed. Richard Morris (revised by A.K. Warder), Oxford: Pāli Text Society (repr.), 1989.

Aṅguttara Nikāya, The, part II, ed. Richard Morris, London: The Pāli Text Society (repr.), 1976.

Aṅguttara-Nikāya, The, parts IV-V, ed. E. Hardy, London: The Pāli Text Society (repr.), 1979.

Aṭṭhasālinī, ed. E. Muller, London: The Pāli Text Society, 1979.

Cullaniddesa, ed. W. Stede, Oxford: The Pāli Text Society (repr.), 1988.

Dhammapada-Aṭṭhakathā I (Devanāgarī), Igatpuri, Nashik: Vipassana Research Institute, 1998.

Dhammapadaṭṭhakathā, vol. IV, ed. H.C. Norman, London: The Pāli Text Society, 1906-14.

Dhammasaṅganī, ed. E. Muller, London: The Pāli Text Society (repr.), 1978.

Dasabhumikasutra et Bodhisattvabhumi (Chapitres Vihara et Bhumi), J. Radher, Paris: Paul Geunther, 1926.

Dīgha Nikāya, The, vols I-II, ed. T.W. Rhys Davids and J.E. Carpenter, London: The Pāli Text Society (repr.), 1975-82.

Dīgha Nikaya, The, vol. III, ed. J.E. Carpenter, Oxford: The Pāli Text Society (repr.), 1992.

Iti-Vuttaka, ed. Ernst Windisch, London: The Pāli Text Society (repr.), 1975.

Jātaka, vols I-VI, ed. V. Fausboll, Oxford: The Pāli Text Society (repr.), 1990-91.

Kāvyaśekhara Mahā Kāvyaya, ed. R.A. Liyanarcci, Colombo: Samayawardhana Book Shop, 2007.

The Khuddaka-Pāṭha Together with Its Commentary Paramatthajotikā I, ed. Helmer Smith, London: Pāli Text Society (repr.), 1978.

Le Traite de la Grande Vertude Sagesse de Naagarjuna, Etienne Lamotte, Louvain: Institut Orientaliste, tome II, 1949.

Mahaniddesa, parts I-II, ed. L. de La Vallee Poussin and E.J. Thomas, London: The Pāli Text Society (repr.), 1978.

Manorathapūraṇī: Buddhaghoṣa's commentary on the Aṅguttara-Nikāya, ed. E. Hardy, Max Walleser and Hermann Kopp, London: The Pāli Text Society, 1963-73.

Milindapañho, ed. V. Trenckner, London: The Pāli Text Society (repr.), 1986.

Majjhima-Nikāya, The, vol. I, ed. V. Trenckner, Oxford: The Pāli Text Society (repr.), 1993.

Majjhima-Nikaya, The, vols II-III, ed. Robert Chalmers, Oxford: The Pāli Text Society (repr.), 1993-94.

Pacittiya-Mahāvagga-Aṭṭhakathā (Devanāgarī), Igatpuri, Nashik: Vipassana Research Institute, 1998.

Paramaṭṭhadīpanī: Dhammapāla's Commentary on the Therīgāthā, ed. E. Muller, London: Pāli Text Society, 1893.

Paramaṭṭhadīpanī: Theragāthā-Aṭṭhakathā, parts I-II (Devanāgarī), Igatpuri, Nashik: Vipassana Research Institute, 1998.

Paramaṭṭhadīpanī: Therīgāthā-Aṭṭhakathā, Igatpuri, Nashik: Vipassana Research Institute, 1998.

Paramaṭṭhadīpanī: Vimānavatthu-Aṭṭhakathā (Devanāgarī), Igatpuri, Nashik: Vipassana Research Institute, 1998.

Paramaṭṭhajotika: Suttanipāta-Aṭṭhakathā, I, Igatpuri, Nashik: Vipassana Research Institute, 1998.

Samantapāsādikā: Buddhaghoṣa's Commentary on the Vinaya Piṭaka, vols I-VIII, ed. Juniro Takakusu, Makoto Nagai and Kogen Mizuno, London: The Pāli Text Society, 1947-75.

Saṃyutta-Nikāya, part III, ed. M. Leon Feer, London: The Pāli Text Society (repr.), 1975.

Saṃyutta-Nikāya, parts I, II, IV-V, ed. M. Leon Fear, Oxford: The Pāli Text Society (repr.), 1989-94.

Sāratthadīpanī Dutiyo Bhāgo: Nidānavagga and Khandhavagga Aṭṭhakathā

(Devanāgarī), Igatpuri, Nashik: Vipassana Research Institute, 1998.

Sumaṅgalavilāsinī: Commentary to the Dīgha Nikāya, 3 vols, ed. T.W. Rhys Davids, J.E. Carpenter and W. Stede, London: Pāli Text Society, 1886–1932.

Sumaṅgalavilāsinī: Sīlakkhandhavagga, Mahāvagga and Pathikavagga Aṭṭhakathā (Devanāgarī), Igatpuri, Nashik: Vipassana Research Institute, 1998.

Sutta-Nipāta, ed. Dines Anderson and Helmer Smith, Oxford: The Pāli Text Society (repr.), 1990.

Thera- and Therī-Gāthā, The, ed. K.R. Norman and L. Alsdorf (2nd edn), Oxford: The Pāli Text Society (repr.), 1990.

Udana, ed. Paul Steinthal, London: The Pāli Text Society (repr.), 1982.

Vimānavatthu and Peṭavatthu, ed. N.A. Jayawickrama, London: The Pāli Text Society, 1977.

Vinaya Piṭakam, The, vols I-II, ed. Hermann Oldenberg, London: The Pāli Text Society (repr.), 1964-77.

Vinaya Piṭakam, The, vols III-IV, ed. Hermann Oldenberg, Oxford: The Pāli Text Society (repr.), 1993.

Visuddhimagga, The, ed. C.A.F. Rhys Davids, London: The Pāli Text Society (repr.), 1975.

Secondary Sources

Amoroso, Henry, 1965, *Sexual Behavior and Customs of the French*, New York: Macfadden Books.

Ard, Ben N., 1989, *Rational Sex Ethics*, New York: Peter Lang Publishing.

Basham, A.L., 1951, *History and Doctrines of the Ajivakas: A Vanished Indian Religion*, London: Luzac.

Beal, Samuel (tr.), 1985, *The Romantic Legend of Sakya Buddha: A Translation of the Chinese Version of the Abhiniskramanasutra*, Delhi: Motilal Banarsidass, (repr.).

Bodhi, Bhikkhu (tr.), 1992, *The All Embracing Net of Views: The Brahmajala Sutta and Its Commentaries*, Kandy: Buddhist Publication Society (repr.), 1992.

——, 2000, *The Connected Discourses of the Buddha: A Translation of the Saṃyutta Nikāya*, Boston: Wisdom Publications.

Burgess, A.W., 1985, *Rape and Sexual Assault: A Research Handbook*, New York: Garland Publishing.

Cabezon, JoséIgnacio (ed.), 1992, *Buddhism, Sexuality, and Gender*, Delhi: Sri Satguru Publications.

Chakravarti, Uma, 1987, *Social Dimension of Early Buddhism*, Delhi: Oxford University Press.

Chalmers, Robert (tr.), 1981, *The Jātaka*, vol. I, London: The Pāli Text Society (repr.).

Clark, Lorenne M.G. and Debra J. Lewis, 1977, *Rape: The Price of Coercive Sexuality*, Toronto: Women's Educational Press.

Cowell, E.B. and W.H.D. Rouse (trs), 1981, *The Jātaka*, vol. VI, London: The Pāli Text Society (repr.).

Dasgupta, S., 1992, *A History of Indian Philosophy*, vol. I, Delhi: Motilal Banarsidass (repr.).

Daw Mya Tin, M.A. (tr.), 1990, *The Dhammapada Verses and Stories*, Varanasi: Central Institute of Higher Tibetan Studies.

Dhirasakera, Jotiya, 1982, *Buddhist Monastic Discipline*, Sri Lanka: Ministry of Higher Education.

Dutt, Sukumar, 1996, *Early Buddhist Monachism*, New Delhi: Munshiram Manoharlal (repr.).

Ford, Clellan S. and Frank A. Beach, 1951, *Patterns of Sexual Behavior*, New York: Ace Star Books (repr.).

Francis, H.T. (tr.), 1981, *The Jātaka*, vol. V, London: The Pāli Text Society (repr.).

Francis, H.T. and R.A. Neil (trs), 1981, *The Jātaka*, vol. III, London: The Pāli Text Society (repr.).

Frauwallner, Erich, 1993, *History of Indian Philosophy*, vol. I, Delhi: Motilal Banarsidass (repr.).

Freud, Sigmund, 1972/1905, *Three Essays on the Theory of Sexuality*, tr. and ed. James Strachey, New York: Avon Books.

Gagnon, J.H. and W. Simon (eds), 1967, *Sexual Deviance*, New York: Harper and Row.

Gamage, Chamindaji, 1998, *Buddhism and Sensuality: As Recorded in the Theravada Canon*, Illinois: Northwestern University.

Gehman, H.S. (tr.), 1974, *Stories of the Departed* (*Petavatthu*), London: The Pāli Text Society (repr.).

Gethin, Rupert, 1998, *The Foundations of Buddhism*, Oxford: Oxford University Press.

Gombrich, Richard F., 2002, *Theravada Buddhism: A Social History from Ancient Benares to Modern Colombo*, London: Routledge (repr.).

Gour, Sir Hari Singh, 1987, *Penal Law of India* (four volumes), rev. M.C. Desi, G. Kumar and R.B. Sethi, Allahabad: Law Publishers.

Govinda, Lama Anagarika, 1991, *The Psychological Attitude of Early Buddhist Philosophy*, Delhi: Motilal Banarsidass (repr.).

Greenwald, Harold, 1970, *The Elegant Prostitute: A Social and Psychoanalytic Study*, New York: Walker.

Grero, C. Ananda, 1996, *An Analysis of the Theravada Vinaya in the Light of Modern Legal Philosophy*, Colombo: Karunaratne and Sons.

Gross, Rita M., 1993, *Buddhism After Patriarchy: A Feminist History, Analysis, and Reconstruction of Buddhism*, Delhi: Sri Satguru Publications.

Hamilton, Sue, 1996, *Identity and Experience: The Constitution of the Human Being According to Early Buddhism*, London: Luzac Oriental.

Harvey, Peter, 1990, *An Introduction to Buddhism: Teachings, History and Practices*, New Delhi: Munshiram Manoharlal.

——, 2000, *An Introduction to Buddhist Ethics, Foundations, Values, and Issues*. Cambridge: Cambridge University Press.

Hensley, Christopher and Richard Tewksbury (eds), 2003, *Sexual Deviance: A Reader*, London: Lynne Rienner.

Herman, Judith Levis and Lisa Hirschman, 1981, *Father-Daughter Incest*, Cambridge (MA), and London: Harvard University Press.

Hiriyanna, M., 1994, *Outlines of Indian Philosophy*, Delhi: Motilal Banarsidass (repr.).

Hirschfield, M., 1935, *Sex in Human Relationships*, tr. John Rodker from French, London: John Lane the Bodley Head.

Holt, John C., 1981, *Discipline: The Canonical Buddhism of the Vinayapitaka*, Delhi: Motilal Banarsidass.

Horner, I.B. (tr.), 1974, *The Minor Anthologies of the Pāli Canon*, part IV, London: The Pāli Text Society (repr.).

——, 1990, *Women Under Primitive Buddhism*, Delhi: Motilal Banarsidass (repr.).

—— (tr.), 1992-93, *The Book of Discipline*, vols I-IV, Oxford: The Pāli Text Society (repr.).

Horton, Anne L., Barry L. Johnson, Lynn M. Roundy and Doran Williams, (eds), 1990, *The Incest Perpetrator: A Family Member No One Wants to Treat*, London: Sage Publications.

Humphreys, Christmas, 1972, *Buddhism*, London: Penguin.

Jayatilleke, K.N., 1975, *The Message of the Buddha*, New York: The Free Press.

Karlen, Arno, 1971, *Sexuality and Homosexuality*, New York: W.W. Norton.

Kalupahana, David J., 1977, *Buddhist Philosophy: A Historical Analysis*, Honolulu: The University of Hawaii, 2nd print.

——, 1992, *The Principles of Buddhist Psychology*, Delhi: Sri Satguru Publications, 1st Indian edn.

——, 1994, *A History of Buddhist Philosophy Continuities and Discontinuities*, Delhi: Mortilal Banarsidass.

Kinsey, Alfred C., Wardell B. Pomeroy and Clyde E. Martin, 1948, *Sexual Behavior in the Human Male*, Philadelphia: W.B. Saunders Co.

Kinsey, Alfred C., Wardell B. Pomeroy, Clyde E. Martin and Paul H. Gebhard, 1953, *Sexual Behavior in the Human Female*, Philadelphia: W.B. Saunders Co.

von Krafft-Ebbing, Richard, 1886, *Psychopathia Sexualis*, Stuttgart: Verlag von Ferdin and Enke.

Lamotte, E., 1949, *Le Traité de la grande vertu de sagesse de Nāgārjuna*, vol. II, Louvain: Bureaux du Muśeon.

Laws, D. Richard and William O'Donohue (eds), 1997, *Sexual Deviance: Theory, Assessment, and Treatment*, New York: The Guilford Press.

Lawson, Annette, 1990, *Adultery: An Analysis of Love and Betrayal*, Oxford: Oxford University Press.

Levin, William C., 1994, *Sociological Ideas: Concepts and Applications*, 4th edn, Belmont: Wadsworth Publishing Company.

Lewinsohn, Richard, 1958, *A History of Sexual Customs*, New York: Premier Books.

Meddegama, Udaya (tr.), 1993, *Anagatavamsa Desana: The Sermon of the Chronicle To-Be*, Delhi: Motilal Banarsidass.

Menuhin, Joel Rice, 1996, *Naked and Erect: Male Sexuality and Feeling*, Wilmette, IL: Chiron Publications.

Merleau-Ponty, Maurice, 1962, *Phenomenology of Perception*, tr. Colin Smith, London: Routledge and Kegan Paul.

Meyer, Johann Jacob, 1930, *Sexual Life in Ancient India*, 2 vols, London: George Routledge and Sons.

Misra, G.S.P., 1995, *Development of Buddhist Ethics*, Delhi: Munshiram Manoharlal (repr.).

Murcott, Susan, 1991, *The First Buddhist Women: Translations and Commentaries on the Therigatha*, Berkeley, CA: Parallax Press.

Nathan, Peter E. and Sandra L. Harris, 1975, *Psychopathology and Society*, New York: McGraw-Hill.

Ñāṇamoli, Bhikkhu (tr.), 1991, *The Path of Purification*, Kandy: Buddhist Publication Society.

Ñāṇamoli, Bhikkhu and Bodhi Bhikkhu (trs), 1995, *The Middle Length Discourses of the Buddha*, Kandy: Buddhist Publication Society.

Narada Thera (tr.), 1993, *The Dhammapada: Pāli Text and Translation with Stories in Brief and Notes*, Taipe: The Corporate Body of the Buddha Educational Foundation (4th edn).

Nevid, J.S., L.F. Rathus and S.A. Rathus, 1995, *Human Sexuality in a World of Diversity*, Boston: Allyn and Bacon.

Norman, K.R. (tr.), 1969, *The Elders' Verses I: Theragatha*, London: Pāli Text Society.

——, 1971, *The Elders' Verses II: Therigatha*, London: Pāli Text Society.

——, 1993, *The Group of Discourses II*, Oxford: The Pāli Text Society.

Nyanaponika Thera, 1992, *The Heart of Buddhist Meditation*, Kandy: Buddhist Publication Society.

Pande, Govind Chandra, 1995, *Studies in the Origins of Buddhism*, Delhi: Motilal Banarsidass (4th rev. edn).

Perera, L.P.N., 1993, *Sexuality in Ancient India: A Study Based on the Pāli Vinayapitaka*, Sri Lanka: The Post Graduate Institute of Pāli and Buddhist Studies, University of Kelaniya.

Posner, Richard A., 1992, *Sex and Reason*, Cambridge: Harvard University Press.

Rahder, Door Johannes, 1926, *Daśabūmikasūtra*, Leuven: J.B. Istas.

Rahula, Walpola, 1982, *What the Buddha Taught*, London: Gorden Fraser (repr.).

Rhys Davids, T.W., 1896, *Buddhism: Its History and Literature*, New York and London: G.P. Putnam's Sons.

——(tr.), 1992, *Dialogues of the Buddha*, part I, Oxford: The Pāli Text Society (repr.).

Rhys Davids, T.W. and Hermann Oldenberg (tr.), 1990, *Vinaya Texts*, part I (The Sacred Books of the East, vol. 13), Delhi: Motilal Banarsidass. (originally 1885).

Rhys Davids, T.W. and C.A.F. Rhys Davids (trs), 1989, *Dialogues of the Buddha*, part II, Oxford: The Pāli Text Society (repr.).

Rouse, W.H.D. (tr.), 1981, *The Jātaka*, vols. II & IV, London: The Pāli Text Society (repr.).

Russell, Diana E.H., 1984, *Sexual Exploitation: Rape, Child Sexual Abuse, and Workplace Harassment*, California: Sage Publications.

Saddhatissa, Hammalawa, 1987, *Buddhist Ethics: The Path to Nirvana*, London: Wisdom Publications.

Simon, William, 1996, *Postmodern Sexualities*, London: Routledge.

Spencer Hardy, R., 1995, *A Manual of Buddhism: In Its Modern Development*, New Delhi: Munshiram Manoharlal (repr.).

Tachibana, S., 1986, *The Ethics of Buddhism*, New Delhi: Cosmo Publications, 1st published 1926.

Thiroux, Jacques P., 1995, *Ethics: Theory and Practice*, Upper Saddle River, NJ: Prentice Hall, 5th edn.

Thomas, E.J., 1993, *The Life of Buddha as Legend and History*, Delhi: Motilal Banarsidass (Indian edn).

Walshe, Maurice (tr.), 1995, *The Long Discourses of the Buddha: A Translation of the Digha Nikaya*, Boston: Wisdom Publication (repr.).

Ward, David A., Timothy J. Carter and Robin D. Perrin, 1994, *Social Deviance: Being, Behaving, and Branding*, Boston: Allyn and Bacon.

Wijayaratna, Mohan, 1990, *Buddhist Monastic Life: According to the Texts of the Theravada Tradition*, Cambridge: Cambridge University Press.

Wilson, Liz, 1996, *Charming Cadavers: Horrific Figurations of the Feminine in Indian Buddhist Hagiographic Literature*, Chicago and London: The University of Chicago Press.

Woodward, F.L. (tr.), 1988-94, *Gradual Sayings*, vols II-V, Oxford: Pāli Text Society (repr.).

——1994, *Kindred-Sayings*, part V, Oxford: Pāli Text Society (repr.).

Articles

Allen, Clifford, 1961, "Perversions, Sexual", in *The Encyclopedia of Sexual Behavior*, ed. A. Ellis and A. Abarbanel, vol. II, New York: Hawthorn Books.

Araji, Sharon K., 1992, "Sexual Violence and Abuse", in *Encyclopedia of Sociology*, Edgar F. Borgatta (editor- in-chief), vol. 4, pp. 1772-79, New York: Macmillan Publishing Company.

Black, D., 2003, "Crime as Social Control", *American Sociological Review*, 48: 34-45; and in *Sexual Deviance: A Reader*, ed. C. Hensley and R. Tewksbury, London: Lynne Rienner Publishers.

Dalla, Rochelle L., 2003, "Exposing the 'Pretty Woman' Myth: A Qualitative Examination of the Lives of Female Streetwalking Prostitutes", in *Sexual Deviance: A Reader*, ed. C. Hensley and R. Tewksbury, pp. 149-66, London: Lynne Rienner Publishers.

Dhirasekera, Jotiya, 1979, "Celibacy", in *Encyclopaedia of Buddhism*, vol. IV, Jotiya Dhirasekera (editor-in-chief), published by the Government of Sri Lanka.

Doctor, Ronald M. and Bryan Neff, 1994, "Sexual Disorders", in *Encyclopedia of Human Behavior*, vol. 4, V.S. Ramachandran (editor-in-chief), San Diego: Academic Press.

Donat, P.L.N. and J. D'Emilio, 1992, "A Feminist Redefinition of Rape and Sexual Assault: Historical Foundations and Change", *Journal of Social Issues*, 48: 9-22.

Ellis, Albert, 1961, "Sex Offenders, the Psychology of ", in *Encyclopaedia of*

Sexual Behavior II, ed. Albert Ellis and A. Abarbanel, pp. 949-55, London: Willliam Heinemann Medical Books.

Felson, Richard and Richard Krohn, 1994, "Motives for Rape", *Journal of Research in Crime and Delinquency*, 1(4): 222-42; and in *Social Deviance, Being, Behaving, and Branding*, ed. David A. Ward, Timothy J. Carter and Robin D. Perrin, Boston: Allyn and Bacon.

Freud, Sigmund, 2001 (1919), A Child Is Being Beaten, in *The Complete Psychological Works of Sigmund Freud*, vol. 17, pp. 179-204, Standard Edition.

Freund, K., 1990, "Courtship Disorders", in *Hand Book of Sexual Assault: Issues, Theories, and Treatment of the Offender*, ed. W.L. Marshal, D.R. Laws and H.E. Barbaree, pp. 195-207, New York: Plenum Press.

Gagnon, John H., 1968, "Sexual Behavior: Deviation: Social Aspects", in *International Encyclopedia of the Social Sciences*, ed. David L. Sills, New York: The Macmillan Company.

Ge, P.H., 1982, "Sexual Behavior, Human", in *Encyclopaedia Britannica, Macropaedia*, vol. 16.

Gethin, R.L.M., 1986, "The Five Khandhas: Their Treatment in the Nikayas and Early Buddhism", *Journal of Indian Philosophy*, 14: 35-53; and 1996, in *Identity and Experience: The Constitution of the Human Being According to Early Buddhism*, ed. Sue Hamilton, London: Luzac Oriental.

Hardman, K., 1997, "A Social Work Group for Prostituted Women with Children", *Social Work with Groups*, 20: 19-31; and 2003, in *Sexual Deviance: A Reader*, ed. C. Hensley and R. Tewksbury, p. 184, London: Lynne Rienner Publishers.

Hudson, Stephen M. and Tony Ward, 1997, "Rape: Psychopathology and Theory", in *Sexual Deviance: Theory, Assessment, and Treatment*, ed. D.R. Laws and W. O'Donohue, pp. 332-55, New York: The Guilford Press.

Jayatilleke, K.N., 1975, *The Message of the Buddha*, London: George Allen and Unwin.

Koss, M.P., C.A. Gidycz and N. Wisneiwski, 1987, "The Scope of Rape: Incidence and Prevalence of Sexual Aggression and Victimization in a National Sample of Higher Education Students", *Journal of Consulting and Clinical Psychology*, 55(2): 162-70.

MacKinnon, Catherine A., 1994, "Rape, Genocide, and Women's Human

Rights", in *Mass Rape: The War Against Women in Bosnia-Herzegovina*, ed. Alexandra Stiglmayer, pp. 183-96, Lincoln, NE: University of Nebraska Press.

McKinney, J.P., 1994, "Sexual Deviations", in *Encyclopedia of Psychology*, ed. Raymond J. Corsini, vol. 3, New York: John Wiley and Sons, 2nd edn.

Milner, Joel S. and Cynthia A. Dopke, 1997, "Paraphilia Not Otherwise Specified: Psychopathology and Theory", in *Sexual Deviance: Theory, Assessment, and Treatment*, ed. D.R. Laws and W. O'Donohue, New York: The Guilford Press.

Murphy, William D., 1997, "Exhibitionism: Pathology and Theory", in *Sexual Deviance: Theory, Assessment, and Treatment*, ed. D.R. Laws and W. O'Donohue, New York: The Guilford Press.

Neu, Jerome, 1995, "Freud and Perversion", in *Philosophical Perspectives on Sex and Love*, ed. Robert M. Stewart, pp. 87-104, New York: Oxford University Press.

Penix, Tomara M., 2008, "Paraphilia Not Otherwise Specified: *Assessment and Treatment*" in *Sexual Deviance* ed. D.R. Laws and W. O'Donohue, 2nd edn, New York: The Guildford Press.

Sanday, Peggy Reeves, 1981, "The Socio-cultural Context of Rape: A Cross-Cultural Study", *Journal of Social Issues*, 37: 5-27; and 1994, in *Social Deviance, Being, Behaving, and Branding*, ed. David A. Ward, Timothy J. Carter and Robin D. Perrin, Boston: Allyn and Bacon.

Schewe, P.A., 1997, "Paraphilia not Otherwise Specified", in *Sexual Deviance*, ed. D.R. Laws and W. O'Donohue, pp. 424-26, 1st edn, New York: Guilford Press.

Stroller, R.J., 1982, "Sexual Deviations", in *Encyclopaedia Britannica Micropaedia*, vol. 16, Chicago: Encyclopaedia Britannica.

Suppe, Fredrick, 1987, "The Diagnostic and Statistical Manual of the American Psychiatric Association: Classifying Sexual Disorders", in *Sexuality and Medicine*, vol. II: *Ethical Viewpoint in Transition*, ed. Earl E. Shelp, Boston: D. Reidel Publishing Company.

Ward, Tony, Julie McCormack, Stephen M. Hudson and Devon Polaschek, 1997, "Rape: Assessment and Treatment", in *Sexual Deviance: Theory, Assessment, and Treatment*, ed. D.R. Laws and W. O'Donohue, New York: The Guilford Press.

Wasserstrom, Richard, 1994, "Is Adultery Immoral?", in *Philosophy and Sex*, ed. Robert Baker and Frederick Elliston, pp. 93-106, New York: Prometheus Books (rev. edn).

Wheeler, S., 1960, "Sex Offences: A Sociological Critique", *Law Contemp. Prob.* 25: 258-78.

Zwilling, Leonard, 1992, "Homosexuality as Seen in Indian Buddhist Texts", in *Buddhism, Sexuality, and Gender*, ed. Jose Ignacio Cabezon, pp. 203-14, Delhi: Sri Satguru Publications.

Dictionaries, Grammar and Encycopaedias

Borgatta, Edgar F. (editor-in-chief), 1992, *Encyclopedia of Sociology*, vol. 4, New York: Macmillan Publishing Company.

Corsini, Raymond J. (ed.), 1994, *Encyclopedia of Psychology*, vol. 3, New York: John Wiley and Sons (2nd edn).

Ellis, Albert and A. Abarbanel (eds), 1961, *The Encyclopaedia of Sexual Behaviour*, vol. II, London: William Heinemann Medical Books.

Encyclopaedia Britannica Macropaedia, vol. 16, Encyclopaedia Britannica, 1982.

Flexner, Stuart Berg and Leonore Crary Hauck (eds), 1993, *Random House Unabridged Dictionary*, New York: Random House.

Hornby, A.S., 2000, *Oxford Advanced Learner's Dictionary of Current English*, Oxford: Oxford University Press, 6th edn.

Malasekera, G.P., 1983, *Dictionary of Pāli Proper Names*, 2 vols, New Delhi: Oriental Books Reprint Corporation, 1st Indian edn.

Morris, William (ed.), 1985, *The American Heritage Dictionary*, 2nd college edn. Boston: Houghton Mifflin Company.

Nyanatiloka, 1991, *Buddhist Dictionary: Manual of Buddhist Terms and Doctrines*, Singapore: Singapore Buddhist Meditation Centre.

Ramachandran, V.S. (editor-in-chief), 1994, *Encyclopedia of Human Behavior*, vol. 4, San Diego: Academic Press.

Rhys Davids, T.W. and William Stede, 1986, *Pāli-English Dictionary*, London: The Pāli Text Society (repr.).

Sills, David L. (ed.), 1968, *International Encyclopedia of the Social Sciences*, New York: Macmillan.

Subhuti, Waskaduwe, 1938, *Abhidhanappadipika* or *Dictionary of Pāli Language*, ed. Waskaduwe Wachissara Thera, Colombo: Maha Bodhi Printing Works.

Whitney, William Dwight, 1885, *The Roots, Verb-Forms, and Primary Derivatives of the Sanskrit Language*, Leipzig: Druck und Verlag von Breitkopf und Hartel.

Williams, M.M., 1990, *A Sanskrit-English Dictionary*, Delhi: Motilal Banarsidass (repr.).

Other Source

Chatthasamgayana CD-ROM, Vipassana Research Institute.

Word Index

Index of Pali Suttas